$\int 4$

J.

THE
KHYBER RIFLES

To Oliver and Dudley,
the good guys in anyone's book

And, of course, to Helen

THE
KHYBER RIFLES

From the British Raj to Al Qaeda

JULES STEWART

SUTTON PUBLISHING

First published in 2005 by
Sutton Publishing Limited · Phoenix Mill
Thrupp · Stroud · Gloucestershire · GL5 2BU

British Library Cataloguing in Publication Data
A catalogue record for this book is available from the British
Library.

ISBN 0 7509 3963 X

Typeset in 12/15 Photina.
Typesetting and origination by
Sutton Publishing Limited.
Printed and bound in England by
J.H. Haynes & Co. Ltd, Sparkford.

Contents

List of Maps and Illustrations

Maps

Black and white illustrations between pages 80 and 81

Foreword

Troubles on the North-West Frontier of Pakistan are with us and will be with us for years to come, and those troubles from time to time involve not only neighbours but also geographically distant peoples. At the end of the sixteenth century the Emperor Akbar had the first carriageable road driven through the Khyber Pass, but he failed in his efforts to control the tribes, resorting as have his successors through the years, to payments to achieve passage for traffic on that road.

Only once have I travelled through the Khyber Pass on that amazing train which Jules Stewart describes, but many, many times by car and I commend his account of the pass, of the peoples who live there and of those charged with maintaining order, to a wider audience than just those interested in the affairs of Afghanistan and Pakistan. I was once invited by the Chief Ministers of the North-West Frontier Province and of Baluchistan to travel from Peshawar to Quetta through the tribal territory and the plans were well advanced for me to make the journey under the protection of tribal lashkars, when the central government in Islamabad intervened and forbade the trip. It is a sensitive area and foreigners who seem to be taking too close an interest arouse suspicions. This book helps us to understand the basis for those suspicions.

When I first saw Jules Stewart's manuscript, it really ended in 1919 with the sad events of the Third Afghan War. We are now presented with a wide-ranging survey of a hundred and fifty years' history, providing the reader with an understanding of the ongoing effort to develop this troubled area on the southern edge of Central Asia. Since 11 September 2001 no one can afford to ignore the problems of this troubled area and I recommend this book to intelligent readers everywhere.

Malcolm Morris, OBE
Australian Ambassador to Pakistan and Afghanistan, 1973–5

Acknowledgements

I would like to express my gratitude to those whose help and guidance made researching and writing this book such an enjoyable undertaking.

In Britain: The helpful archive staff at the British Library India Office, Royal Geographical Society and London School of Oriental and African Studies, Helen Crisp for her all-round support, Major John Girling, Robin Hodson, Colonel Tony Streather and Graham Wontner-Smith for sharing their Frontier experiences with me, Mark Baillie for his useful suggestions, Peter Hopkirk for his guidance and encouragement, my agent Duncan McAra and the team at Sutton Publishing.

In Pakistan: Khyber Rifles Commandant Colonel Muhammad Riaz Shahid, Colonel Syed Akbar Husain for making the right people available, Faisal Haq Khan for his companionship and for cutting through red tape, Captain Shafiullah Khan and Major Farooq Nasir Pirzada for their invaluable help with researching the project, National Bank of Pakistan Chairman Ali Raza for his logistic support, Zubyr and Durdana Soomro for their hospitality, and my fearless driver Akbar.

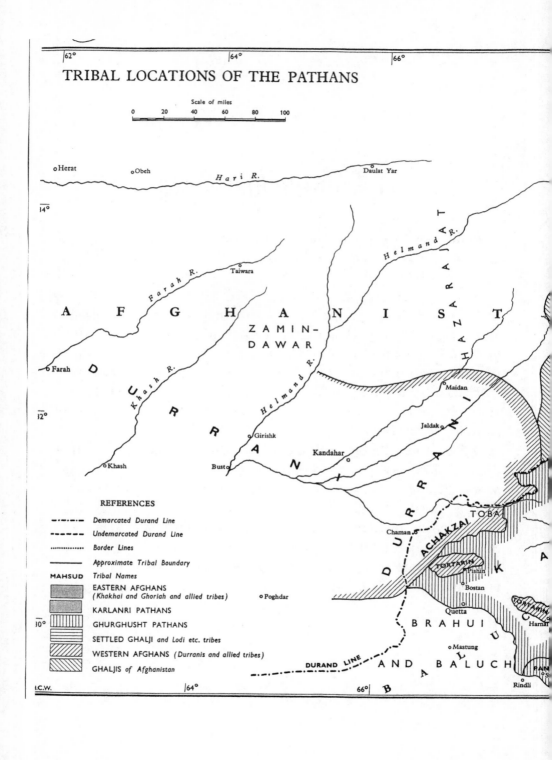

TRIBAL LOCATIONS OF THE PATHANS

Scale of miles

0   20   40   60   80   100

62°   64°   66°

oHerat   oObeh   *Hari R.*   Daulat Yar

14°

Farah R.   Taiwara   *Helmand R.*

A   F   G   H   A   N   I   S   T

ZAMIN-
DAWAR

Khash R.   *Helmand R.*   Maidan

oFarah   D   U   R   Jaldak   H A Z A R A J A T

12°   R   oGirishk   Kandahar

oKhash   Busto   R   A   N   I

TOBA

REFERENCES   Chaman   ACHAKZAI   K

—·—·—·— Demarcated Durand Line   TORTARIN   Pishin

— — — — — Undemarcated Durand Line   Bostan

············· Border Lines   A

————— Approximate Tribal Boundary   Quetta   TORTARIN

MAHSUD Tribal Names   Harnai

EASTERN AFGHANS   BRAHUI   C
(Khakhai and Ghoriah and allied tribes)   oPoghdar

KARLANRI PATHANS   oMastung

30°   GHURGHUSHT PATHANS   L

SETTLED GHALJI and Lodi etc. tribes   U

WESTERN AFGHANS (Durranis and allied tribes)   DURAND LINE   AND B A L U C H

GHALJIS of Afghanistan   B   Rindli

I.C.W.   64°   66°

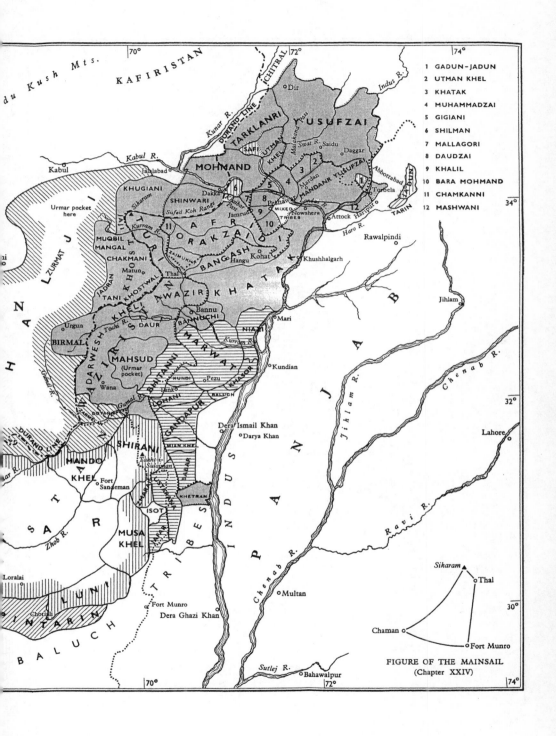

FIGURE OF THE MAINSAIL
(Chapter XXIV)

1 GADUN-JADUN
2 UTMAN KHEL
3 KHATAK
4 MUHAMMADZAI
5 GIGIANI
6 SHILMAN
7 MALLAGORI
8 DAUDZAI
9 KHALIL
10 BARA MOHMAND
11 CHAMKANNI
12 MASHWANI

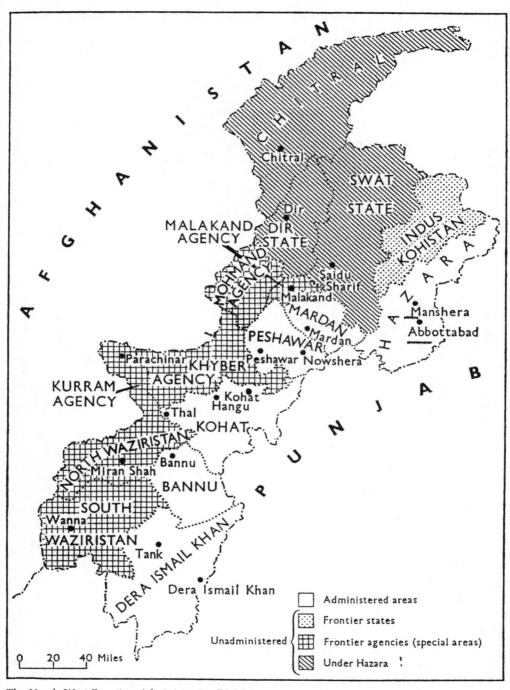

The North-West Frontier: Administrative Divisions

Within the map:

AFGHANISTAN

CHITRAL

Chitral

SWAT
STATE

Dir

MALAKAND
AGENCY

DIR
STATE

MOHMAND
AGENCY

INDUS
KOHISTAN

Saidu
Sharif

Malakand

MARDAN

H A Z A R A

Manshera

Abbottabad

PESHAWAR

Mardan

Parachinar

Peshawar   Nowshera

KHYBER
AGENCY

KURRAM
AGENCY

Kohat
Hangu

Thal

KOHAT

P U N J A B

NORTH WAZIRISTAN

Miran Shah   Bannu

BANNU

SOUTH

Wanna

WAZIRISTAN

Tank

DERA ISMAIL KHAN

Dera Ismail Khan

Administered areas

Frontier states

Unadministered { Frontier agencies (special areas)

Under Hazara !

0   20   40 Miles

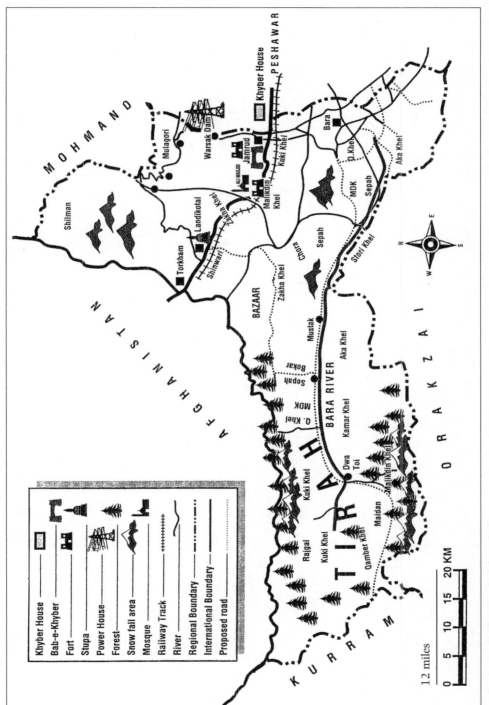

Tirah: the Forbidden Land of the Afridis

CHAPTER ONE

'To stop is dangerous, to recede ruin'

The summit of the Khyber Pass rises 3,600 feet above sea level, a barren, rock-strewn wasteland swept in winter by blasts of icy spindrift, baked in summer by temperatures that soar above 110°F. Perched on a rocky promontory near the summit stands Michni Fort, the most remote outpost of the legendary tribal militia, the Khyber Rifles. Below to the west lies a land drenched in the blood of Greek, Persian, Moghul, British, Russian and American invaders. From here, one's gaze is drawn across the desolate Afghan flatlands stretching to the western horizon, beyond which lurk the eternal snows of the Hindu Kush. Gazing down from Michni, it is hard to repress a shudder at the dark and sombre defiles of this pass, so pregnant with disaster. They invoke an uncomfortable reminder of the fate that befell those who throughout history have entertained thoughts of Afghan conquest. The fanatical *mullahs* who preach jihad to their brethren must be endowed with magical powers, to have so effectively sprinkled amnesia dust in the eyes of each successive wave of invaders. For the US forces now engaged in the futile exercise of dropping bombs on rocks in Afghanistan arrived only twelve years after the mighty Soviet Red Army trudged home exhausted and humiliated, and a century and a half after the British Raj suffered its costliest ever military disaster, a few desperate miles from the Khyber Pass.

The British displayed more tenacity than even the armies of Genghis Khan and Tamerlane in their determination to subjugate the wild Afghan tribesmen. In 1878, thirty-six years after Britain's calamity on the retreat from Kabul, the army once again crossed the Khyber. This time it was determined that British soldiers would not be exposed to surprise attack on the road. To ensure the army safe passage into enemy territory it was necessary to secure the Khyber Pass, the strategic route between Afghanistan and British India. But instead of stationing regular troops on the inhospitable and dangerous cliffs that tower over the road, the British came up with an ingenious scheme: why not recruit the local tribesmen into the fold, offering them the incentive of paid employment in the Government of India plus the freedom to use their weapons with impunity? After all, the Pathans knew every sniper's nest above the pass like the back of their hands, and their long-barrel matchlocks could easily out-range British breech-loading Sniders. Thus was born the rag-tag embryo of what was to become the Khyber Rifles, the guardians of the Khyber Pass.

With the raising of the first of the Frontier Corps the British found that the tribesmen's loyalty could in part be bought, in part commanded by officers of a very special calibre, men who spoke their language and understood their ways. The government had made significant strides in dealing with the Pathans since that fateful day in 1842 when the army marched out of the gates of Kabul to its destruction, leaving in its wake a legacy of arrogance and ineptitude. But the experience had been gained at a terribly high cost.

On a bitter January morning, a rider slumped across a dying pony was spotted stumbling across the Afghan plain towards the shortly-to-be-besieged British garrison of Jalalabad, 90 miles east of Kabul. William Brydon was a 33-year-old Scottish surgeon attached to the doomed Army of the Indus, commanded by Major-General William Elphinstone, an ageing soldier crippled by gout, an ailment that he had hoped to cure by taking the posting to India. From the outset grave doubts had been expressed about the General's suitability for the task of leading an army against so cunning an adversary as the Afghan. Elphinstone's previous battle experience had been at Waterloo twenty-six years before.

Brydon was close to gasping his last when a detachment of cavalry officers galloped from the fort to escort him to safety. He was rushed to the infirmary where the garrison's surgeon worked feverishly to stem the flow of blood from multiple sword cuts to his hand, knee and head, with a musket ball wound in his leg for good measure. That evening, hunched by the fire in the officers' mess, Brydon savoured his first proper meal in more than a week. As for his wounds, 'how, and when, these happened,' he recounted in a numbed state of mind, 'I know not'. But Brydon did retain an appallingly vivid recollection of what he had endured during the seven-day retreat from Kabul, a tale that filled his listeners round the fire with a stunned horror. It was the tale of a massacre, the slaughter of more than 16,000 men of the once victorious Army of the Indus, including wives and children and thousands of camp-followers, who on a freezing January morning had tramped out of Kabul, jubilant with the prospect of returning home to the warmth and civilisation of India. In spite of the knee-deep snow that turned each step into a gruelling struggle, the retreating British were confident of reaching safety ninety miles away at Jalalabad in a fortnight's march. Instead, the entire column perished within three days of abandoning Kabul.

The British forces garrisoned in Kabul had been lulled into a state of complacency by the ease with which the Afghans had been beaten into submission by their new masters in 1838, one year after the royal teenager Victoria had ascended to the throne of England. The first two years in Kabul passed without major incident, and with mulberry blossoming in spring the troops, no longer an expeditionary force, were settling down as an army of occupation. Bungalows were erected, gardens laid out, wives sent for, and not a soul among them could anticipate the calamity that lay in waiting like a tiger crouched in a thicket. The enemy king

Dost Mohammed had surrendered in November 1840 and was given honourable asylum in India. The British Lion roared with victory, and all was well.

The melancholy events that enfolded on the march from Kabul in 1842 came about largely as a result of the East India Company seeking to cut back on expenditures. One of history's earliest episodes of corporate downsizing was to touch off a major human and political cataclysm. With wisdom that may be generously described as dubious, the cost-conscious government *babus* in Calcutta had decided to reduce the subsidies that were doled out each year to the Khyber tribal chieftains. These allowances were given on the tribesmen's commitment to keep open the lines of communication with the army and its outposts across the border in Afghanistan. The British could generally rely on the tribal *maliks* to keep their word, that is so long as the baksheesh kept rolling in. But directly the bribes dried up, the all too predictable outcome was an immediate Pathan uprising. Revolt swept swiftly and suddenly across Kabul in November 1841. The incapacity of the British command to deal with the situation was surpassed only by the treachery of the Afghans. The British Envoy Sir William Macnaghten, a fastidious, pinched-mouth career bureaucrat, had taken it upon himself to break the news to the tribesmen: following orders from the East India Company he announced abruptly to the maliks assembled in *jirga*, the government subsidy was to be slashed from £8,000 to £4,000. The tribal leaders went away to ponder this piece of intelligence, and their response was to summarily cut off the key road connection to and from British India, the Khyber Pass. A tidal wave of horsemen fell upon every caravan that ventured up the road, looting the baggage trains and spreading havoc among the camel drivers. Spurred on by the Dost Mohammed's favourite son, Akbar Khan, a slight, feline creature with a wispy moustache and almond eyes, who bore a deep hatred for the *feringhee*, the flames of revolt spread up and down the Frontier, to finally engulf the unsuspecting British forces and their families in Kabul, where the situation was deteriorating by the hour.

Kabul was now effectively cut off from the powerful garrison at Jalalabad. Another British Envoy to the city, the adventurer Alexander Burnes who had attempted to negotiate an alliance with Dost Mohammed, was the first high-profile figure in the cantonments to fall victim to the mob. On 2 November the Afghans torched the Residency, hacked Burnes to pieces, along with two British officers and all the *sepoy* guards inside. The kindly but doddering Elphinstone, when told of the assassination, took pen in hand and wrote to Macnaghten: 'We must see what morning brings and then think what can be done.' Macnaghten barely had time to ponder his commander's soothing words. As the government's caretaker administrator, Macnaghten was looking forward to taking up his new appointment as Governor of Bombay. He arranged to meet Akbar Khan for truce talks at a spot by the banks of the Kabul river, a quarter mile from the Residency. No sooner had Macnaghten alighted from his horse, he was brutally murdered in the presence of the amir's nephew. The crafty Afghan, who was in his early twenties, disclosed to the attending mob that the British envoy was plotting to abduct a tribal chief, and that was provocation enough for the tribesmen to fall upon Macnaghten. To the delight of the Afghans already intoxicated with the scent of British blood, Akbar Khan ordered Macnaghten's head to be paraded through the city on a pole. As for the rest of the hapless Envoy's remains, the rabble took it upon itself to hang Macnaghten's headless corpse from a hook at the entrance to the bazaar.

The game was now well and truly up. This supreme humiliation of the British master roused the horde to even loftier enterprises. The frenzied tribesmen next laid siege to the cantonments, the vulnerable bungalows and barracks where the British had foolishly chosen to hold up instead of behind the secure hilltop walls of the Bala Hissar citadel. The well-defended palace-fortress was occupied by Shah Shujah, the despised weakling the British had placed on the Afghan throne after the Governor-General Lord Auckland engineered Dost Mohammed's removal. Britain's amir-in-waiting, however, made the fatal mistake of taking his position too seriously. He haughtily refused to allow the British, his benefactors and only realistic source of protection, to take up residence in the Bala Hissar. Shah Shujah suffered his inevitable fate: he fell to Akbar Khan's dagger as soon as the army trudged out the city gates on the ill-fated retreat from Kabul. To give Elphinstone his due, he had recommended the building of a fort for the garrison, but this proposal clashed with the tight-fisted policies of the East India Company's bean counters, who rejected the army's request for £2,400 to carry out the works. After all, the occupation of Kabul was already costing the Honourable Company £1 million a year. Lieutenant Vincent Eyre, one of the few British survivors of the Afghan disaster, observed with some irony that 'The credit of having selected a site for the cantonments, or controlled the execution of its works, is not a distinction now likely to be claimed exclusively by anyone.'[1] Eyre, the garrison's Deputy Commissary of Ordnance, expresses in his memoirs of captivity under Dost Mohammed a stark wonder of how the government could have 'in a half-conquered country' left their forces in so extraordinary and injudicious a military outpost as the exposed cantonments:

> The position eventually fixed upon for our magazine and cantonments was a piece of low swampy ground, commanded on all sides by hills or forts. It consisted of a low rampart and a narrow ditch in the form of a parallelogram . . . 1000 yards long and 600 broad, with round flanking bastions at each corner, every one of which was commanded by some fort or hill.[2]

The Mission compound, which served as the residence of the envoy, officers and assistants of the occupation force, was a death trap. Its very existence 'rendered the whole face of the cantonments, to which it was annexed, nugatory for purposes of defence'. With a doddering old man like Elphinstone at the helm, the garrison's predicament could hardly have been more desperate. Eyre lavishes praise on his commanding officer's professional acumen, his courtesy and kindly attitude towards all ranks. But of Elphinstone the leader of men, he sadly notes, 'He had, indeed, but one unhappy fault as a general – the result, probably, of age and infirmity – and this was a want of confidence in his own judgement, leading him to prefer everybody's opinion to his own . . . until he was at a loss which course to take.' In the end, Elphinstone's dithering and indecision 'proved the ruin of us all'.[3]

Most of Elphinstone's contemporaries tended to agree that defending the Kabul garrison was too overwhelming a task for him to take on in his deteriorated state of mind and body. The ominous clouds gathering over the Army of the Indus and its civilian charges was, in the opinion of the indomitable Lady Sale 'enfeebling the powers of (Elphinstone's) mind'. Lady Florentina Sale was the embodiment of Victorian self-confidence and pluck. Her husband, Sir Frederick Sale, was dispatched to command the garrison at Jalalabad, while she remained at Kabul Cantonment with the main body of the army. This *grande dame* had nothing but contempt for what she dismissed as 'reprehensible croaking' by British officers who spent their time bemoaning the imminence of disaster. When the Afghan mob finally attacked and scaled the walls of one fortification using poles picked up from the ground as ladders, Lady Sale snorted, 'A child with a stick might have repulsed them.'[4]

With tragic inevitability, Elphinstone capitulated to Akbar Khan's threats and agreed to withdraw his army from Kabul. This decision precipitated the most calamitous defeat ever to befall a British fighting force: a 16,000-strong column betrayed and exterminated by an Afghan rabble-rouser, who moreover had personally guaranteed the retreating column safe conduct to India.

Before Elphinstone and his army were permitted to abandon Kabul that freezing January morning, the amir demanded six hostages be delivered to ensure certain pledges undertaken by the British officials. The prisoners were later to be liberated by Major-General George Pollock, but fortunate as they were to escape the ghastly fate awaiting those who marched with Elphinstone, their months in captivity could hardly be described as a bed of roses. Captain James Airey recalls in his diaries that on the day the prisoners rode out of Kabul in the company of their liberator General Pollock, he was alarmed to learn of a 'reverse' suffered by the Second Division in the Khyber Pass. The report was in fact erroneous. The British forces managed to rout the Afghans who had attempted to block the advance of the Army of Retribution. But it was distressing news for a group of officers anticipating a triumphant march home after ten months of confinement in the hands of their bloodthirsty captors. 'You cannot conceive how glad I am to have left Afghanistan,' Airey writes:

I always hated it and the last ten months were a period of anxiety that was anything but pleasant. During the first five or six months we poor hostages were never certain how long we should have our heads on our shoulders, for the people of Kabul used to often to assemble around the house in which we were and insist on our being brought out to be killed. Had it not been for the man in whose custody we had been placed, who defended us at the risk of his own ruin, we should have all been murdered.

Airey adds with some understatement, 'It is rather a disagreeable sensation at first to be awakened in the morning by the cries of people insisting on having your blood.'[5]

Eyre was another of the lucky survivors who was taken back into captivity to join the small band of British hostages left behind after the departure of Elphinstone's column. His account of the journey is one of the few contemporary tales of the full horror of the carnage that befell the once-proud Army of the Indus:

The retreating army had marched over the same ground on the previous day, and terrible was the spectacle presented to our eyes along the whole line of road. The snow was absolutely dyed with streaks and patches of blood for whole miles, and at every step we encountered the mangled bodies of British and Hindoostanee soldiers, and helpless camp followers, lying side by side, victims of one treacherous undistinguishing fate, the red stream of life still tricking from many a gaping wound inflicted by the merciless Afghan knife. Here and there small groups of miserable, starving and frost-bitten wretches, amongst whom were many women and children, were still permitted to cling to life, perhaps only because death would in their case have been a mercy.[6]

Eyre raised a cry of outrage at the horrors he witnessed on that march, never doubting that 'these events will assuredly rouse the British Lion from his repose'. As indeed they did.

Retaliation was swift and deadly. Pollock avenged the annihilation of Elphinstone's army by forcing the Khyber Pass with 14,000 men and delivering Akbar Khan a resounding defeat in two hard-fought battles. The army then marched on to Kabul, reaching the city gates on 16 September, where in language that Pollock quite accurately surmised the Afghans would understand, he proceeded to blow up the bazaar. On 12 October Kabul was evacuated and the army retired to India, once again by way of the Khyber Pass. By express desire of Lord Ellenborough the troops had seized as war booty the gates of Mahmud of Ghazni's tomb, thought to be the ones that had been removed from the temple of Somnath in Gujarat in AD 1025. In fact they were of a later date and quite worthless. Nevertheless, the British Army had, in keeping with tradition, won the last battle. The rebel Akbar Khan made good his escape but not before he had deprived his conquerors of the pleasure of having his father's usurper Shah Shujah murdered as he stepped out of the Bala Hissar. A twist of political fate saw Dost Mohammed, Britain's former arch-enemy, who was later to prove himself one of Afghanistan's most enlightened potentates, brought out of his gilded exile in Delhi in 1843 and restored to the throne, where he ruled for twenty more years, dying in 1863 at the age of 80 and still in possession of power. There seemed to be no objection to Akbar Khan reappearing on the scene as his father's *wazir* (or Chief Minister) until his death four years later at the early age of 29. Auckland could now reassure the mandarins at the East India Company that Afghanistan basked in a reign of tranquillity and stability. Britain had an ally on the throne, one who could be trusted to resist any threat of attack by the tsar's armies. For it was of course Russia's overtures to Dost Mohammed that had served as the pretext for the British invasion of Afghanistan, despite the fact that St Petersburg stood squarely on the sidelines during the disastrous events leading up to and during the First Afghan War. Burnes's mission to Kabul was to negotiate a friendship treaty with Afghanistan and determine the extent of Russian intrigues in the amir's court. Burnes had arrived in Kabul in 1837, at a time when Dost Mohammed was in a state of despair over the pincer thrust closing in on his empire, with the Persians, backed by the Russians, laying siege to Herat and the Sikhs holding the sacred city of Peshawar. Burnes failed to obtain an alliance with the Afghan ruler, thus leaving the British in a state of high anxiety over the arrival of a rival mission to Kabul in the person of a young Cossack officer, Captain Ivan Vitkevich, who had been received with pomp and splendour by Dost Mohammed. The government was now fully convinced that the amir constituted a menace to the security of India and therefore had decided to act. This, notwithstanding the fact that so outstandingly unsuccessful was this Russian mission that no sooner had Vitkevich returned home he destroyed his papers and put a revolver to his head. The passivity of Russia in the First Afghan War and the later débâcle on the road to Jalalabad showed to what disastrous an extent the government had miscalculated the tsarist threat.

One of the hostages set free by the amir was Lieutenant Robert Warburton, an Anglo-Irish officer in the Indian Army, who was in command of eighty Punjabi sepoys. On his release Warburton was most probably relieved to learn that these recruits, untrained fighting men of doubtful fidelity, would not be returning to Kabul.

Two years before, Warburton had taken as his bride an Afghan princess, a niece of Dost Mohammed. While the slaughter on the road to Jalalabad was taking its grim toll on the Army of the Indus, the amir's son Akbar Khan found out that this noble-woman, in his fanatical eyes a traitor who had defiled herself by marrying an infidel and an enemy of his people, was in hiding somewhere in Kabul. Akbar spent months chasing his prey. But the woman, who had many confidants in the serpentine alleyways of Kabul, managed to escape his net and was able to join her liberated husband in the tiny British garrison at Ghilzai. There, on 11 July, she gave birth to a son who was christened Robert, after his father.

That event, which was to have such a pivotal impact on Frontier history, took place before the badly shaken Government of India had woken to a fact of military life: defending the empire west of the Indus would require the presence of a frontline force to garrison the Khyber and other vulnerable invasion routes from Afghanistan. More than thirty years were to pass before the first dashing native Frontier levies came into being. When that day arrived, the man called in to raise the Khyber Rifles, the first of these corps, fell to the son of an Anglo-Irish Indian Army officer and an Afghan princess, Captain (later Colonel Sir) Robert Warburton.

The Afghan War of 1839–42 was the first time Britain had come up against the Pathan tribes of the Frontier, seasoned, fanatical warriors who made up the bulk of the amir's fighting forces. The massacre on the Kabul road symbolised the loss of innocence for an imperial army that for more than eighty years, since the day of Robert Clive's victory at Plassey on the steaming plains of Bengal, had rolled victoriously westward across the subcontinent. The North-West Frontier was destined to remain a vexatious thorn in the British Lion's side for yet another century, roughly spanning the period from Queen Victoria's accession to the throne until the evening in 1947 when the Union Flag was lowered for the last time over the Khyber Pass.

The Pathans revealed themselves as a different sort of adversary from the native fighting forces the British had encountered east of the Indus. These tribesmen of the hills were not easily bought off, much less converted to the cause of the Raj, and they certainly were not to be subdued for long by force of arms. But the government recognised the urgent need to fortify the North-West Frontier in order to safeguard the integrity of India's most remote and volatile border, in particular the vital passes that could serve as invasion routes for Afghan as well as Russian armies.

Auckland, an aristocrat who cut a dashing figure in society, was a life-long bachelor who relied on his two adoring sisters to carry the burden of the social affairs he so detested. To the Governor-General went the misfortune of presiding over the calamity of the First Afghan War. The North-West Frontier was by this time a key piece in Britain's jigsaw of imperial strategy, and Auckland was as fearful as was the rest of government of Russia's hidden agenda in Afghanistan. Sadly, he was the obvious scapegoat for the disaster that wiped out Elphinstone's army, and was therefore recalled to London soon after General Pollock routed the amir's forces.

In the aftermath of the war, Britain's push to the North-West was directed mainly at the Sikhs, against whom the army waged two successful campaigns. Then came the 1857 Mutiny, and this calamity put a damper on aggressive territorial expansion for more than two decades. Under the viceroyship of John Lawrence, a pious and severe administrator whose chief interests were forestry, sanitation, railways and irrigation, British India turned its attention to retrenchment and reform. Lawrence favoured a 'close border' system, which on the North-West Frontier meant holding the line short of tribal territory. A decade or so later, the brilliant soldier and 'Master of Baluchistan', Captain Robert Sandeman, planted the seeds of what was later to flourish as the 'forward policy', a return to territorial expansionism that defines the life-blood of empire. Sandeman had something of the precursor in him when he enlisted local Baluchi guides to deal with a spate of banditry plaguing the Dera Ghazi Khan district, an arid wasteland that fell under his jurisdiction as Deputy

Commissioner. Although the confrontation was settled in a peaceful council with the maliks, the image of a British officer riding off on a military mission in the company of loyal tribesmen could be taken as the embryo of a future Frontier force.

By this time the government was forced to acknowledge that leaving the vast, uncharted tribal territory to its own devices as a buffer against the intrigues of Afghanistan and the advance of Russia, was no longer a tenable strategy. The Viceroy Lord Lytton bemoaned the fact that British officers who ventured a mile or two into this no man's land were unlikely to be seen alive again.

This explains the volte-face from a policy of stagnation to a return to imperial expansion eagerly embraced by the hawks that had come to roost on the ramparts of Whitehall. The prevailing view in the India Office was that the North-West Frontier must at all costs be made secure against the threat of Russian invasion. Britain's sensitivity to Russian movements in Central Asia was so acute that in 1891 the army organised a punitive expedition against the mir of Hunza for having allowed Cossack troops to reconnoitre his mountain kingdom. Sir Frederick Roberts, later Lord Roberts of Kandahar, was at that time Commander-in-Chief in India. 'Fighting Bob' Roberts commanded an extraordinary level of respect from the ranks, and he was an immensely popular military hero also affectionately known to his troops, British and Indian alike, as the 'Lion of Kandahar'. Such was Roberts' prestige with the sepoys that when he retired from service in 1893 the Muslim soldiers under his command, who included numerous tribesmen from the Frontier, sent him off with a public address dripping with breathtaking adulation:

We, the Mahomedans of the Punjab, have dared to approach Your Excellency with eyes tear-bedimmed, but a face smiling. The departure of a noble and well-loved General like yourself from our country is in itself a fact that naturally fills our eyes with tears . . . A boon for which the Natives of India will always remember your name with gratitude, is that you have fully relied upon, and placed your confidence in, the Natives, thus uniting them more firmly to the British Crown, making them more loyal, and establishing the good relations between the Rulers and the Ruled on a firmer footing to their mutual good.[7]

Roberts was thoroughly mistrustful of the tsar's designs on India. He makes mention in his memoirs of one Colonel Yanoff, who had crossed the Hindu Kush with his Cossacks by the Korabhut Pass, advancing as far as the borders of Kashmir. Even more outrageous was the Russians' treatment of two British officers found journeying along the road to India by way of the Pamirs and Gilgit, who were ordered to leave what the leaders of the Cossack party claimed to be 'newly acquired Russian territory'. Roberts writes: 'As this was a distinct breach of the promise made by the Russian government, and an infringement of the boundary line as agreed to between England and Russia in 1873, it was necessary to take steps to prevent any recurrence of such interference.'[8] Hence a small force was despatched to this almost inaccessible region to carry out the 'brilliant little Hunza-Naga campaign' and punish the mir who, Roberts notes with indignation, 'had openly declared himself in favour of Russia'. So while Warburton was earning his spurs as a promising young cadet, Britain was busily getting herself embroiled in another lather over the 'Russian menace', a conflict that would once again put the army on the march across the North-West Frontier passes into Afghanistan.

Britain's forward policy in the North-West Frontier, which in its broadest sense can be defined as securing control of the border up to the Durand Line,* aimed to set up a military and political buffer against Russian aggression. The scheme was conceived in the wake of an unprecedented official visit to India by the Prince of Wales, later to be crowned Edward VII. In fact, the strategy of pressing ever westward was inspired by Clive himself, the historic 'father' of the forward policy who after his brilliant victory at Plassey had proclaimed, 'To stop is dangerous, to recede ruin.' The plan was to neutralise the single most

---

* The frontier demarcation between Afghanistan and British India that came into being in 1893.

dangerous obstacle to Britain 'realising its destiny in Central Asia', namely Russia. Indian Army strategists saw in this mission an opportunity to push the dominion of British India right up to the North-West Frontier, thus securing the border with Afghanistan and, while they were about it, perhaps take some key outposts west of the Khyber.

In 1874 Britain was at the zenith of her imperial power. The archetypal Victorian, Benjamin Disraeli, had just been returned to a second term as Prime Minister, and the only figure of relevance to raise a voice against expansionism was the Viceroy Lord Northbrook, a man of impeccable India credentials whose grandfather had been chairman of the East India Company. Northbrook's un-Victorian-like restraint, however, was by no means an insurmountable obstacle for the likes of Disraeli's hardline Governor-General of India, Lord Salisbury. The chief India administrator managed to hound Northbrook out of office, with a relentless bombardment of telegrams demanding that British agents be stationed on Afghan soil in order to keep a watchful eye on Russian movements in Central Asia, a diktat that Salisbury knew would fly in the face of Northbrook's close border proclivities. Northbrook, resentful as were most viceroys of being bossed about by politicians comfortably perched in the ivory towers of Whitehall 6,000 miles away, threw in the towel and returned to his Hampshire estates to enjoy his considerable fortune and outstanding collection of paintings amassed by his family, the Baring banking dynasty. Northbrook's replacement, the talented linguist and poet Edward Robert Bulwer Lytton, later ennobled to the peerage as Lord Lytton, arrived in Calcutta in time to help celebrate the magnificence of Queen Victoria's proclamation as Empress of India, a title he clearly intended to see carried forward to the subcontinent's remotest boundaries – and beyond.

The Disraeli-Salisbury-Lytton triumvirate lost no time in pursuing their forward policy by demanding that the Afghan ruler Sher Ali allow a British mission to take up residence at the court of Kabul. While these negotiations were in progress a piece of intelligence landed at Government House in Calcutta that sent the General Staff's antennae flying about: Sher Ali had been wining and dining an official delegation from St Petersburg led by General Nikolai Stolietoff. What was even more galling, the tsar's emissaries had travelled to Kabul at the behest of the amir himself. According to a contemporary report by Major Reginald Mitford the Viceroy's reaction was to call for a 'total cessation of all official intercourse with the Afghan capital'. Lytton was never happy to accept the settled district of the North-West Frontier as India's boundary with Afghanistan, and he squarely aligned himself with those who bemoaned the close border policy as a total failure. Shortly thereafter, Calcutta was to heave a sigh of relief when the amir broke his official silence to announce that, after all, he would be delighted to receive a British mission. In reality, the crafty amir was simply seeking to keep his options open. Sher Ali was testing the temperature of the water, trying to decide which of the great foreign powers in Asia, Russia or Britain, would come up with the best deal. Taking the amir at his word, Lytton despatched a mission through the Khyber Pass, only to have it intercepted by Afghan troops and turned back at Ali Masjid fort. It is unlikely the British grasped the significance in the Afghans having chosen this spot to confront their intruders – an old Moghul proverb has it that 'He who holds Ali Masjid rules at Delhi.'

Sher Ali, suspecting that Britain's friendly advances might conceal a more shadowy agenda, perhaps even a secret plan to occupy or break-up his kingdom, sent a detachment of troops to the Khyber Pass to halt the advance of a party led by Sir Neville Chamberlain. Brigadier-General Chamberlain, now 58 and a seasoned veteran of the Mutiny as well as several hard-fought Frontier campaigns, took this as an affront to his personal dignity. He fired off a telegram trumpeting his outrage to the Secretary of State for India, who quickly responded in kind, with Disraeli's consent: the Khyber Pass was to be cleared immediately of these insolent Afghans. The exchange of entreaties, and eventual open threats between Kabul and Calcutta, eventually boiled down to an ultimatum from the British camp: let Chamberlain's mission pass unhindered through the Khyber by 20 November or suffer the consequences. Predictably, Sher Ali was no longer in a conciliatory mood. The deadline passed without any signs of withdrawal by the Afghan troops. Thus, on 21 November, with the onset of winter, the government activated Plan B. An army of nearly 30,000 British and native troops marched across the border into Afghanistan, preceded by a message cabled by the Viceroy to the War Office in London, stating with exquisite pomposity, *Jacta est alea*, the die is cast. The Second Afghan War was under way.

The army moved forward in three columns. The first came up from the south, from Quetta to Kandahar, the line of defence chosen by Roberts to repel any Russian attack on India through Afghanistan. The second column advanced across a central front into the Kurram valley. The third marched north from Peshawar through the Khyber Pass to Jalalabad. What is today a Khyber Rifles outpost, Ali Masjid, came close to becoming the scene of disaster for the 15,000-man northern column advancing through the Khyber under the command of Sir Samuel Browne. The fortress commands a formidable defensive position above the pass, and at that spot nearly 4,000 enemy troops and native tribesmen lay in waiting for the Peshawar Valley Field Force. Browne, the one-armed veteran of the 1857 Sepoy Mutiny, saved the day by outmanoeuvring the Afghan forces. He ordered one of his brigades to mount a flanking manoeuvre and then simultaneously launched a frontal infantry attack, setting the Afghans on the run at bayonet point. The other two columns achieved their objectives and within three months the British expeditionary force was camped in the snow outside the gates of Kabul. Sher Ali fled to Turkestan, where he was shortly to die. His son Yakub Khan, known to the amir as 'that ill-starred wretch', assumed the throne and finding himself outgunned, he promptly capitulated to the conquering British. Victory was sealed in the treaty of Gandamak, in May 1879, 'after much of the delay and equivocation inseparable from dealing with Asiatics', recalls an official. The amir was forced to cede a wide swathe of borderland, including the jewel in the crown, the 32-mile length of the Khyber Pass. For good measure, he also 'consented' to receive a British resident at his court. Disraeli's policy objectives had been achieved, the key strategic route between both countries was finally in British hands, and once more the might of British arms basked in glory. But not for long.

On a brisk autumn morning in September 1879 the commander of the newly installed Kabul Cantonment, the exaltedly-named Major Sir Pierre Louis Napoleon Cavagnari, an Anglo-Frenchman whose father had served as one of Napoleon's generals, along with his party of eighty fighting men were going about their morning drill and barracks duties. Without warning, the Residency came under siege by a sword- and musket-wielding mob of fanatical Kabulis. Finding they could not storm the place, the attackers set fire to the doorway below, and when that gave way they stormed in and overwhelmed the defenders. With the connivance of Yakub Khan, the screaming multitude cut down the garrison, leaving not a man alive. Thus was fulfilled the gory prophecy of former Viceroy Sir John Lawrence, who had warned that by taking up residency in Kabul Cavagnari and his men 'will all be murdered – every one of them'. The British, it seems, had not learnt the lessons of their past dealings with the Afghans. They had once again fallen victim to the amir's treachery.

The task of redeeming British battle honours fell to Roberts, the legendary military hero who, at the very moment Cavagnari and his troops were being butchered in Kabul, was marching his troops back to India across Afghanistan's mountain wilderness. The amir, sensing that he had perhaps ventured into deep water, fired off a letter dripping with cynicism, in the hope that the Government of India might forestall reprisals for his duplicity in the Residency bloodbath. 'I am grieved with this confusing state of things,' Yakub Khan wrote. 'It is almost beyond conception. By this misfortune I have lost my friend, the Envoy, and also my kingdom. I am terribly grieved and perplexed.'[9] Roberts was unmoved by this piece of mendacity. When informed of the outrage that had befallen Cavagnari and his men, he swiftly turned his column round and marched his 7,500 men to Kabul, where he informed the amir that he was out of a job. Yakub Khan was ousted from Kabul with the same apparent ease that the Taliban were ejected from the capital 133 years later. But within three months it was to appear just as deceptive a victory. Almost immediately, the handful of tribal warlords who had melted into the hills with their fighters ahead of Roberts' arrival staged a mass uprising. After several days of desperate fighting, Roberts found himself boxed into the same corner as his predecessor Elphinstone nearly four decades before, only this time sheltered behind thick walls to defend himself against the Afghan rabble. The news of the army's plight sped to Calcutta where Lytton, contemplating the hopelessness of the Afghan adventure, threw up his hands in despair and demanded 'a way out of that rat-trap'. The Viceroy was only too delighted to negotiate the evacuation of Roberts' troops with almost any Afghan potentate, although he refused to deal with the deposed and truculent Yakub Khan. At last an agreement was hammered out to hand over the throne to Abdur Rahman Khan, a nephew of Sher Ali. His mission accomplished, Roberts gathered his army together and departed Kabul, having been spared Elphinstone's ghastly ordeal. The Government of India's Afghan policy was back to its normal shambolic state and apart from having won control of the Khyber Pass and several other, less significant territorial gains, the Second Afghan War drew to an inglorious conclusion.

Within a few years, however, the forward policy once again began to gather momentum. Robin Hodson, formerly with the Khyber Agency, notes that the British presence was spread considerably throughout the tribal territories. 'The permanent occupation of Quetta, in what was to become Baluchistan, was recognised, and the boundary extended to the foot of the Khojak range, halfway to Kandahar,' he writes. 'In the north, our jurisdiction was extended to the Peiwar Kotal at the head of the

Kurram valley, and to Landi Khana at the eastern end of the Khyber Pass.'[10] In 1891 the Samana range was occupied to bring the Orakzai tribe under control, and a year later the Kurram valley was placed in British hands. 'The Forward Policy had become a reality that advocated a firm occupation of this mountainous country to ensure the tranquillity of the settled districts down to the Indus,' Hodson explains. Never again would a viceroy have to lament, as did Lytton in 1877, that the country within a day's ride of Peshawar 'is an absolute *terra incognita* and that there is absolutely no security for British life a mile or two beyond our border'.

In 1919 Britain managed to get dragged into yet another full-blown conflict with Afghanistan, the third war in less than a century. This time it was the Amir Amanullah, a jovial, aggressive personality who enjoyed strutting about in top-boots and whipcord riding breeches, who opened hostilities against the Government of Delhi (the capital was moved from Calcutta in 1912), ostensibly on the pretext of a disputed tract of land below the Khyber Pass. The events leading up to this war were of a more complex nature than in the previous two conflicts. By the early twentieth century British politicians of vision had grasped the reality that time was running out on the Raj. India was ablaze with pro-independence demonstrations, often degenerating into full-blown street riots. The most infamous of these disorders took place in the Punjab city of Amritsar, on a scorching April morning when Gurkha troops under the orders of Brigadier-General Rex Dyer opened fire on a gathering of several thousand supporters of Mahatma Gandhi, killing almost 400 people. Amanullah, who had assumed the Afghan throne after his father's assassination, was a weak and vainglorious individual who, despite his avowed hatred of the British had accepted the hospitality of the Lord Mayor of London at the Guildhall a few months before he launched his invasion of British India. On the dubious pretext of preventing a spillover of Indian nationalist violence into Afghanistan, but in reality with designs on capturing Peshawar, Amanullah rushed troops to the border. The

27-year-old amir's strategy was to exploit the wave of Congress Party outrage over the Amritsar massacre. In fact, very few of the victims at Amritsar were Muslims, so the killing could not by any stretch of the imagination be seen as an act of sectarian violence or threat to Afghan citizens.

Nevertheless, any excuse was valid for rattling the British while enhancing the amir's prestige among the Frontier tribes by standing up to the Raj. Amanullah obviously harboured designs on the tribal lands between the political border and Peshawar, a territory that Afghan rulers have always claimed as their historic national territory. Amanullah achieved his initial objective of rallying support for a confrontation with Britain. While Afridi tribesmen began running amuck in the bazaars of Peshawar, Afghan *lashkars* saddled their mounts in readiness for a strike against the Khyber Pass outposts.

Major-General Sir George Roos-Keppel, of British-Dutch descent, answered to the role model of the soldier-scholar, in the tradition of Alexander. The Khyber Rifles Commandant had written a grammar of the Pushtu language, and was a prolific academic who translated arcane Pushtu works, such as the *History of Sultan Mahmud of Ghazni*. Roos-Keppel served as President of the Government's Committee of Examinations in the Pathan language. Such was his passion for Pathan culture that he co-founded Islamia College, a sumptuous grouping of red sandstone colonial buildings in a setting of palm groves, now the undergraduate school of Peshawar University. Photos of Roos-Keppel in silk turban and ermine-collared greatcoat, his hooded eyes gazing sternly upon the world from above a formidable handlebar moustache, reveal a man possessed of Churchillian self-confidence.

In 1919 Roos-Keppel held the position of Chief Commissioner of the North-West Frontier Province and was looking forward to 'a quiet summer', as he informed the Viceroy Lord Chelmsford in one of his weekly despatches. Alas, the soldier who had commanded the Khyber Rifles for twelve years, a man fully at ease conversing with the Pathans in their own language, should have spotted the danger signals brewing along the Frontier. On 3 May, with the blistering summer heat at its fiercest, Afghan army units slipped across the border and swiftly stormed and occupied the village of Bagh in the Khyber Pass. With the advantage of surprise on their side, the Afghans swarmed down on British territory, virtually unopposed. This was undeclared warfare, as well as a highly dangerous gambit for the amir whose game plan was to stir up a jihad among the tribes. Within a few days the British commanders had awoken from their summer stupor and were busily mustering a force to launch a counter-attack. But the campaign to dislodge the Afghan invaders was put together hastily and in haphazard fashion. From the outset, the army found itself fighting a rearguard action whose objective was to keep open the lines of communication through the Khyber Pass, while repelling waves of vigorous harassment from the Pathan tribesmen who were clearly impressed by the amir's brazen attack on the British masters.

The Third Afghan War occupies a curious place in the annals of military campaigns. What started out as almost a medieval siege ended with a foretaste of what was to become the most dreaded feature of modern warfare. It was decided that one of the first retaliatory actions would necessarily be the capture of the key Afghan fort of Spin Baldak. Brigadier Francis 'Ted' Hughes, then a 22-year-old subaltern in the 1st Gurkhas, recalls in his memoirs that the High Command, 'acting doubtless on the excellent principle that if you can't surprise the enemy it is better to surprise your own side than no one at all, supplied little or no information about the fort and its garrison'.[11] Hughes's regiment was ordered to take the south side of the of the fort's 15ft high outer wall in what was to be the last occasion when a British Army unit used scaling ladders. 'The plan was first to place the scaling ladders in the ditch, so that the regiment could climb down one side and then up the other,' he explains. 'Then the men were meant to climb the wall, haul up the ladders, climb down, go through the ditch, and then climb the next wall. The Gurkhas

were greatly diverted by this simple plan and declared that
nothing like it had been seen since the siege of Jerusalem.'
Hughes says that everything was to be done in deathly silence:

> Indeed, the only sounds were the crashing of ammunition boxes
> and entrenching tools as the mules threw their loads, and the
> thudding of hooves as they bolted into the night. Every few
> seconds the air was split by the yells of some officer urging the
> men to greater silence or the despairing call of some NCO who
> had lost his section. A sound as of corrugated iron being
> dropped from a great height denoted that the scaling ladders
> were being loaded onto the carts: with these two exceptions, no
> one would have had an inkling that several thousand armed
> men were pressing forward to the fray.[12]

As things turned out, the scaling ladders were too short even for
descending into the ditches, but fortunately the Afghan garrison
commander had no stomach for a fight in the fort and retreated
with his unit to the hills. The British occupied the fort for a
month, strengthened the defences and improved the water supply.
Then they handed it back to the Afghans.

The Viceroy, who had served in India in the First World War,
could see that Amanullah's mischief merited a vigorous response,
something more on the order of major surgery than a localised
punitive action. The Royal Air Force was called out, a tactic the
Afghans considered highly unsporting. But the use of air power
for the first time on the Frontier rendered this 'war' a fairly cut-
and-dried affair. Unlike the carpet bombing of Taliban strongholds
by US Air Force B-52s, on this occasion an RAF Handley Page
aircraft was sent over Kabul, from which the navigator lobbed a
single bomb on the city to persuade Amanullah that the stakes
had been raised beyond his limit. This did the trick, for the amir
quickly saw the light. Exactly one month to the day after
embarking on his adventure in the Khyber, Amanullah raised the
white flag. He called off his forces, although for the triumphant
British it looked like something short of a pyrrhic victory, for the

amir managed to exact a promise from government to grant his country full independence. Up to then Afghanistan's foreign affairs and defence had come under the auspices of British India.

The North-West Frontier remained the scene of regular dust-ups between British forces and Pathan tribesmen until August 1947, when the sun finally set on the Raj. What the former colonial masters bequeathed to the state of Pakistan was an untamed no man's land where in some places even the British Army, in all the years it fought to keep the peace on the Frontier, had failed to penetrate. That Pakistan has managed to maintain an uneasy status quo with its Frontier citizens is due solely to a cautious policy of non-interference in tribal matters. The Pathans collect 'good behaviour' allowances today from Islamabad as they did in the past from the British, while Pakistan exercises minimal jurisdiction over the tribes. The government writ does not run in these lands. No arrest can be made, no crime logged unless it takes place on a state road. Less than 10 per cent of some 600 federal laws apply in tribal territory. Ten yards off the road there is only tribal justice and the blood feud. This is a reality that the US forces and their allies in Afghanistan, who at the time of writing are heavily engaged in the country, could do well to take into consideration. If 'history is a pattern of timeless moments,' as T.S. Eliot wrote in his *Four Quartets*, Western political leaders might reflect on Britain's three bloody conflicts in Afghanistan, spanning a period of eight decades, nearly a hundred years' war, and which served up no lasting spoils whatsoever. When debating military action in Afghanistan, the politicians would do well to heed the counsel of the Duke of Wellington, somewhat of a practitioner in the art of soldiering, who stood firm against the British invasion of 1839. An advance into Afghanistan, warned the Iron Duke, would mean 'a perennial march into that country'.

CHAPTER TWO

'The Earth is full of anger'

In the barren, forbidding mountains of Central Asia there is a line of demarcation between civilisation and barbarism. Stretching to the west lie the steppes that spawned the ravaging hordes of Genghis Khan and Tamerlane, wild horsemen who swept across the land, leaving in their dust cloud a trail of rotting corpses. To the east, beyond the Indus, unfold the fertile plains of India, whose highly refined people assimilated with little effort the benefits of Western enlightenment. The invaders from Central Asia looked upon the high passes that straddle these two civilisations as their gateway to India, while for those who dwelt east of the Indus, this no man's land stood as their first line of defence against the Asian marauders. For more than two thousand years, none of these natural invasion routes has been more deeply soaked in the blood of conflict than the Khyber Pass.

We were south and west of the entrance to the Pass by midnight. Everyone was on the alert. Ahead of us we could see faintly the V in the mountains against the sky. That was the Khyber, battleground of centuries of invaders. It looked dark, grim and slightly forbidding, as it loomed, sullen and gloomy, ahead; and it seemed to contract from the wide, free desert where there was room to spare, into a narrow defile, bordered by towering crags of ominous outline. Suddenly I felt very insignificant and, I am not ashamed to admit, rather scared, for our party was such a small one to try to crash this monumental barrier.'[1]

Thus describes Major John Fox of the Special Investigation Branch his mission through the pass in 1945, in hot pursuit of a gang of Afghan arms smugglers.

The Khyber has a way of imposing its dark grandeur on those who stand before its lofty walls. Fox's apprehension at entering the pass was shared by great soldiers and intrepid travellers alike, who throughout history have taken their courage in both hands to embark on the crossing.

Bab-e-Khyber is the name of the fortified arch, inaugurated with great pomp in 1963 by Pakistan's former military ruler Field Marshal Muhammad Ayub Khan, that today bridges the road entrance to the Khyber Pass. Once past this police checkpoint, the ancient excitement of the Khyber springs to life. In winter, the roadside bustles with crowds of Afghan nomads, Ghilzai, Powindah and Koochi tribesmen, noisily driving their camels, mules and cattle down to the fertile pastureland of the Indus valley. In the warmer months, Afridi tribesmen traditionally meet up for an afternoon stroll, chatting as they amble along the roadside, AK-47 assault rifles slung under their arms, always at the ready. The men keep a vigilant eye on the cluster of houses that stand in the distant fields, mud dwellings whose walls are pierced with loop-holes to defend their inhabitants against raiders. They are virtual fortresses, designed to settle blood feuds from the comfort of one's home. The houses have no windows in the outer walls, but the towers have parapets and rifle slits. A Pathan engaged in one of these blood feuds may be a man of means, and if so he may hire a *dushmani*, a professional tunneller, who will dig below an enemy's house and blow it up with dynamite, a few sticks always kept within arm's reach in a tribesman's home. This practice was picked up from the British sappers who built the railway and bridges in the Khyber. The road leading up to Landi Kotal, the high point of the pass, is cluttered with bearded, hawk-nosed tribesman whizzing past on noisy, high-powered Japanese motorbikes, while others lounge on *charpoys* by the roadside cafés, their gaze fixed on television screens blaring out ear-splitting Bollywood films. This indulgence in Western domesticity paints a deceptive picture, for the Khyber tribesmen of today remain 'wild, lawless, intolerant of foreign rule as of old, and as fiercely jealous of their ancient rights'.[2]

Looking up at Fort Jamrud at the mouth of the pass, there rises a forbidding rampart of barren mountains some two miles in the distance. Little sign of habitation is visible anywhere in the hills that stand stark and grim under the blazing sun. The hills are of a yellowish grey hue, and they are sparsely dotted here and there with scrubby bushes clinging precariously to life. The road passes Jamrud and then climbs through a steep valley into hills that quickly and unnervingly close in on all sides. The valley is short and steep, and the road almost at once begins its ascent in a long series of curves and loops to Shahgai ridge, then following a gentler stretch along the ridge to Fort Ali Masjid, where the way seems to be barred by a massive range. After the steep ascent to this fortress the traveller is confronted with a Biblical landscape as the road rises to its final height of 3,600 feet above sea level. Here, the bleak, dusty spurs of the Spin Ghar range draw nearer, yielding the first glimpses of the old British military railway, a wonder of engineering that threads its way across culverts and through tunnels to the Afghan border. The road has now left shale country and has reached blue limestone, full of cracks, fissures and a magnificent gorge, though the stream is nearly dry except once or twice a year during a flash storm. The waterway that flows through the gorge has its source at the bustling town of Landi Kotal at the summit of the pass. From there the road follows the stream into the main valley of the Khyber that now begins to open out until it is half a mile wide or more in places. The valley rises at a 2 per cent gradient, or a two feet rise in every hundred feet travelled. Here cultivated fields come into view, dotted with more Afridi villages surrounded by high square mud walls, some with embrasures along the top, and always with loop-holed places for riflemen. The road then wends its way down to Torkham and the dusty barren plains of Afghanistan.

The scrub hills that tower above the road and the old riverbed caravan routes abound with the vestiges of history, from the ancient Buddhist stupas of Kafir Kot and Shopla, to the stone insignia of legendary British regiments, the Lancaster and York, the Gordon Highlanders and others, men who fought and died in long-forgotten battles defending the empire's remotest frontier. Few today would associate the Khyber Pass with those British regiments that from time to time were called into action against rebellious tribesmen or Afghan regulars. The enduring celebrity of the Khyber Rifles is a different story. This was the original native levy raised by the British to guard the most critical gap on India's vulnerable and volatile North-West Frontier. Few will have heard of the Zhob Militia, the Gilgit Scouts or the Kurram Militia. But the name 'Khyber Rifles' is another matter, and if it strikes a familiar chord, this is almost certainly because of the corps' association with the pass they guard. This oldest of Frontier corps is to many a household name because the pass is steeped in history and strife, and because the men who call themselves 'the Guardians of the Khyber Pass' are still there. The veteran Frontiersman Lieutenant-Colonel Henry Crocker once remarked that if the romance of the East is to be found in India, 'then surely the romance of India centres in the Khyber Pass'.[3]

The American adventurer and writer Lowell Thomas, who crossed the Khyber Pass en route to Afghanistan in the 1930s, was another of those Western travellers who fell under the Frontier's romantic spell. He noted that in spite of the hardships and the likelihood of meeting an unseemly end, there were British officers who had spent all their lives in the Khyber region and left it not by choice but only by necessity. 'Who shall say in what the fascination lies?' Thomas speculates in an outpouring of hyperbole:

The grey hills that jag into the turquoise sky, the little green valleys, the mournful beauty of the dawns and twilights, the majestic cirque of hills that girds the fertile plains of Peshawar, the sunlit plain of Kohat as it stretches out from the (Khyber) Pass, the desolate gorges and snowy saltpetre of the river by Bahadur Khel – these things weave a spell, in recollection anyway, that will hold the memory when many more beautiful scenes are forgotten.[4]

The Khyber Rifles were originally thrust into the public eye by Talbot Mundy's gushing 1917 novel *King of the Khyber Rifles*. Apart from its title, the book makes very little reference to the Khyber Rifles, and only then in the most dripping prose: 'He was a *jezailchi* (musket-carrying tribesman) of the Khyber Rifles, hook-nosed as an osprey, black-bearded, with white teeth glistening out of a gap in the darkness of his lower face.' The novel's plot was focused more on the Khyber Pass ('as much British as the air is an eagle's') than the men who volunteered to defend it. The reader is offered the tale of the fictional caves of Khinjan in the Khyber Pass. 'Spies had been sent in, but none had ever returned. There was one woman, though, who apparently had access to the caves – Yasmini, beautiful, clever, an exquisite dancer, mistress of many languages. She was, perhaps, on the British side. Could she be trusted?' The mission to verify Yasmini's loyalty fell to Captain Athelstan King, 'a member of the Indian Secret Service, with India in his blood for seven generations.' King makes his way to the Khyber Pass and the dreaded caves, where big trouble awaits him. Mundy's hero 'knew he had to escape, had to win. What he didn't know was the price of success.'

Mundy was sadly not to reap the rewards of his melodrama's eventual success, for it took until 1953 for Hollywood to pick up on the commercial potential of the Khyber Pass, and that was thirteen years after Mundy's death. Extraordinarily, it was nearly twenty years before Twentieth Century Fox's original film script was able to ply its tortuous course through a tangle of political bureaucracy, premiering at last with Tyrone Power in the role of the dauntless Captain King, rechristened more plausibly 'Alan', who plays a role that in almost no respect bears any resemblance to the book's original story, apart from its setting in the pass. The

British Board of Film Censors, the India Office and Twentieth Century Fox fell into a protracted wrangle over the film script. The British were fearful of antagonising the Indian public with yet another tribute to imperialist superiority, as had been the case with *The Drum*, a jingoist film of the first order set in the North-West Frontier, whose screening touched off riots in the streets of Bombay and Madras. Of *King of the Khyber Rifles*, an India Office memo of 1936 stated: 'We would much prefer that this film should not be produced if it is possible to stop it.' The Whitehall view was, in the end, that the film could go ahead if certain objectionable passages were excluded. For instance, the bombing of a village on the North-West Frontier, the shooting of a wounded officer by a Pathan fanatic, and the sequence in which a tribesman brings in his own father's head in a bag. The British were understandably anxious to avoid antagonising the Pathans of the Frontier at a time when nationalist agitation was running high and Germany was emerging as an imminent menace to Britain and the empire. A much sanitised version of the script finally met with India Office approval, following concerns that the film 'was treading on dangerous ground'. Twentieth Century Fox acquiesced to the government's demands: 'The synopsis already reviewed will be considerably amended, and the passages which you consider as objectionable, will certainly be excluded,' the company conveyed through the Board of Censors to the India Office Military Department.

The 'Carry On' series of comedies of the 1960s brought the Khyber Rifles back into public focus with *Carry on up the Khyber*, a harmless bit of buffoonery about British Army escapades among farcical Pathan tribesmen and their promiscuous womenfolk. The film reinforces the obvious fact that the literary and celluloid interpretations of the Khyber Rifles and the pass they defend have served up a light entertainment version of reality. These historical flights of fancy notwithstanding, the popular association of the name Khyber with high romance and intrigue is accurate enough, more so of the pass itself than the men in khaki *shalwar kameez* and red beret who stand guard over it. Whatever is known of the Khyber Rifles comes largely through the history of this 32-mile-long pass, a land, in Kipling's words, 'filled with anger'.

The Khyber Pass has been the scene of bloody conflict from the time of the first British advance into its brooding ravines in 1839. From that day, skirmishes between British Army troops and Pathan warriors became an almost monthly event. The clashes began to build in ferocity, with Afridi lashkars falling upon patrols and undefended settlements, followed by retaliatory raids in tribal territory by the army, until both sides finally locked horns in the Bazar Valley Expedition mounted to punish sections of the Afridis. In this engagement the army took the unprecedented step of sending elephants through the pass to carry field guns with the troops – the first time since the days of Babur that these beasts had been used for military purposes. The animals required up to 400 pounds of forage daily, which posed a logistical nightmare for the transport officers. (Army records also mention that the elephants proved useful in demolishing the homes of rebellious tribesmen, a simple task given their mud construction. Khyber villagers, even those affluent souls engaged in the lucrative arms or drugs trade, still prefer to build their homes of mud, and for a very practical reason. One of the punishments the council of maliks and elders, known as the jirga, imposes on those found guilty of breaking tribal law is to have their homes demolished. It obviously requires less work to rebuild a mud house than one constructed of concrete or timber, which in any event is a rare commodity in the parched lands of the Khyber.)

In 1878, when war with Kabul was looking imminent, Colonel Robert Warburton, Political Officer Khyber, took the initiative to open negotiations with those Afridi clans that had shown themselves willing to reach an understanding with the British. A deal was struck on 20 November of that year: in return for a monthly allowance of 6,550 rupees, the tribal maliks agreed to allow their men to guard the Khyber Pass in each clan's respective limits and 'restrain their fellow tribesmen from molesting the highway'. The following day, General Sir Samuel Browne, with a force of twelve infantry battalions, one brigade of cavalry, five batteries of field guns and four columns of sappers, opened hostilities with Afghanistan by forcing the Khyber Pass in the first stage of the army's advance on Kabul. Soon after Browne's columns had crossed into Afghanistan, the native fighters were organised into a corps of Jezailchis of about 250 men, partly Khyber Afridis and partly inhabitants of the Peshawar valley. The corps was armed with muzzle-loading *jezails*, and its duties were to assist in escorting convoys and repelling attacks in the pass. This marked the first time in recorded history that the pass had fallen under the control of a foreign military command – not that some of the world's most formidable fighting forces had failed to give it their best shot over the centuries.

The wisdom of Warburton's initiative was never doubted, particularly in later years when the Khyber Rifles were obliged to bear the full impact of armed insurrection by their Afridi kinsmen. 'The Khyber Pass has to be kept open to us,' declared General Sir William Lockhart, who led a punitive expedition into Tirah following the 1897 Pathan insurrection. Lockhart acknowledged the pass to be the key trade route between the Punjab and Afghanistan. But, the General argued with foresight, its commercial value was far outweighed by its strategic significance 'in the event of military intervention in that country becoming necessary', as had been the case on two occasions in the past and was to be again in twenty years' time. 'The defile of the Khyber Pass should be guarded by irregular troops raised locally. It must be remembered that, in undertaking military operations in Afghanistan, the friendly attitude of the Frontier tribes would be of much greater moment than the absolute safety of any single pass, however important. If the attitude were friendly, the Pass would be secure in any case.'[5]

The historian Charles Allen writes,

The Pakhtuns say that when Allah created the world he had a pile of rocks left over, out of which he created Afghanistan. Some fifteen miles west of Peshawar, that pile of rocks is cut by a dark ravine out of which a river debouches onto the plain. This is the mouth of the Khyber Pass, although pass suggests a high crossing-point over a mountain range, whereas this is really a trail that leads up the bed of a river which has cut itself a deep, narrow defile of more than twenty miles through the mountains. Although only one of a number of fissures in the mountain chain which provides India with a natural defensive wall to west and north, the Khyber has always provided the subcontinent with its main invasion and trade route. It also long served as the chief highway between what the Afghans had come to regard as their respective summer and winter capitals, Kabul and Peshawar. Yet even the Afghans were forced to recognised that passage through the Khyber could only be obtained with the agreement of its guardians, the local Khybari tribesmen, who had held it for centuries and who made their living by exacting heavy tolls from every traveller. To secure safe passage through the Khyber without the approval of the Khyber tribes meant holding the high ground on both sides of the caravan trail. But before high ground can be held it has to be seized and picquets set up on all the strategic points – an enormous undertaking in the case of the Khyber Pass, which is serrated by scores of ravines and side-valleys and overlooked by hundreds of peaks and crags. Many conquerors with mighty armies have come this way, but all have found that, if they failed to pay their dues, they suffer for it.[6]

The Khyber Pass has always been the stage-set for historical drama. Long before the first Persian carpet merchants despatched their wares across the rocky desert tracks of Afghanistan, the Khyber served as an invasion route for the armies of Central Asian conquerors, from Alexander the Great to Babur, the first Moghul emperor of India. Since the earliest days of trade in this region, the camel caravans from Persia, China and the bustling markets of Central Asia that traversed the Silk Road found their natural gateway to India through the Khyber. 'Through the centuries these old hills have watched endless processions filing along their valleys, armies and traders, the pomp and panoply of war, and the peaceful caravan of the trader,' Crocker observed on his travels in 1931. 'Their rocky walls have witnessed the tramp of the legions and the weary feet of countless thousands of beasts of burden bearing the commerce of Bokhara, Afghanistan and Peshawar through the mountain passes.'[7]

Nearly two and a half millennia after Alexander's generals marched through its narrow corridor, the Khyber still fulfils the dual role of trade route and battlefield. From time to time camels can still be seen plodding their way along the caravan route that today runs adjacent to a deafening stream of roaring, psychedelically decorated lorries rumbling back and forth on the metalled road across the Afghan-Pakistan border. The lorries are laden to the brim with imported goods on their way to the *baras*, the smugglers' markets in the Pakistani border towns below the pass. A staggering variety of goods lay stacked by the roadside shops at Karkhano Market, from factory-fresh Sony television sets to Marks & Spencer menswear, not to overlook the array of Kalashnikovs and automatic pistols on offer in the arms bazaar. Here the customer can sit down in the comfort of an air-conditioned shop to negotiate the purchase of smuggled domestic appliances, illegal Scotch whisky or heroin. Goods landed at Karachi are transported across Pakistan, up the Khyber Pass into Afghanistan, usually by homicidal lorry drivers stoked up on hashish. Once delivered to the 'importer' the lorries are turned round and sent back across the border to Karkhano, where that 21in Sony TV, for instance, can be purchased for the equivalent of £200, a considerable saving over the normal £400 retail price. The Khyber Agency's Bara district provides unmolested passage for lorries at several points, as a safe haven for smuggled good shipped back into the country from Afghanistan. The sordid affair that sees millions of arms and drug dollars change hands every month yields windfall profits for the local constabulary and bureaucrats, who turn a blind eye to the traffic. Even a casual labourer employed to keep a record of incoming goods can earn £2,000 a year, in a country with an average income of around

£300. Officials working hand-in-glove with the smugglers, by allowing the lorry convoys safe passage into Pakistan, can pocket up to £450 in a single day.

At Michni Post, a few miles beyond the bustling bazaar, a different genre of import is stacked against the fortress's courtyard wall, a grim reminder of the Khyber Rifles' ongoing role as a frontline defence force on Pakistan's vulnerable western border. Here the visitor finds rows of Russian shell casings, fired at Michni and other Khyber Rifles outposts when the Soviet Army was waging its hopeless war against the Afghan mujahedin. With blatant disregard for national boundaries, the Russian artillery batteries would regularly open fire on the guerrillas fleeing across the Khyber to their safe havens in Pakistan. The Soviets were not the only aggressors to consider the border region an open target. Within a month of the 11 September terrorist attack on the United States, with the Taliban scattered and driven into hiding, the victorious Northern Alliance troops kept the Khyber Rifles border guards on their toes. One November afternoon, Khyber Rifles troops had their lunch abruptly disrupted when a salvo of rockets fired from a distance of 500 yards slammed into two checkpoints near the Torkham border crossing. This was accompanied by a volley of several hundred rounds of automatic weapon fire from the surrounding hills. No one took responsibility for the attacks – no one had to, for as far as the Khyber Rifles are concerned, everyone to the west of Torkham is a potential enemy.

The Hindu Kush, or 'the point where the Hindu perishes', soars to more than 20,000 feet across the frozen wastes stretching north of Kabul. Given the inhospitable climate and terrain of this pre-Himalayan range, whose snow-bound passes are closed to travellers for many months of the year, ancient migrations of peoples, as well as invading armies, followed a southerly route into India. This took the caravans through an arid but negotiable land towards the Khyber Pass, that crucial breach in the hills cutting across the old Silk Route connecting South and Central Asia with Europe. The pass was once floridly described by *The Times* as 'that floodgate through which the overflow of swarming hordes or military monarchy has again and again poured down into Hindustan'. While the pass now serves as a major trade artery between the newly independent Central Asian republics and Pakistan, as a strategic outpost its military role stretches back more than 2,000 years in recorded history. The Persian ruler Cyrus is said to have marched an army through the pass in the sixth century BC, staging a raid on Gandhara, or modern-day Peshawar. Legend places the first passage through the Khyber Pass even further back in time, to the first Aryan caravans trundling their way eastward from Central Asia, some 4,000 to 6,000 years ago. There are no written records to substantiate these events, but in the case of Alexander the Great, it is a fact that in 327 BC the young Macedonian king crossed the Indus at Attock, the fortification that takes its name from *atak*, the north-west limit of empire that was established in the sixteenth century under the reign of Moghul Emperor Akbar. Alexander's invasion was spearheaded by a Macedonian army of 120,000 men deployed in two divisions, one under Alexander's own command, consisting of 30,000 picked, light-armed troops led by General Craterus, and the other, the main army, consisting of some 90,000 foot soldiers and cavalry under Generals Hephaestin and Perdiceas. The great advancing host spent months tramping across the bleakness of Afghanistan, then over the foothills of the mighty Safed Koh range, the men's gaze fixed rapaciously on the lush valleys of the Indus beyond the mountain barrier. Alexander may have taken to heart his readings of Herodotus when he took the decision to send Hephaestin and Perdicas through the Khyber Pass with the main body of the army, choosing himself to lead the smaller élite force across the more northerly Kunnar valley and Sapnaska Pass. The Greek historian testifies that in the Gandhara area west of the Indus, there dwelt a tribe known as the Apey Reti (the modern Afridis), and he warned all travellers of their ferocity and bravery in battle. Alexander may well have considered it necessary to send the larger, more heavily armed segment of his army to breach the Khyber Pass. After pacifying the Swat valley, whose surviving inhabitants fled in terror to a high rock retreat called Aornos, Alexander swung his column southward to link up with his two generals. He joined them after sixteen encampments, from where he began the crossing of the Indus and the invasion of India proper.

Alexander's sojourn in India was short-lived, resembling more a raiding party on a grand scale than an imperial invader bent on staking a permanent claim beyond his kingdom. He overran the Punjab after several hard-won battles, but here his men would go no farther. The Greeks had had enough of this alien and inhospitable land, and they longed to go home. Eschewing the arduous and perilous route back across the hills, Alexander led his men back to Macedonia through the desert regions of modern Baluchistan, southern Afghanistan and Persia.

Some chroniclers argue that Alexander's southern columns were the last of the ancient invaders to traverse the Khyber, at least until 1525 when Babur, at the head of a host of Persian and Turkistan soldiers of fortune, went rampaging across the pass to meet the Sultan of Delhi on the field of battle at Panipat. As the victorious Babur, now proclaimed Emperor of India, went about laying the foundations of his dynasty, the Khyber Pass gradually became more of a regular point of transit in the Moghul's own territory. Babur and his successors attached great strategic importance to control of the pass, but they were singularly unsuccessful in their attempts to hold it. Those of Babur's descendants who believed that forcing the pass was synonymous with subduing its inhabitants were soon to learn that this was untrue, often at a high cost. Never had the pass ran so deep with blood as in 1672 when the Pathan leader Aurangzeb waylaid the Amir of Kabul Mohammed Amin Khan, as he confidently led his army of 40,000 men, along with elephants and thousands of women and children through the Khyber. There were no survivors.

Those who followed in Alexander's wake, conquerors such as Mahmud of Ghazni and Akbar, as well as various Moghul forces, battled through the Khyber on their path of conquest to and from the Indus valley. The last recorded crossing of the pass by one of the great Central Asian invaders of India, before the arrival of the British, was that of Nadir Shah. In 1739 he captured and sacked Delhi and returned in triumph and majesty laden with loot equal to three years' imperial revenue. Strapped to the army's lead elephant festooned with silk and gold embroidered caparisons was one of history's most splendorous battle trophies, the Peacock Throne. Nadir Shah's homecoming took him once more through the Khyber Pass and across Afghanistan to Persia, where he was assassinated.

Once the formalities are disposed of, it is an easy drive on a tarmac road from Peshawar up to Fort Michni, the hilltop outpost overlooking the arid Afghan badlands three miles in the distance. Smartly turned-out sentries patrol Michni's crenellated perimeter, keeping an anxious vigil on the Torkham border crossing, a marksman's badge pinned to their khaki tunics trimmed with green velvet facings, ten inches from the edge of the cuff of the left sleeve, in accordance with the regulation dress code. In winter months the men's faces glisten from the ointment they use to protect themselves against the ferocious winds howling up the pass from the Afghan plains. At dusk, when darkness descends on the hills, the sentries gratefully hand over to the night watch and retire to a small mess hall for their evening meal, as an uneasy silence settles on the pass, and no man dares venture abroad unarmed. 'Every night at dusk the Pass is closed to all traffic, and those who look forward to seeing another day are careful to spend the night behind the walls of a fort or a caravanserai,' noted an early twentieth-century traveller in his diary.[8]

The Khyber Rifles have emblazoned on their regimental coat of arms the motto 'Guardians of the Khyber Pass' above crossed Afridi daggers superimposed on a replica of Fort Jamrud. Every element of the crest has its historical origin and can be explained in that context, except one – *Khyber*. No one can say for certain where the name comes from. As far as the Pushtun-speaking tribes that inhabit the region are concerned, it is a meaningless

name, much like the name *Buddha* means nothing to any Tibetan.
Scholars claim that *Khyber* is a word of ancient Hebrew origin
signifying 'fortification'. This has yet to be linguistically
substantiated, but some scholars point out that the Hebrew word
herev, meaning 'sword', is a noun derived form the verbal root
harav, 'to attack', and thus could have a kinship with the modern
word Khyber. A fort known as 'Khyber' lies some 40 miles west of
Medina in Saudi Arabia. It was used as a stronghold by warring
Israelite tribes in pre-Islamic days. The Khyber Pass itself is ringed
with hilltop army outposts, where until recently the Khyber Rifles
and the Taliban border guards kept an eye on one another across
the barbed wire checkpoint. Like all previous Afghan regimes, the
Taliban had never relinquished their claim to parts of North-West
Frontier territory. This is what confers on the Khyber its
credentials as a frontline outpost. The black-turbaned Muslim
fanatics no longer patrol the border, but it would be naïve to
assume that they represented the last threat the Khyber Rifles will
have to face on the Frontier.

The pass itself is full of legend, most of it a product of tribal
folktales. A mammoth boulder balances precariously on the hill
overlooking the mosque at Ali Masjid, which lies beside a
perennial stream of clear water. The Pathans believe that when
this spot was visited by the fourth caliph of Islam, Hazrat Ali, a
female pagan called Khyberai Bibi crept up on him while he was
at prayer. She hurled the boulder down from her perch above the
pass, but Hazrat Ali caught it in time and flung it back up,
slaying the demon. The huge rock lodged itself in the hillside,
where it sits today. There is a spot a few miles up the road called
the Haunted Picquet, where a small detachment of Khyber Rifles
on road patrol duty had constructed a *sangar* (stone breastwork),
in which they bedded down for the night. As they slept huddled
by the fire, a handful of Afridis crept up on the sangar planning
to cut the throats of its inhabitants and make off with the
soldiers' coveted rifles. When they broke cover and found no
sentry outside to raise the alarm, the tribesmen rushed the shelter
and discovered to their delight that all the men were lying in their

camp beds – stone cold dead. The soldiers had let their coke fire burn through the night and had gassed themselves.

Buddhism spread westwards through the pass to Afghanistan, where legend has it the Indian sage Padmasambava, or Guru Rinpoche as he is known to the Tibetans, was born in a lotus flower in a lake near Bamayan. The stone foundation of a vanished Buddhist stupa can be found on a low hillock near Ali Masjid, and another a little farther along the road at the village of Sultan Khel. The local tribesmen look upon these Buddhist relics as evil spots, haunted by spirits. They believe that whoever goes near these unbelievers' tombs at night will be found dead in the morning. This is a difficult superstition to disprove, since the only people to venture into the Khyber after dark are those most likely to be perpetrating murder. The Pathans also claim that the pass is inhabited by ghost caravans and other sorts of spirits, many of which are said to be four-footed creatures that rush about singly or in troops, breathing harshly and noisily. The Pathans believe that witches and wizards use these demons to carry out their acts of hatred.

If one seeks the ghosts of imperial Britain in the Indian subcontinent, their spectral cries can be heard most terrifyingly in the wind racing up the Khyber Pass, where over the decades tens of thousands of Indian Army troops and Pathans have perished on a battlefield that today still marks the barrier between tribal lawlessness and constituted order. The Khyber Pass and the native troops who stand guard over its approaches, have come to symbolise in the imagination of the West all that is dashing and romantic about the North-West Frontier. The visitors' book in the Khyber Rifles' mess at Landi Kotal reads like a *Who's Who* of the past hundred years. World statesmen, royalty, politicians and Hollywood celebrities, from Winston Churchill to Princess Anne, UN Secretary General Kofi Annan and film star Robert de Niro, have added their signatures to the cracked leather-bound book. They all came to savour one of the most glorious symbols of the

Great Game. Rudyard Kipling was another distinguished visitor who 'took a walk into the Khyber', and had the dubious honour of being shot at, although 'not in malice'.

For roughly 150 years to the time of Partition in 1947, British India's borders remained impregnable to attack by sea. As for land incursions, the subcontinent's eastern frontier was buffered by Burma, which proved itself an effective killing field for all comers, including the Japanese Imperial Army during the Second World War. To the north, the Himalaya stood as a formidable deterrent to invasion, taking into account the logistical nightmare of marching an army across this frozen mountain wasteland at any time of year, quite apart from keeping open supply lines and communications. Only to the west was the empire vulnerable, and it was Britain's misfortune that this territory was teeming with hostile tribesmen. The North-West Frontier was, in fact, the only corner of empire that the British never succeeded in pacifying.

The Khyber Pass began to loom large in the thoughts of British India in 1839, the year in which the army scored a crushing, definitive defeat on the Sikhs. With the annexation of the Punjab, the government found itself, at least on paper, lord and master of the wild North-West Frontier and the largely desolate, uncharted belt of tribal territory, 300 long and 100 miles across, that lies wedged between the administrative border and the Durand Line. Though he would never dare admit it, the vanquished Sikh ruler Ranjit Singh was probably delighted to see the British walk off with this troublesome corner of his empire, infested as it is with warlike and hostile Pathan tribes. In their push to expand India's borders, British administrators from Lord Auckland to Curzon came to view the Frontier as the vulnerable soft underbelly of the Raj. Their dilemma was how to devise a strategy for pacifying these lawless tribal lands.

There was no doubt in anyone's mind that whatever the sacrifices, the Khyber Pass was of vital strategic importance and needed to be garrisoned. In the late nineteenth century an idea began to take hold, inspired in part by the close call Major-

General Sir Samuel Browne's column had in the pass at the outbreak of the Second Afghan War, when the army almost met with disaster in skirmishes with Afghan regulars. Perhaps, army strategists suggested, it was not necessary to commit British troops to the Khyber Pass after all. Could not the job be done by trained and commissioned Afridi tribesmen who after all, loved nothing better than the chance to fire a rifle? The redoubtable Frontiersman Robert Warburton was the man destined to bring to fruition the government's new Frontier strategy. Hence the Khyber Rifles were brought into existence because the pass needed to be made secure for military operations in 1878, and thereafter as a safe buffer against Afghanistan and a trade route between Central Asia and India.

Warburton had great admiration for the Pathans as peerless warriors and trusted servants. This view placed him very much in the minority with British soldiers and officials, most of whom held the tribesmen in utter contempt. But Warburton, as a fluent Pushtu speaker and half-Afghan by birth, found himself at home among his wild kinsmen of the Khyber hills. He saw in the Afridis and the other Khyber tribes the potential to form an élite corps of Frontier guardians, men who knew every twist and turning of the mountainous terrain they would be called upon to patrol and guard, men who had a deep respect for the officer sahib's qualities of leadership. Warburton's gamble paid off. The fledgling Khyber Rifles, the first native levy to be raised on the Frontier, went under the microscope as a template for other corps of Frontier irregulars. Within a decade the Khyber Rifles were behaving 'splendidly' against rebellious tribesmen, in actions such as the Black Mountain campaigns, for which they were awarded decorations by the Viceroy himself. They also had no qualms about firing on their own kith and kin, just so long as they were given the opportunity to engage in their cherished pastime of fighting.

The fragility of this *entente cordiale* became apparent as soon as the lion tamer stepped foot outside the den. Once Warburton had departed the scene, it took only three months for the tribal warlords to rally their men for another strike at the British. The Pathan's loyalty stems from his respect for strong leadership, and Warburton's absence left a void which the Khyber Rifles, lacking the support of their revered Political Officer Sahib, struggled to fill. The Khyber Rifles were the only Frontier corps to volunteer for service outside their home territory. The British were happy to despatch them to any theatre of operations, for they knew these men could be trusted to deal with raiders and shoot down tribesmen found staging raids in the settled territories, cutting telegraph wires or damaging the roads. 'Much depends on the character of the British officers with whom the Pathan comes into contact,' says William Barton, who after serving as Commandant of the Khyber Rifles, stayed on in the Frontier government into the 1930s. 'He adores force and he will give a qualified loyalty in normal times to a British government that is prepared to show strength.' But the Pathan will not be intimidated, and in the late nineteenth century the tribes were told by their mullahs, through the machinations of the Amir of Kabul, that the feringhees were plotting to seize their tribal homelands. With that, the Frontier went up in flames.

Heartbroken, Warburton was recalled to the Khyber to deal with the conflict. He was 55 years old, a remarkable achievement in itself taking into account the harsh conditions of the Frontier, as well as his many years of devotion to this insalubrious territory, which rewarded him with chronic dysentery. The rebellious Afridis were punished and an uneasy peace was restored to the Frontier. But Warburton tells of how he was dumbfounded by what he termed 'this hideous disaster', coming after so many years of faithful guardianship. 'It makes me quite sad to think how easily the labour of years – of a lifetime – can be ruined and destroyed in a few days,' he wrote in a letter to a friend, shortly before his death. Taking into account the British Army's failure to come to the rescue of the besieged Khyber garrisons during the Pathan uprising, it came as no surprise that when the tribes once again took up arms *en masse* in 1919, many of the Khyber Rifles recruits melted away before their onslaught. This stands as the one ugly blemish on an otherwise spotless military record. Twenty-five years were to pass before the corps was resuscitated under its original guise. By that time, Warburton had been many years in his grave.

Sir Olaf Caröe, the last British Governor of the North-West Frontier Province before the handover to Pakistan, recounts that around the time the Khyber Rifles were raised in 1878, the government was in a state of panic over Russia's 1,000-mile push eastward across Central Asia. Something had to be done to secure India's border with Afghanistan, and for starters the obvious stop-gap measure was to send in more troops. But it was also necessary to ensure the loyalty of the Pathan tribes, whose sympathies lay more with Kabul than with the British. 'A scheme was propounded by [Viceroy] Lytton with a view to giving the central government a more direct control over Frontier administration and policy, and improving the relations of the districts with their trans-border neighbours,' he writes.[9]

The much-feared Russian menace kept the Khyber on a state of high alert from the day it passed into British hands in 1879 to the departure of the Raj nearly seventy years later. 'Russia...was causing trouble around the world and there was always the threat of Russian expansion through Afghanistan and the Khyber Pass to the Indian Ocean.' This account comes from Francis Ingall, the dashing brigadier of the Bengal Lancers who served on the Frontier in the 1930s, and who later went on to carve out a successful stage and film career in America. 'Therefore, in my day the bulk of the Army, both British and Indian, was in the north, though other units were stationed all over India.'[10] Troops garrisoned in the Khyber region lived in a state of permanent readiness. Ingall compares conditions on the Frontier with those the US cavalry had to contend with before the subjugation of the American Indian tribes. Indeed, during the First World War, keeping the peace on the North-West Frontier tied down four British Army divisions that were sorely needed elsewhere.

Extending government control to the tribal territories, as well as another more ambitious scheme to extend the North-West Frontier boundaries from Peshawar to the sea, were summarily shelved when Britain launched its second invasion of Afghanistan. If the Pathan tribes acknowledged no more than a cursory allegiance to Kabul, their loyalty to the Government of India was nil. After twenty years' soldiering on the North-West Frontier, George B. Scott came to the conclusion that the tribes occupying this tract of country 'had never given more than shadowy allegiance to the amirs (of Afghanistan) at any time, had raided their neighbours on both sides and caused much friction with the Indian government.'[11] Curzon quickly realised that that not even imperial Britain would ever be able to establish effective control over the more than two million inhabitants of the tribal territories. He therefore designated the region a march-land, a buffer state between the official Durand Line border with Afghanistan and India proper. The effect of this decision was to exacerbate the inherent flaw written into the original boundary treaty, which had left the tribes sitting outside the jurisdiction of both countries. 'Though perhaps in the circumstances the best line possible,' remarked a British administrative official of the day, Sir William Fraser-Tytler, 'the Durand Line has few advantages and many defects. It is illogical from the point of view of ethnography, of strategy and of geography.'[12]

The cavalier manner in which Britain went about fixing the boundary between its newly acquired northern territories and neighbouring Afghanistan, was one of the catalysts that brought the Khyber Rifles into being, as a template for eventually raising half a dozen other corps of native irregulars up and down the Frontier. For the Frontier, a relatively tiny tract of land in the vastness of the empire, was nevertheless Britain's 'imperial migraine'. The history of the British Empire, unlike that of most European states, has little to do with frontiers. The pervasive operation of British sea power from the sixteenth century onwards, and the good relations between Canada and the United States established after Sir Robert Peel settled outstanding border troubles in 1842 and 1846, left British territory, from a diplomatic standpoint, without land borders save at one point, India's North-West Frontier.

That the Government of India took such pains to seek a formal settlement of the border question – having flattened the Sikh armies and sent their Afghan allies packing – was a reflection of Whitehall's deep-rooted fear of the threat lurking in the uncharted territories beyond Afghanistan. From the first half of the nineteenth century, the commencement of the first Great Game period, Russia's relentless push through Central Asia right up to Afghanistan's northern frontier, where Cossack cavalry were observed patrolling the banks of the Oxus, had filled the Government of India with a cold dread. In 1878 a report was received in Calcutta that caused little amusement at Army GHQ. Russia's Imperial Chancellor, Prince Aleksandr Gorchakov, had just pointed a loaded pistol at the heart of the British Empire. With astonishing audacity, the Russian nobleman made clear his threat in a policy manifesto published in the *Journal de St Petersbourg*. Russia, too, had borders to protect and the motherland's security could only be guaranteed by gobbling up the lawless khanites of Central Asia. True to his word, within five years Tashkent and Samarkand had fallen to the tsar's imperial forces. Now the Russian bear hungrily poked its snout across the banks of the Oxus.

Finally, in 1893, the Viceroy despatched a mission to Kabul to 'negotiate' with Amir Abdur Rahman Khan the demarcation of his country's border with India. A few contemporary observers were quick to point out that the presence of a surveyor or a topographer in the British negotiating team, led by Sir Mortimer Durand, might have helped to avoid some of the bloody conflicts that were to plague the Frontier forces for decades to come, indeed right up to Britain's departure from newly independent Pakistan half a century later. As they sipped green tea in Kabul's royal citadel, the Bala Hissar, the amir warned his guests of the dire consequences in store for the British if they included the Khyber tribes inside Indian territory. 'If you should cut them (the border tribes) out of my dominions . . . you will always be engaged in fighting or other trouble with them, and they will always go on plundering,' the potentate warned. But the government was in no mood to compromise with the Afghans, who after all had allied themselves with the Sikh armies in the Punjab war. Thus the amir was obliged to affix his stone seal to a treaty that for the first time defined the spheres of influence of both powers across a land stretching from the snow-capped Hindu Kush to the desert wastes of Baluchistan. Colonel Sir Thomas Holdich, the officer in charge of the survey, stood alone in raising his voice in protest, when he warned that setting the boundary behind the tribes effectively handed them a sanctuary on a platter. With the border slicing through the tribal lands, marauders were free to attack the British settlements at will and gallop back to their Afghan asylum laden with arms and booty. But empires abhor a vacuum and British India was no exception. Ignoring the spoil-sport Holdich, the British team was soon at work pounding boundary markers into the greyish hills north and south of the Khyber Pass.

'In 1893 for the first time it became possible to think of, and refer to, a tribal belt under British control between Afghanistan and the administered border of India, a belt of which the limits were defined on both sides, east and west, and well known to all concerned,' wrote Caröe, whose job it was to keep the peace on the North-West Frontier until the handover to Pakistan. 'There was no longer a no-man's-land of uncertain extent, and both authorities could now think and act with greater precision.' Caröe stresses the crucial point that Britain's territorial ambitions, at least officially, never extended beyond the Frontier. 'It is true that the agreement did not describe the line as the boundary of India, but as the frontier of the Amir's dominions and the line beyond which neither side would exercise interference. This was because the British government did not intend to absorb the tribes into their administrative system, only to extend their own, and exclude the Amir's authority in the territory east and south of the line.'[13]

The government had erected a legitimate goal post on the unprotected borderland along its North-West Frontier. One of the ironies of Durand's efforts, however, was that the British terror of tsarist invasion touched off two Afghan campaigns that cost more than 20,000 British and Indian lives, without the Russians having fired a shot.

Alas, Holdich's dire predictions were borne out within months of signing the demarcation treaty. Bedlam suddenly erupted along the Frontier, as hordes of enraged tribesmen came charging over the hills to lay siege to the garrison of Chitral to the north of the Khyber. The fort came under fierce attack even as the demarcation commission was erecting its boundary pillars. In an outburst of bravado before two British officers being held hostage by the attackers, the Pathan tribal chieftain Umra Khan made clear what he had in store for the feringhees who would fashion themselves rulers of the Frontier. 'I have just received a letter from the commander-in-chief of the Afghan army,' he boasted. 'His proposal is that I shall invade the Peshawar valley by way of the Malakand with 30,000 men and that he will co-operate through the Khyber Pass with 10,000 more.' Amir Abdur Rahman Khan must have been sniggering up his sleeve.

Far from pacifying the tribes through force of arms, the Khyber Pass remained a gauntlet that even today must be negotiated at the traveller's peril and under his sole responsibility. In 1875 the new Viceroy, Lord Lytton, remarked that the only semblance of safety through the Khyber lay in not straying from the road into tribal territory. William Barton noted that the presence of armed men on peaks overlooking the Khyber road was 'eloquent testimony of the dangers that threaten human life in these dark ravines'. On his journey up the pass, Barton was impressed by the stark landscape only 10 miles outside the manicured lawns of Peshawar, where 'the desert is divided from the sown, and emerald green gives way to drab monotony'. The perfect setting, Barton envisaged, for blood feuds and tribal enmities, the exchange of rifle shots between rival homesteads. If the traveller is 'fortunate', he might be able to observe 'a miniature battle in progress, as one drives along, protected by the immutable law that there must be no firing over the road, for the British road is sacrosanct'. Barton discovered to his dismay that the volume of crime had spiralled to an appalling level on the Frontier. While in 1902 the number of serious crimes such as murder and 'grievous bodily harm against British and Indians' stood at 709, by 1929 it had almost trebled to 2,045. At the end of his inspection tour, Barton felt compelled to report back to Delhi that, 'With its population of two and a quarter millions, only this tale of crime stamps the Frontier province as the most lawless country on the face of the earth.' In any event, from gun battles to roaring convoys of contraband-carrying lorries, life on the Khyber comes to standstill in the hours of darkness. 'Traffic in the Khyber Pass closes at sunset when the picquets are withdrawn,' Barton observed. 'After dusk the authorities no longer guarantee the safety of the traveller.' (Nothing has changed in that respect, since today the Political Agent's permit for travel in the Khyber ominously states, 'The foreigner shall not travel before sunrise and after sunset.'[14])

As recent as 1983, when the travel writer Geoffrey Moorhouse was about to embark on his journey from Fort Jamrud through the pass, the local *tahsildar* (district official) saw him off with this sobering word of advice: 'Enjoy the trip, but if he (the *khassadar* escort) tells you to take cover, please do take cover.' Anyone on a visit to the Khyber Rifles will note, with mixed feelings of reassurance and apprehension, that when stopping en route for snapshots or a look around the bazaars, the mandatory khassadar in black shalwar kameez is never more than a few paces away, his Kalashnikovs cocked and at the ready.

Ian Hay observed on his travels in the North-West Frontier Province in 1930, during the period the Khyber Rifles were disbanded, that these provisional guardians of the pass, had they not been raised as irregular armed constabulary, would have been 'irregular armed bandits'. 'The British Government,' he remarked, 'with its usual uncanny instinct for turning poachers into gamekeepers, has diverted them into the paths of usefulness by giving them a regular job, of which they are inordinately proud, and the rudiments of discipline. They are only employed by day, or the Khyber Pass closes, like Kensington Gardens, at dusk.' Hay further noted on his tour of the tribal lands, 'The first thing the British Government does when trouble breaks out on the North-West Frontier is to close the Khyber Pass – much as a prudent householder turns off the gas at the meter on the first alarm of fire.'[15]

Apart from trading rifle fire with Pathans and the constant threat of hostilities with Afghanistan, or the ultimate horror of Russian invasion, those who served in the Khyber could be assured of two things. First, as soldiers, at some point in their career they would be called upon to test their mettle against the tribal warriors. Secondly, the longer they stayed on, the slimmer their chances of having 'Died Peacefully' inscribed on their tombstone. In fact, there are no such entries at all for British servants of the Raj in the burial registers of Peshawar from 1856 onward, when the causes of death began to be listed. The odd musket ball from a tribesman's jezail was almost a rare occurrence by comparison, and for some it might have come as a welcome and swift escape from the sort of tortures a Frontiersman was obliged to endure, ranging from rabid dogs and 120°F plus heat to poisonous water and clouds of ravenous mosquitoes.

The list of killer diseases that plagued the Khyber reads with almost medieval grotesqueness and in terms that suggest a grisly existence for the servicemen and their families: 'abscess of brain', 'acute dilation of the heart', 'hysterical mania' and 'sarcoma of testis' to name a few of the ghastly afflictions. And this quite apart from the violent deaths brought on by 'effects of a hornet's sting', 'murder by Kuttack Afridis in Palm Tree Hill, only a few bones recovered', 'scald (sic)' and 'accidental poisoning, prussic acid being administered by mistake'. In the three weeks from 16 September to 5 October 1869, forty-seven Britons died on the Frontier, every one of them of cholera, while in the summer of 1920 every recorded death was caused by heatstroke. In this hellish environment it is hardly surprising to find the cemetery's tombstones liberally sprinkled with inscriptions such as 'asphyxia from hanging – temporary insanity' and 'delirium tremens assisted by an attempt at suicide'.[16] Small wonder that Indian Army officers serving on the North-West Frontier were given three months' 'privilege leave' on full pay every year, compared with two months for soldiers stationed elsewhere in the subcontinent.

British officialdom adopted a predictably pragmatic approach to the hardships of life in the Khyber, when after the defeat of the Afghans in 1879 they managed to wrest political sovereignty over the pass from the amir. The first step was to construct a proper road from Peshawar to the line of demarcation with Afghanistan, fortify it and lay down the Pax Britannica, made more achievable by the distribution of those monthly bribes to the Khyber tribes. Next came the rule of law, which in essence stated: 'You can blow one another to pieces in settling your blood feuds, but let no man dare to fire across the road, for the highway is British territory, and is therefore sacrosanct'.

The Pathans could be relied upon to comply with this prohibition, at least most of the time. In fact, their enthusiasm for British law could rise to levels of macabre irony, as was the case in 1921 when Latif Khan of the Zakha Khel clan led his men in a revenge attack on a village in the Ali Masjid gorge, a place inhabited by a fellow tribesman, Sultan Khan, with whom Latif Khan had a blood feud. Piling into a caravan of taxis hired in Peshawar, and armed with sticks of dynamite and fuses stolen from the railway magazine, Latif Khan and his kinsmen sped through the night towards the unsuspecting village, the powers of darkness sliding the Khyber ridges to and fro to let murder pass. The devastating dynamite attack set the houses alight, and all Latif Khan's men needed to do was to bide their time outside the village gate to gun down every man, woman and child that ran screaming from the inferno. The following morning, with the charred remains of the village still smouldering, Latif Khan turned up at the Political Agent's office in Peshawar to ask forgiveness. For, as the burly tribesman contritely admitted, in the confusion of the previous night's massacre some of his men had inadvertently fired across the road, a misdemeanour for which he was prepared to pay a fine.

Crocker was impressed to find on his wanderings through the Khyber that as late as 1931, this decree proclaiming the sanctity of the open road still commanded the Afridis' respect.

It has been explained to us that the road itself only is British, but nowhere else, and that we cannot move a yard off the road without the escort of a *khassadar*. In Tribal Territory the inhabitants are free to shoot each other up as much as they please without interference from us, but woe betide anyone who fires across the roads or railway. Our Political Agents insist on the Peace of the Road being strictly preserved, and every man who offends in this respect is fined 2,000 rupees. Our *khassadar* told us with great gusto of a man who was run in for firing across the road at a certain spot. He said it was the wrong place, and volunteered to show the Political Agent where he had fired. On examination it was discovered that he had not only fired across the camel road but the motor road as well, and the railway in addition. That one shot cost him 6,000 rupees, a pretty useful morning's work.[17]

In due course there came that great civilising force of empire, the railway. The idea of laying a railway line through the Khyber Pass, one of history's great romantic engineering projects, had put out shoots as early as 1842 when Captain Sir Guildford Molesworth, a veteran of the First Afghan War, looked at the possibility of running a narrow-gauge line from Peshawar to the Afghan border. The project was shelved for lack of a bridge over the Indus river crossing at Attock, that would enable the line to be brought up from Rawalpindi. Another survey was carried out in 1890 when the railway line had reached Peshawar, and a decade later the smoke-belching coal burners stood poised at Jamrud for their assault on the pass. In 1905 Major George Roos-Keppel, Commandant of the Khyber Rifles, was asked to prepare 'a scheme for the guarding of the Kabul River Railway'. Roos-Keppel submitted his report in a tone of characteristic military precision. 'At present the Khyber Rifles (strength 1,250 rifles) guards the Khyber Pass road from Jamrud to Torkham, a distance of 25 miles,' he quipped. 'This works out at 50 miles per rifle. The length of the line of the Kabul River Railway from the point where it will leave British territory, near Warsak, to its probable terminus somewhere in the neighbouring state of Smatzai is, by either alignment, 35 miles.'[18] Roos-Keppel was fully aware of the fact that running a railway line through tribal territory, particularly that of the hostile Zakha Khel clan, was hardly going to encourage the tribesmen to put out bunting.

A separate Levy Corps to guard this line would require to be very strong, as it would necessarily be self-contained and would provide its own supports in case of emergency. On the scale of rifles per mile sanctioned for the Khyber the strength of the new corps would be roughly 1,750 rifles. This might be reduced to some extent but not very largely, as the line of the railway is very exposed to attack, especially from the north. A separate corps would require to be about 1,100 or 1,200 strong.

But there was an alternative to raising this separate corps, a more logical scheme that at the same time would enhance the commandant's prestige at GHQ. 'If, however, we take advantage of the existing Khyber Rifles and enlarge this corps to hold the Kabul river line in addition to the Khyber Pass,' he put forward with impeccable reason, 'concentrating the re-organised corps at Landi Kotal, where it is possible to promptly support either line, we can effect large economies both in cost of administration and in personnel, and the result will be in every way more satisfactory.'

The Khyber Rifles at that time was organised in two battalions of six companies each and one troop of *sowars* (cavalry troops), led by six British officers. Roos-Keppel proposed an increase in his force of six to fifteen companies of infantry and 100 to 200 sowars, depending on the route chosen for the railway. The least complicated way to make this addition was, at first sight, to raise a third battalion of six to nine companies on the model of the existing two battalions. Roos-Keppel declared himself contrary to this solution which, he explained to the Governor-General of the North-West Frontier Province who he knew was bent on holding the line on costs, would result in the appointment of 'three independent adjutants and quartermasters establishments, three sets of workshops, three hospitals and three lots of recruits being trained simultaneously'. He reminded his superiors that the construction of the railway was unpopular and the line would be open to attack by the Mohmands from the north, the Afghans from the west and the Afridis from the south. The best and simplest organisation, he reasoned, complete with economy of administration, would be a compromise of three wings of six or seven companies each, with a corps staff that would perform the duties of the adjutants' and quartermasters' departments for the three wings. Roos-Keppel presented a cost analysis for reorganising the Khyber Rifles, amounting to an annual increase in expenditure of 85,000 rupees. The commandant went into great detail, shedding some light in passing on the extent to which the British valued the services of their native officers. A British commandant of the Khyber Rifles, including his expatriate allowances, was paid 1,317 rupees and 23 anna per month. The pay package for a native commandant came to 300 rupees per month. Alas, Roos-Keppel's plan never saw the light of day, for the Frontier was once again starting to smoulder. The Zakha Khel clan began raiding across the border from the Bazar valley, and the lashkars even staged a daring raid on Peshawar itself. This uprising south of the Khyber Pass brought a renewal of attacks from the Mohmands to the north. The unrest simmered up and down the Frontier, culminating, in 1919, with an official declaration of war against Afghanistan, leaving nearly ten turbulent years to pass before the Khyber Railway became a reality.

On a crisp winter's morning in 1920, an eccentric individual pitched up at the Political Agent's office in Peshawar to discuss the disposition of the Khyber tribes towards the idea of running a railway through their jealously coveted territory. Victor Bayley, for whom life in the trenches during the First World War had 'destroyed any romantic notions about being shot at', was not encouraged on his first visit to the Frontier, when in his hotel room he contemplated two notices, one of which read, 'In case of burglary ring up No. 743'. The other, 'In case of raid ring up No. 492'.

Bayley was a railway engineer, who had been sent to Peshawar to build a rail line through the Khyber Pass. 'I had built railways elsewhere, but never had I encountered anything like this,' he reminisces:

The line curved to and fro and at one place actually crossed above itself in its serpentine progress. After Shahgai the steepness of the gradient eased off a bit and there was a stretch of level. Thereafter it rose steadily to the summit of Landi Kotal, where I was to go and live. From Landi Kotal the line dropped sharply through a series of tunnels, and once more effected a great zigzag to Landi Khana at the frontier of Afghanistan.[19]

The line that was eventually completed required thirty-four tunnels in 30 miles, and their aggregate length was only 3 miles. They were all nearly on sharp curves and on steep gradients, so that they were really spirals. It was a truly remarkable piece of engineering for its day.

In spite of the obstacles, the Indian Government was dead set on realising this long overdue project of extending the Indian railway system to the most remotest gates of British territory. Never again would the army have to suffer the humiliating inability to mobilise troops quickly in the face of invasion by Afghan forces, as had been the case in 1919 when war broke out with Afghanistan.

Sir Francis Humphrys, Political Officer of the Khyber Agency, informed his guest that the whole of his proposed railway lay in a no man's land, where there existed no law and order other than tribal custom. 'He explained,' Bayley recalls, 'that there was a belt of tribal territory between Afghanistan and the North-West Frontier Province of India. This is not part of the British Empire, but lies wholly outside it, while the whole of the Khyber Pass lies in tribal territory.'

Bayley decided that it was now time for him to meet these dreaded Afridis, and enquire face to face just why they were so staunchly opposed to the construction of a railway through the Khyber Pass. In particular, he sought an audience with Sher Ali Khan, 'a stout old ruffian of the formidable Zakha Khel clan', who steadfastly refused to hear anything about the British project. Bayley found himself one afternoon sitting cross-legged on a charpoy in Sher Ali's home, surrounded by a roomful of grizzled tribesmen armed to the teeth, while he explained to the old malik through an interpreter that he was the engineer who had come to the Khyber to build a railway through it 'as ordered by the Sirkar'.

'What folly is this?' the old chieftain growled. 'A railway through *our* lands!' At this point, the tribesmen all sprang up, brandishing rifles and shouting that a railway was forbidden. 'Things didn't look at all nice,' Bayley recalls. The engineer attempted in vain to persuade his host of the advantages the railway would bring to their territory: cheapening of foodstuffs, ease of communication, and other strides forward into the modern era. It all fell on deaf ears. Then some imp of mischief took hold, Bayley writes. With a slow smile, he explained that the gradient would be steep and the train would travel slowly, passing close to the malik's doors. There were, he grinned, rich opportunities for looting the trains. When this was translated into Pushtu, the tribesmen broke into a roar of laughter, with shouts all round of 'Yes! Build the railway and loot the trains!' Presently refreshments appeared, cakes, hard-boiled eggs, fruit and tea. Bayley was beginning to make some headway.

Well might the Brigadier Khyber District marvel at the perseverance with which the Afridi railway construction workers went about patching up traces of storm damage on the line, when three years later he paid a visit to the Khyber Pass in the company of chief engineer Victor Bayley. 'I can't work out how you got these ruffians to work on the line,' the Brigadier remarked in wonder. 'Only three years ago the mere mention of a railway brought the tribesmen out like a swarm of angry bees. Nowadays that's all changed, and an Afridi I was talking to the other day actually spoke of *our railway*. They positively take a pride in it.' Their railway indeed, Bayley might have replied, had he at the time been inspired by the same imp of mischief that whispered into his ear during his meeting with Sher Ali.

The railway line inched its way up the Khyber Pass towards the Afghan border at an agonising quarter mile per day, a fraction of the pace it would have taken to lay the track on flat prairie land. The work was held to a snail's pace by almost every conceivable obstacle that Nature and Man could conspire to throw at Bayley and his Afridi labourers. Work in the tunnels was made more treacherous by large hidden volumes of water, which without warning would convert the shale into slippery mud. The drills suddenly sank without resistance into sodden wet mush, opening the floodgates to a gushing wall of slime. Nevertheless, work progressed throughout the night to keep the project on schedule. Given the dangers lurking in the pass after sunset, Bayley and his staff never dared to venture out at night, leaving the tribesmen excavators to work unsupervised in the tunnels under an incessant rain of mud and water, often within a few inches of timbers groaning with the pressure of the disturbed mountain squeezing in upon them. 'And all the while there was the haunting fear of attack on our works by raiders out for loot, or by an enemy at blood feud with the contractor,' Bayley says. He found that his jest advising the tribesmen to build the railway and then loot the trains had been taken to heart, and this well before the last sleeper was bolted into place. The sleepers were in fact much valued by the Pathans for building their villages, as was to be expected in a timberless land like the Khyber. Bags of Portland cement were also highly prized, and any portable object made of steel or iron was considered fair game. By this time Bayley had been seduced by the

Khyber. He recalls the danger that was present everywhere, from flood above ground to the unpredictable tribesmen. 'And yet I loved it all, and could not leave it,' he says. 'The cruel fascination of the Frontier had caught me. No money could have tempted me to go, and a fierce determination to defy all the forces in opposition drove me on.' The railway that was to render British India impregnable from land attack resembled not so much a transport system as a line of fortification. The station buildings were in fact built as mini-fortresses. This is indicated by one of the instructions on an architect's drawing of the time: 'Combined Booking Office Window and Machine Gun Loophole'. Then came the day in November 1925, five years after the first spike was hammered in at Jamrud, that the Khyber Railway locomotive came puffing up to the top of the pass to Landi Kotal where the last fish-bolts were inserted and the nuts screwed home.

The opening ceremony was to take place six months later, when the line would be completed to the Afghan border, a project costing in total 21 million rupees. Bayley learnt to his delight that the Viceroy, the gaunt, quixotic figure of Lord Erwin, was to preside over the event. Then came the news that the Viceroy would be unable to attend the opening, as his wife was very ill. Bayley took the news in his stride, his thoughts fixed on the remaining line to be laid to the Afghan border. Shortly after the official opening, the strain of more than five years of ceaseless toil on the Frontier caught up with Bayley. He was invalided back to England, but the North-West Frontier had worked its magic on Bayley, who in later years was inspired to produce two schmaltzy novels based on his adventures as the intrepid Khyber Railway chief engineer, *Carfax of the Khyber* and *Khyber Contraband*.

The Khyber Railway line was extended to Landi Khana in April 1926, 2 miles short of the Durand Line. This section of the line was closed in 1932, and all public services ceased in the 1980s at the time of the Soviet invasion of Afghanistan. Today the railway operates sporadically as a tourist attraction, depending on the temperature of the political climate. Two 1920s steam engines push-pull the coaches through thirty-four tunnels and across ninety-two bridges and culverts, a climb of nearly 4,000 feet up to Landi Kotal, where visitors are entertained by sword dancers on the lawn at Khyber Rifles headquarters. Passengers on the three luxury coaches would have to strain their imagination to catch the echoes of Afridi workers drilling at night in the tunnel walls, or the tribesmen's brethren stealthily creeping up to the goods wagons, or chief engineer Victor Bayley enthusing over his intrepid scheme with a gin and tonic at the Peshawar Club.

The Khyber Pass was and presumably always will be a no man's land. It is not only the tribesmen's hostility to outsiders that makes this a dangerous place. The many Pathan clans that inhabit the territory are careful not to tread on one another's domain. Blood feuds between rival clans and even families within the same tribe are as commonplace today as in centuries past.

The country today called Afghanistan was in the nineteenth century, and to a considerable extent remains a patchwork of tribal fiefdoms, bearing only the loosest semblance of national cohesion, despite sharing thousands of miles of border with fearsome neighbours like the Tajiks and Uzbeks. The Government of Pakistan retains nominal sovereignty over the tribal lands bordering the Khyber Pass, but like the British before them, Islamabad's jurisdiction barely extends a few yards on either side of the road. There is evidence that imposing the rule of law on the Pathans, if such a task was ever seriously envisaged by any government, is becoming an ever more difficult business. The triumph of the Taliban in the mid-1990s came close to eliminating the North-West Frontier's former identity. The hundreds of thousands of Afghan refugees who poured across the Khyber Pass brought about a tendency for the tribes to set up small autonomous emirates on Pakistani soil. In short, there exists a clear risk of the border slipping back to its blurred origins, as when the British first set foot in the region and encountered a hotchpotch of migratory hill tribes taking orders from no one, much less from an Englishwoman seated on a throne 4,000 miles away.

CHAPTER THREE

'These misguided, ignorant yet plucky barbarians'

Was it a secret British love affair with the untamed and unconquerable tribesmen of the Khyber hills, or, more prosaically, the grinding, colossal bureaucracy of empire keeping its files updated, that accounted for the outpouring of those millions of documents that were produced during the occupation of the North-West Frontier? In all probability there was nothing glamorous about it at all, merely an army of government functionaries determined to leave no stone unturned in their meticulous organisation of empire. This was the sort of zeal that in 1910 produced for the General Staff Army Headquarters an official dictionary of the Pathan tribes of the Frontier. Some seventy years after the Raj first came violently up against the Pathans, in the days of the First Afghan War, the boffins of the Indian Civil Service brought out what must still stand as the definitive ethnic cataloguing of the North-West Frontier tribes. The volume that emerged from Superintendent Government Printing nearly one hundred years ago could have flowed from the pen of a Kafka, in what amounts to a labyrinthine, inverted pyramid of social hierarchy. The Pathans, we are told, organise their society from the tribe, to the clan of the tribe, to the division of the clan, to the sub-division of the division, to the section of the sub-division, all the way down to other minor fractions of the section. 'Thus, (standing the pyramid upright) the Dado Khel are a minor fraction of the Dreplara section, of the Khugrogi sub-division, of the Nasrudding division, of the Zakha Khel clan, of the Afridi tribe.' This must truly stand as a courageous effort by the British to document what Kipling called 'the ravel of the inter-tribal complications across the Border'.

Fascination with the Pathan tribes there was, but in the eyes of most British administrators this did not equate to a very high esteem of the tribesmen as a breed. On the contrary, the Pathans were generally dismissed as contemptible barbarians. 'Now these tribes are savages, noble savages perhaps, and not without some tincture of virtue and generosity, but still absolutely barbarians nevertheless,' opines the Secretary to the Chief Commissioner of the Punjab in a memorandum to his boss in 1855.

They have nothing approaching to government or civil institutions. They have, for the most part, no education. They have nominally a religion, but Mahomedanism, as understood by them, is no better, or perhaps is actually worse than the creeds of the wildest race on earth. In their eyes the one great commandment is blood for blood, and fire and sword for all infidels, that is, for all people not Mahomedans.[1]

The official Record of Expeditions against the Pathans tribes displays the battle scars of military leaders unaccustomed to the savagery of Frontier warfare. '(The Pathan) is bloodthirsty, cruel and vindictive in the highest degree,' the report states:

He does not know what truth or faith is, inasmuch that the saying *Afghan be iman* [the Pathan is supreme] has passed into a proverb among his neighbours. And though he is not without a courage of a sort, and is often reckless of his life, he would scorn to face an enemy whom he could stab from behind, or meet him on equal terms if it were possible to take advantage of him, however meanly.[2]

Half a century and numerous punitive expeditions later, British sentiment had, if anything, hardened against their tribal neighbours. 'Of the moral attributes of the Afridis (the Khyber tribe) it is quite impossible to say anything in praise,' concludes an official government report.

> Ruthless, cowardly robbery and cold-blooded, treacherous murder are to an Afridi the salt of life. Brought up from his earliest childhood amid scenes of appalling treachery and merciless revenge, nothing can ever change him: as he has lived – a shameless, cruel savage – so he dies. And it would seem that, notwithstanding their long intercourse with the British, and that very large numbers of them are, or have been, in our service, and must have learned in some poor way what faith and mercy, and justice are, yet the Afridi's character today is no better than it was in the days of his father.[3]

This breathtaking appraisal is, unsurprisingly, founded on imperious ignorance liberally seasoned with hypocrisy. For when the chips were down, the British had no misgivings about turning to the tribes for help. The raising of the Khyber Rifles for the purpose of safeguarding the pass on the eve of war with Afghanistan stands as a classic example. Who but the Pathans, that race of 'savages' and 'barbarians', men who knew every inch of their tribal homeland like the backs of their hands, could be trusted to defend British interests against the hostility of their own people? Yet the prevailing opinion of the tribesmen, from the officers' mess to official historical records, was almost always one of consummate scorn. It comes as no surprise that Winston Churchill held some rather strong views of his own on the Pathans. The young officer of the 4th Hussars, who by the time he was 25 had taken part in three campaigns on the North-West Frontier, refers to the inhabitants of the tribal territories as 'that pestilential race'. Churchill pulled no punches in branding the Pathans a people who ranked 'amongst the most miserable and brutal creatures on earth'. But when not regaling his newspaper readers at home with such grandiloquent outbursts, Churchill was capable of articulating more dispassionate and edifying sentiments about his adversaries, and his observations of Pathan life were not far off the mark.

Amid these scenes of savage brilliancy (on the Frontier) there dwells a race whose qualities seem to harmonise with their environment. Except at harvest time, when self-preservation enjoins a temporary truce, the Pathan tribes are always engaged in a private or public war. Every man is a warrior, a politician and a theologian. Every large house is a real feudal fortress made, it is true, only of sun-baked clay, but with battlements, turrets, loopholes, flanking towers, drawbridges, etc., complete. Every village has its defence. Every family cultivates its vendetta, every clan its feud. The numerous tribes and combinations of tribes all have their accounts to settle with one another. Nothing is ever forgotten, and very few debts are left unpaid.[4]

There are reasons why blood feuds have since time immemorial been a basic part of Pathan life. One of these is the bellicose character of the tribesmen. They have been described as 'possibly the most ferocious, independent, and warlike race ever known' and hyperbole apart, the assertion contains a good deal of truth. One could hardly imagine a Swedish or a Dutch solicitor practising in London, upping sticks to return home to settle a blood feud simply because he was the last living member of his line. Yet this is precisely what a Pathan lawyer, highly regarded in his profession, did in the 1970s. The Pakistani cricketer Imran Khan, who is of a distinguished Pathan family, tells the story of a case in the Tirah in the 1870s, when the tail of a horse belonging to an Afridi tribesman's guest was cut off as a joke by the tribesman's cousins. So furious was the Afridi at this insult to his guest that he shot dead both cousins. That touched off a blood feud which a century later had claimed more than a hundred lives. 'The Pathan tribes love nothing better than a good gun battle,' recalls a British officer who served in the Khyber Rifles before Partition. 'The Pashtu word for patrol is *gasht*, and when the Pathan recruits heard that magic word they raced like the devil for their rifles, and we were off. This was their overriding passion, to shoot at somebody.' The patrols normally marched about the unsettled tribal districts, one or two companies of men travelling quickly 20 or 30 miles out from their fort. Sometimes the patrols would run into a bit of sniping, in which case they would happily return the fire, but the principal *raison d'être* of *gashting*, at least as far as the British were concerned, was to go out and show the flag among the tribes.

Patrolling with native troops was highly popular with officers as well. Gashting was one of the earliest professional activities to draw a travel allowance. Officers of the Khyber Rifles and other Scouts units, who were usually seconded from their regular Indian Army regiment, were paid eight anna per mile while out on gasht, hence the incentive to ride out as far as practicable from the garrison. In later days, when the militias were formally established under the Frontier Corps, officers drew an extra 150 to 750 rupees per month special hazard allowance for serving on the Frontier. Serving in the regular Indian Army could also be a profitable experience. On permanent transfer from one appointment to another, an officer was provided with a first-class rail warrant and in addition three and a half times the first class rail fare to his new destination was paid into his account. The idea, conceived in Victorian days, was that an army officer should not be out of pocket for the cost of conveyance of his heavy baggage and furniture, as well as any horses, servants and family accompanying him.

There is another powerful force kindling unrelenting tribal blood feuds – *Pakhtunwali*, the Pathans' code of honour. Life on the Frontier is governed by this tribal code, under which each man is bound to abide by three precepts. The first rule is that fugitives – Osama bin Laden would be no exception – must without question be granted safety in one's home. Similarly, the Pathan is obliged to grant hospitality to all who seek it, friend or foe. However, the visitor should be forewarned that while he can rest easy while under a Pathan's roof, once he puts a foot outside the door he is considered fair game. Major William Broadfoot, in a report delivered to the Royal Geographical Society on his experiences with a surveying expedition in unexplored tribal territory in 1884, says that he 'went amongst a set of murderers unharmed because a guest'. Yet in the same breath, he makes cursory reference to the slaughter of 'one hundred of the men of my party one night', as soon as they were back on the road. Lastly, there is the law of retaliation, or *badal*, the most sacred of the Pathans' three principal maxims. This normally takes the form of blood feuds, often inherited from past generations, arising from murders, violations of safe conduct or disputes about debts, or inheritance, or tribal quarrels over land or water. Rivalry over women is another common cause of feuding. In the case of adultery, amputation of the nose was the very least a wife could expect from her aggrieved husband in the way of punishment. But death was considered a perfectly legitimate penalty as well. Kipling's stories of Frontier life were inspired by what he saw and was told on his travels to the tribal lands. In *Soldiers Three*, he recounts in 'Dray Wara Yow Dee' the tribulations of the Pathan who beheaded his unfaithful wife and then spent the rest of his days in pursuit of his enemy Daoud Shah. 'There shall be no harm befall Daoud Shah till I come,' prays the nameless seeker of vengeance. 'For I would fain kill him quick and whole with the life sticking firm in his body. A pomegranate is sweetest when the cloves break away unwilling from the rind. Let it be in the daytime, that I may see his face, and my delight may be crowned.'

The Pathans' relentless pursuit of revenge and terrifying predilection for cruelty were the two traits that stood out in the minds of British veterans of the Frontier. The novelist John Masters spent several years with the 4th Gurkhas, during which time he took part in a number of savage Frontier skirmishes and set battles with the tribesmen. 'They [the Pathans] never took prisoners but mutilated and beheaded any wounded or dead who fell into their hands,' he recalls in his memoirs of the Frontier. 'They took advantage of the rules to disguise themselves as peaceful passers-by, or as women. They simulated death and pounced on anyone foolish enough to relax his guard.' A British Army officer lay severely wounded after a sharp battle, and when he was found next day, 'he had been castrated and flayed, probably while alive, and his skin lay pegged out on the rocks not far from camp.' Masters tells that if the Pathans captured any soldiers other than Muslims, and especially if the prisoners were Sikhs or British, they would routinely castrate and behead them. 'Both these operations were frequently done by the women. Sometimes they would torture prisoners with the death of a thousand cuts, pushing grass and thorns into each wound as it was made.'[5]

The British had the highest regard for the Pathan as a foe, which is why they eagerly embraced the idea of bringing them into the fold as gamekeepers. Charles Chevenix Trench tells a story that illustrates Pathan bravery and disregard for personal safety on the battlefield, on an occasion when Scouts were engaged in a fierce battle with tribal lashkars:

> We set out next morning and encountered the lashkar about five miles south of the fort . . . It was an indecisive sort of action, both sides shooting at one another from parallel ridges, neither able to gain an advantage. I saw one Scout wounded far down the forward slope. One of his tribe ran down to rescue him. It was a terribly hot day, and the hillside was very steep. He slung the wounded man across his shoulder and staggered up the hill, but soon had to put him down, rest and have a drink. Then he picked up his friend and struggled up a few more yards before again putting him down. He eventually reached the top, with two bullets in him.[6]

There was a temptation among outsiders who came into conflict with the Pathan to describe him as a savage, ruthless opponent, ready to break his word when it suited him, a turbulent rebel and generally an abominable nuisance. It is worth keeping in mind, however, what motivated the Pathan tribesmen to act in so savage a fashion. Olaf Caröe, who along with Warburton had a better grasp of Pathan life and customs than almost any other Frontier administrator, makes note of a singular truth: 'These men, whether fighting (the Moghul emperor) Shah Jahan or the British, were defending the freedom of their homes. Had we in 1940 had to fight on the beaches, it is to be hoped our battle would have been as ruthless and as bloody as theirs.'[7] Caröe might have added that the Pathans, unlike more 'advanced' societies, did not have recourse to gas chambers, napalm or cluster bombs, and that those who did never hesitated to use them.

Earlier conquerors usually took a rather less enlightened view of their foe, and felt compelled to deal with the tribesmen using the sort of tactics they would understand. A puzzling structure lies a couple of hundred yards south of the Khyber road, not far from Michni Post. It is known locally as Tamerlane's Prison, but could more accurately be described as a kind of medieval 'blender'. In reality this was a gruesome execution device built by the Tartar warlord in the fourteenth century and designed to strike terror into the hearts of his Pathan foes. A blockhouse sits on top of a hill and is connected on one side to a slide, which is itself enclosed on both sides and was in Tamerlane's day fitted with blades just long enough to slice through a man's body without stopping his descent. Victims were hurled on to these slides and their quartered remains were left to rot in a mud pit at the bottom, as a stark warning to any tribesmen harbouring seditious inclinations.

> For if there are qualities in the Border people which are less than amiable, it must be understood that they were shaped by the kind of continuous ordeal . . . that reached its peak in the sixteenth century, when great numbers of the people inhabiting the Frontier territory lived by despoiling each other, when the great Border tribes . . . feuded continuously among themselves, when robbery and blackmail were everyday professions, when raiding, arson, kidnapping, murder and extortion were an important part of the social system.[8]

Here we have a vivid sketch of tribal life on the North-West Frontier, one which any British administrator of the day would have no doubt endorsed as painfully accurate. Indeed, the words echo the tone of countless government reports portraying the cruelty and lawlessness of Pathan life, great boxes of which sit gathering dust in the archives of the British Library's India Office. Yet the quote is not from some Frontier official bemoaning the latest outrage committed by a tribal raiding party: it comes instead from the pen of George MacDonald Fraser in his history of the Anglo-Scottish reivers, the murderous rival clans on either side of the Border, and the March Wardens, the sixteenth-century equivalent of the Khyber Rifles and the other Frontier militias that waged war on this great community of brigands. 'The Border reivers were aggressive, ruthless, violent people, notoriously quick on the draw, ready and occasionally eager to kill in action, when life or property or honour were at stake,' writes MacDonald Fraser. 'They were a brave people, and risked their lives readily enough. When they had to die, they appear to have done so without undue dramatics or bogus defiance, that would have been wasted anyway. They lived in a society where deadly family feud was common, and when they were engaged in feud they killed frequently and brutally.' If Pathan society today still largely conforms to this picture, it is because their homeland became an enclave between two sovereign states, Afghanistan and India. There never arose the question of annexing the tribal territories or putting the tribes under one flag, as was the case with the union of Scotland and England when the rulers of both countries crushed the reivers. The Frontier answers to its name on either side of the Torkham border crossing, notwithstanding both countries' (Pakistan in place of British India) nominal claim to sovereignty over their respective portions of the Pathan homeland. The Pathan asks only one thing of the outside world, to be left alone.

In 1901 the Viceroy Lord Curzon took it upon himself to remove the Frontier from the jurisdiction of the Punjab Government and carve out a separate entity, the North-West Frontier Province. His Frontier policy, as set forth in his Budget Speech of 1904, was summed up in a few words: 'Withdrawal of British troops from advanced positions, employment of tribal forces in defence of tribal country, concentration of British forces in British territory behind them as a safeguard and a support, improvement of communications in the rear.' Curzon was always very doubtful of the wisdom of having commissioners acting directly under the central government in their dealings with the tribes beyond the administered border. 'Curzon developed his case in characteristic fashion,' writes Caröe. 'First came a siting shot, followed by sharp single shots on the bull's-eye, culminating in a salvo of concentrated rapid fire.' In a series of letters to Whitehall, the 41-year-old Viceroy reminded his bosses that he was responsible for dealing with the Pathans, but that he was hamstrung by having to conduct his policy through 'the elaborate machinery of a provincial government, to which the Frontier and its problems are necessarily something of side-shows, acting as an intermediary.' With a barrister's flourish, the Old Etonian summed up his case:

> The result is that in ordinary times the Punjab government does the Frontier work and dictates the policy without any interference from the supreme government at all, but that in extraordinary times the whole control is taken over by the Government of India acting through agents who are not its own, while the Punjab government, dispossessed and sulky, stands on one side, criticising everything that is done.

One can imagine the young aristocrat exclaiming with a toss of his gallant head, 'And with this, I lay down my pen.' Curzon got his way, over the vigorous protests of the Lieutenant-Governor of the Punjab, Sir Macworth Young. In reality, there was nothing new in the idea. At least thirty years before, the proposal for a separate Frontier province had been put forward by Warburton and the Viceroy Lord Lytton. But it took the perseverance and single-mindedness of Curzon to turn it into a reality, ignoring all political opposition to his plan. The new jurisdiction covered the tribal territories up to the Durand Line, which effectively enabled the government to withdraw the more than 10,000 troops it had stationed along 200 miles of administrative border with Afghanistan. The Khyber Rifles benefited from this new arrangement, as the army's withdrawal meant the government was obliged to beef up the fighting strength of the native corps, and this also spawned some of the other famous tribal levies of the Frontier, such as the South Waziristan Scouts and the Kurram Militia. The irregular forces raised to guard the Frontier adopted the names of Militia, Scouts and Rifles. There are subtle distinctions between the three types of corps. Apart from the proper Frontier Forces, the government created khassadars as local police at the disposal of the Political Agents in the several tribal agencies. The militias were and today remain support units for the armed forces, whose recruits are local tribesmen from each area. Most of these militia units gradually adopted the title of scouts, which more accurately describes their role as gathering information on tribal affairs and protecting troop movements through hostile territory by manning picquets and guarding the roads. The title of rifles was used to distinguish Indian Army regiments that carried lighter equipment and moved faster over the Frontier's hilly terrain than heavy infantry units. The Khyber levy was re-christened 'rifles' simply because this was the only weapon they carried.

Curzon considered the previous system, under which the Government of the Punjab took responsibility for tribal policy and all decisions had to be channelled through Lahore before reaching the viceroy's attention, as a dangerous aberration. He held himself ultimately responsible for Frontier security and was determined to remove the obstacle of a subordinate government interfering in matters of Frontier security. The new province contained the whole of the Pathan tribal territory, together with the five settled districts of Hazara, Peshawar, Kohat, Bannu and Dera Ismail Khan. It was presided over by a Chief Commissioner, Sir Harold Deane, one of the few British administrators who commanded the trust and respect of the Pathans, and who reported directly to the Viceroy. Curzon's radical shake-up of the Frontier passed unheralded, if given any notice at all, by the tribes. 'Neither Mughal, Durrani (Afghan royal dynasty) nor Sikh had dared to penetrate deeper than the fringes of his (the Pathan's) territory, and when they did as much as that they paid heavily for their presumption,' says Major-General James Elliott, who spent some twenty years of his army career on the Frontier. 'After the arrival of the British the Pathan came to accept the minor punitive expedition, but at any suggestion that this might lead up to permanent occupation a whole tribe would be up in arms.'[9] This is how punishments came to be infamously known as 'butcher and bolt' operations. An early European traveller was told by the Pathans, 'We are content with alarms, and we are content with blood, but we will never be content with a master.' The Pathan bowed his heads to no man, regardless of rank or lineage. Pandit Nehru came close to learning this basic truth the hard way when in 1946 he went to the Frontier to address a tribal jirga. Major Robin Hodson was there to chaperone India's future prime minister on his tour.

The Mahsud jirga assembled that day on the Residency lawn to hear what he had to say,' recalls Hodson. 'To my astonishment Nehru rose to his feet (it was customary for holders of jirgas to sit with tribesmen squatting on the ground in front of the chairs) and advanced with his arms in the air as though he were addressing a political rally in Allahabad. When his voice reached a crescendo, he announced that he had come to free the tribes from the slavery of British imperialism. At that the entire jirga rose in anger and (tribal elder) Mehr Dil advanced on Nehru with raised umbrella saying "We are not slaves", and tried to strike him, adding, "Come here again and we will circumcise you". The proceedings then broke up in disorder and the Mahsuds raged out of the camp.[10]

The incident brings to mind a remark by a visiting British journalist in the 1950s, who described the North-West Frontier as 'the last free place on earth'. The Pathans have time and again shown their determination to keep it so.

The Nehru incident lends credibility to the jingoist theory put forth by the early twentieth-century soldier-historian George B. Scott, who said that the Pathans worshipped strong men, but that they would never be dictated to by an assembly of Indian intelligentsia, drawn exclusively from non-military races. 'They want a man, and preferably an Englishman, to rule over them,' he wrote. 'If also a soldier by profession, so much the better.'[11] The Frontier tribes in fact wanted no man to rule over them, Englishman or otherwise. Yet Scott's argument contains a grain of truth: the Pathans saw the British defeat the Afghans and the Sikhs in hard pitched battles, and thus the fair-haired invaders merited the tribes' highest regard. They could do business with the British warrior race, but they would never be dictated to by the likes of Gandhi, a man they perceived as a limp-wristed Hindu intellectual.

The British produced administrators from time to time, men like Warburton and Carõe, who could galvanise the Pathans' respect by dealing with the tribesmen in their own language and exhibiting some sympathy for their ways. When that was lacking, the army could temporarily bring them to heel by force of arms. Whatever views the British may have harboured about the tribes, and these were in the main scathingly negative, political realities of the day dictated that some arrangement of peaceful coexistence was needed to minimise the threat of Frontier instability. There was no question of subduing the tribes, and punitive expeditions took the form of hit-and-run missions. The army never entertained the folly of attempting to permanently occupy the tribal territories. Once the job was done and the offenders had been brought to their knees the troops departed, and the tribesmen quietly clambered back to their feet.

'Our dealings with the Pathans was a gentleman's game, you know,' recalls another British Army officer of the period. 'No matter how poor a Pathan was, he may meet the King of England or the Viceroy of India, but he'd look him straight in the eye and shake hands with him as if to say I'm as good a man as you are.'

What has yet to be unravelled is the mystery surrounding the origin of the people Kipling referred to as 'a few thousand gentlemen of Jewish extraction who lived across the border, and answered to the name of Pathan'. The Pathans account for some 20 million souls living mainly in the border region between Afghanistan and Pakistan, and thus make up the world's most numerous tribal confederacy. Though the diaspora set in motion more than twenty years ago, first by the Soviet and more recently the American invasions of Afghanistan, has sent millions fleeing across the border to neighbouring Pakistan, the Pathans still comprise nearly 40 per cent of Afghanistan's population. This number could slowly creep back to the pre-war level of 51 per cent, provided the homeward bound flood of refugees is not halted by some new calamity. Anthropologists put forward the theory that these people migrated across the Central Asian steppes with the Aryan hordes that descended on the Indus valley a millennium or so before Alexander's army marched through the Khyber Pass in 327 BC. The assumption is that these migratory tribes settled in the hills along the Frontier and grew harder and fiercer with years of rugged mountain life and snowy winters, as well as internecine strife. As so often occurs in tribal societies, the question of ethnic origin is far less of a mystery to the people in question than to the ethnologist struggling to decipher their ancestral roots. There is an abundance of folklore that addresses the riddle of the Pathans' genealogy. Most Pathans call themselves *Ben-i-Israel*, or 'sons of Israel', thus claiming to be descendants of the ten lost tribes, a theory that gained widespread support among historians a century or so ago. The Afghan royal family holds to a tradition by which their origins can be traced to the tribe of Benjamin and the family of Saul, the first king of Israel. The common belief is that Saul had a son called Jeremiah, and that he in turn had a son called Afghana. Jeremiah died at about the same time as Saul, and Afghana was brought up by King David of the Israelites. Some centuries later in the story appears the name of Bakhtunnasar (Nebuchanezzar) and the tradition runs that at the time of the dispersal of the tribes of Israel, not all the Hebrew ancestors of the Afghans returned to Jerusalem as was commonly believed. Instead, some of them withdrew to the mountains of Ghor (modern Hazarajat), the birthplace of Qays bin Rashid, and others to the lands around Mecca. Both these tribal colonies came to be known as *Ben-i-Israel* or *Ben-i-Afghana*.

With the rise of Islam in the seventh century, Mohammed sent his follower Khaled ibn Waleed to the 'sons of Israel' to spread the word of Islam among the pagan Afghan tribes. The Prophet's emissary succeeded in his mission and returned to Mohammed with an Afghan deputation, now converted to Islam. The Pathans of today seek to link their obscure beginnings, intermingling history and myth, with David, Solomon and Saul, the great patriarchs of the ancient Hebrews. There are in fact traces of archaeological evidence to support the theory of Jewish origin. Gravestones have been discovered near Herat bearing Persian and Hebrew names, while the Kabul Museum, before it was demolished by the Taliban, contained a black stone unearthed in Kandahar with Hebrew inscriptions carved in it. Given the lack of tribal unity among the Pathans, the diversity of tales of their origins comes as no surprise. While the Afridis represent the principal proponents of the Jewish origin theory, others adhere to the concept of Aryan genealogy, and still others are happy to consider themselves descendants of the Arabs, Persians or Greeks. The Mohmands, for instance, firmly believe they can trace their ancestry back to followers of the Prophet Mohammed, while other tribes bear names with clear links to biblical genealogy. Shinwari, for instance, comes from Simeon, Yusufzai translates as 'sons of Joseph', the suffix '*zai*' being a corruption of the Pathan word *zoe*, meaning 'son', and *Afridi* is itself a derivative of 'Ephraim'. The last of the Pathan tribes was converted to Islam in the tenth century AD, and they cling to their religion with the same fanatic zeal with which they defend their homeland.

Leaving aside discrepancies over genealogical roots, the Pathans share a common structure as a political rather than an ethnic unit, with a conglomeration of clans bound together by allegiance to a malik. The various tribes contain a nucleus of two, three or more clans descended from a common ancestor. When a clan or a portion of a clan finds itself at odds with its brethren, as is often the case (the Pushtu word *tabur* is used indistinctly for cousin and enemy), it will claim the protection of a neighbouring malik. The clan then becomes his *hamsayas*, or dwellers beneath the same shade, and the malik is bound to protect them and they to obey him.

The Pathans who gave the Indian Army its most biting headache were the Afridis, 'those lean but muscular men, with long, gaunt faces, careful shots and skirmishers, patiently awaiting the chance of an easy shot at the enemy'. The Afridis comprise the largest and most belligerent of the Frontier tribes, and they came to make up the backbone of the Khyber Rifles. Like the Wazirs, Mahsuds, Mohmands and other Frontier tribes, the Afridis are divided into several clans, in their case eight in total. Of these, six are known collectively as the Khyber Afridis. They are the Kuki, Malikdin, Kambar, Kamar and Zakka Khels, and the Sipahs. The Aka and Adam Khels, on the other hand, claim as their territory lands lying outside the Khyber district. 'This is the most powerful of the Frontier tribes,' says Captain Hugh Nevill, who campaigned on the North-West Frontier a century ago and thus takes no pains to promote a more charitable sentiment towards the tribes than that held by most of his brother officers. 'The members of it are endowed with many martial qualities, but are rapacious, untrustworthy, and lawless by nature.'[12]

The Afridis control the Khyber Pass and they also hold sway over the fertile Tirah valley to the north-west of the pass, 'the bit that no one ever penetrated, and which is today a main poppy growing area', says a former British officer who served in the Khyber. The Tirah is still home to black bear, leopard and jackal, among other wild species that roam the deep forests of deodar, fir and walnut. The Frontier historian David Dichter observes that even in the 1960s less information was available from inside sources about this independent tribal area than about any other on the Frontier. 'Acting as self-appointed guardians of the Khyber are the Afridis, estimated at 200,000 strong,' he says.

The eight powerful sections that make up the Afridi nation have long held centre stage in the drama of Frontier politics by their control of three important passes, their fighting strength and the inaccessibility of their mountainous homeland. Even today they constitute one of the most formidable fighting units on the Frontier, and the fact that they are one of the few large tribes capable of concerted action makes them an even more potent force. Besides dominating the vicinity of the Khyber, the Afridis also hold most of the rest of the Agency, which includes portions of the main Safed Koh range.[13]

Tirah, a land of isolated alpine forests criss-crossed by mule tracks and no metalled roads, was the scene of some of the bloodiest punitive expeditions undertaken by British troops. It was almost inevitable that the Afridis, arguably the most formidable opponents the British Army had to face on the Frontier, would clash with the empire in its push to the north-west. The vital strategic roads linking Peshawar, a city that the tribesmen look upon as home territory, with Kabul and Kohat, run for more than 10 miles through a salient of Afridi territory.

Britain's first encounter with the Khyber Afridis took place around the time of the First Afghan War. It was common coin for British officials serving in the Khyber Agency to denounce the Afridis as untrustworthy and treacherous brigands, yet there are no recorded cases of any Britons, who have stayed among the tribesmen as guests, being molested by their hosts. British officers of Pathan regiments were full of tales of the tribesmen's devotion and loyalty, often under trying circumstances, as occurred during expeditions against their own people, and in the Ambela Campaign of 1863, when fanatical mullahs went about denouncing the Afridis in the army's ranks as renegades and infidels. George Scott recalls that in 1841–2, when the news of the Kabul disaster was spread abroad and every tribe from Kabul to Peshawar rose against the British, 'the Corps of Afridi Levies, from Pesh Bolak in the Jalalabad valley, escorted Lieutenant Ferris and other officers safely through the hills to Peshawar'. Scott recounts an example of Afridi loyalty by men who took part in a punitive expedition against their own tribe, when on returning to camp, an orderly was fired upon by three men in some long grass near a cave. The orderly, fixing his bayonet, rushed into the grass and shot and bayoneted all three men. As he was examining their faces, a British officer came rushing up to commend the man's courage and said he would bring his conduct to the notice of the general. 'Not a word Sahib, for that one is my cousin.' The orderly had to wait several months before he dared to collect his Order of Merit.

There is, of course, another side to this story, one that portrays the 'noble savage' as at times somewhat wanting in nobility. It was an Afridi fanatic who in 1853 stabbed Frederick Mackeson in front of his house in an act of treachery. In that year it fell to the newly appointed commissioner in Peshawar, Sir Herbert Edwardes, to deal with the first open conflict between government and the Afridis, when the army was obliged to mount a full-scale invasion of Afridi territory in retaliation for raids on villages in the Khyber hills. Likewise, the most infamous outrage ever committed against a British official in India, the assassination of the Viceroy Lord Mayo in 1852 while on a visit to a penal colony, was the work of an embittered Afridi convict. Former soldier Sher Ali, hailed by one of his British officers as 'a man of fine physique, ruddy complexion, cheery manner, always ready for a joke or a laugh', was serving a life sentence for murder in the Andaman Islands prison, known to the criminal class as the 'Black Water'. Ironically, on the day of his sentencing, Ali had begged to be executed instead of being transported to the notorious disease-ridden penal colony. He later got his wish.

The first open hostilities between the Afridis and the British broke out in 1854, in a series of raids and counter-raids that had their roots in a demand for tribal allowances from the government. The British forces on this occasion proved themselves second-to-none in employing tactics of ruthlessness. For although the army as a rule refrained from the ungentlemanly pastime of dismembering wounded soldiers on the battlefield, it did manage to bring the tribesmen to their knees by carrying off their cattle and blockading trade routes with neighbouring tribes for an entire year, thus literally starving out the enemy.

Relations with the Afridis marked a sharp improvement after Britain's victory in the Second Afghan War. As at any polo match in Central Asia, the spectators will always cheer the winning side, so it was with the tribesmen of the Frontier, who bowed to the victor in a show of arms. The British now came to trust in the Afridis who stood guard over the Khyber Pass in their guise as the newly raised Jezailchis, and with justification. The army marched home through the pass without incident in late summer of 1880. An official account of the event records with satisfaction, 'The Pass remained quiet, and there were no attempts, even on the part of isolated fanatics or bad characters, to plunder stores or molest the camps at night.' Army commanders now felt comfortable enough with their Afridi allies to contemplate a complete withdrawal of regular troops from the pass, leaving responsibility for guarding the road wholly in the hands of the embryonic Khyber Rifles. In September 1880, after the uneventful return to India of the Afghan expeditionary force, the army decided to pull its troops out of their last remaining garrisons in Ali Masjid and Landi Kotal, 'if satisfactory arrangements could be made to keep the Pass open under the independent and exclusive charge of the tribes'.

There was only one way to secure these 'satisfactory arrangements', and this was through the tribal jirga, an institution so powerfully entrenched in Pathan custom that in 1872 the British introduced legislation allowing a magistrate to withdraw a case and submit it for arbitration by this council of elders and headmen. Therefore no time was lost in despatching envoys throughout Khyber territory, summoning the heads of the various Afridi clans to a meeting with the Political Officer in Peshawar. The maliks and dignitaries set off from their mountain villages and by the end of the month more than 300 had assembled in the city. The government's proposal to hand over the guardianship of the pass to the tribesmen met with an enthusiastic response from the Afridis. Above all, they cherished the idea of clearing their homeland of foreign troops. The jirga is a genuinely democratic institution that governs by majority consent, so it wasn't until January of the following year that the maliks who had attended the Peshawar gathering were able to exact an agreement from all the Afridi Khyber clans. This, of course, required a call to another grand council. So once again the dusty road to Peshawar was churned up by hundreds of tribal representatives converging on the Khyber capital.

Squatting on the ground in the traditional semicircle, one by one the chieftains rose to their feet and stepped forward to the Political Officer's table to affix their seals to the pact. The protocol contained nine basic terms. The government agreed to recognise the independence of the Afridis, provided they refrained from allowing any power other than Great Britain to interfere in their affairs, a veiled reference to Afghanistan's expansionist ambitions, and indirectly to the ever-present Russian threat. The Afridis were to undertake to maintain order throughout the Khyber, in exchange for a mutually acceptable sum of yearly allowances. All matters concerning arrangements in the Khyber Pass were to be submitted to a general meeting of representatives from all the tribal sections. No traveller was to enter the pass without an order from the Political Agent, a rule that remains in force today, specifically stating that the visitor is to vacate the pass 'between the hours of sundown and sunrise'. The tribes would not require military aid from India, a formality that hardly needed rubber-stamping given the Afridis' fierce determination, shown time and again throughout history, to defend their homeland, not to mention the fact that the tribesmen also ran their own flourishing arms manufacturing industry.

The sixth condition set out the terms for the creation of a corps that was to be the embryo of the Khyber Rifles. For here the government sought to ensure that the Khyber Pass came under the protection of native levies, answerable to the government but independent of the regular army. 'The Afridis are to furnish such a number of Jezailchis as the government might direct,' the clause

Colonel Sir Robert Warburton. Political Officer Khyber Agency, the man responsible for raising the Khyber Rifles in 1878. (*Photo: W & D Downey*)

Sir Aslam Khan, the Khyber Rifles' first Muslim Commandant. (*National Army Museum*)

The Khyber Pass from the summit of Ali Musjid. (*The Graphic*, 7 June 1879)

British and Indian regimental
badges in the Khyber Pass.
(*Author's Collection*)

Lieutenant-General Sir Samuel Browne, commanding the forces in the Khyber Pass. (*Illustrated London News*, 14 December 1879)

Ali Musjid fort in the Khyber Pass, captured by General Browne, 22 November 1878. (*The Graphic*, 30 November 1878)

Dignitaries at Landi Kotal. Seated in first row, left to right: Sir Aslam Khan (Khyber Rifles Commandant), Major George White (Gordon Highlanders), Lord Elgin (Viceroy), William Cunningham (Commandant Peshawar), Colonel Sir Robert Warburton (Political Officer, Khyber). (*British Library*)

Entrance to the Khyber Pass and Jamrud fort. (*Illustrated London News*, 5 October 1878)

Landi Kotal garrison, Khyber Pass. (*British Library*)

An Afridi picquet in the Khyber Pass. (*The Graphic*, 7 June 1879)

A Khyber Jezailchi, a forerunner of the Khyber Rifles. (*National Army Museum*)

A Pathan sniper in the Khyber Pass. (*National Army Museum*)

Camel caravan, or *kafila*, winding its way up the Khyber Pass. (*British Library*)

The author at the entrance to the Khyber Pass. (*Author's Collection*)

Bab-e-Khyber arch, the gateway to the Khyber Pass. (*Author's Collection*)

Escort of kassadars at Khyber Agency headquarters, Peshawar. (*Author's Collection*)

Colonel Tony Streather, who escorted dignitaries up the Khyber Pass. (*Photo: John Cleare*)

Graham Wontner-Smith today in Surrey, England. (*Courtesy Graham Wontner-Smith*)

Khyber Rifles at Torkham checkpoint, Afghan-Pakistan border crossing. (*Author's Collection*)

The vast bleakness of the Khyber Pass, unchanged through the centuries. (*Author's Collection*)

stated, 'with headquarters at Jamrud, to be subject to political inspection and to be paid by the British Government, but not to constitute a government force.' The agreement also stipulated that all tolls and taxes collected in the Khyber belonged to the government. Offences on the road were to be dealt with by a general jirga reporting to the government. Lastly, the tribe was to 'abstain from committing outrages' in British territory. There were a number of additional minor arrangements contained in the treaty, mainly in reference to the custody of Ali Masjid fort and other outposts in the Khyber Pass. The territorial limits of tribal responsibility were set between Landi Khana on the west, a stone's throw from the Afghan border, and Jamrud on the east, sitting at the entrance to the pass. For agreeing to abide by all these conditions, the Afridi clans were to receive subsidies totalling 7,155 rupees per month, the size of the allotments increasing in proportion to the relative nuisance factor of each clan. Hence the Shinwaris, who inhabit a portion of the Khyber valley and some of the eastern valleys of the Safed Koh, were considered 'a quiet, well-behaved set as a rule, who are well aware how much their prosperity depends on their good conduct'. So this peaceful lot received 805 rupees per month. The intractable Zakka Khels, on the other hand, who more than any other clan had been the target of the army's many punitive expeditions into tribal territory, were bought off with an allowance of 1,700 rupees.

The Zakka Khels are one of the most powerful and turbulent clans in the Khyber Agency. They always took the hardest stand against British control because their villages lie a long distance from the settled border area. They are also a more self-sufficient people than their brother clans, hence their trade with British-controlled territory was negligible. Their homeland, today as in the past, occupies part of the Khyber Pass road, from a ravine to the west of the Gurgurra outpost to a spot near Garhi Lala Baig, at which point the Shinwari clan takes over. The Zakka Khels' territory is by far the most extensive and politically sensitive in the Khyber, covering as it does the whole of the Bazar valley and a large part of forbidden Tirah, traditionally the region's prime poppy growing area. The clan's geo-strategic location effectively places it in control of the Khyber Pass and allows the Zakha Khels to travel throughout the Khyber Agency without having to step foot on land belonging to any other Afridi clan. Even Warburton, who almost alone among Khyber officials of his day could muster words of praise for the Afridis, wrote of his contempt for this particular section, which he dismissed as 'the greatest thieves, housebreakers, robbers and raiders amongst all the Khyber clans, their word or promise never being believed or trusted by their Afridi brethren without a substantial security being taken for its fulfilment'.[14] It was, after all, the Zakka Khels who had galvanised the Afridis and other Pathan tribes into insurrection up and down the Frontier in 1897, and it was this same clan that never accepted the terms of submission laid down by the government, preferring to continue to stage raids and commit atrocities in the settled districts long after the formal end to hostilities. The outrages in fact became an almost daily occurrence in the early years of the twentieth century, for in 1907 the Zakka Khels persuaded the Amir of Afghanistan to supply them with an illegal shipment of arms, which they used to step up their attacks across the administrative border. It is hardly surprising that the other Afridi clans have always taken pains to remain on good terms with their warlike Zakka Khels clansmen. Hence not a word of protest was raised when the government decided to grant the Zakka Khels the lion's share of the Khyber allowances.

The ill-fated Colonel Mackeson would have bestowed his blessing on this government initiative. 'The Afridis are a most avaricious race, desperately fond of money,' he wrote, shortly before he fell victim to an Afridi assassin's dagger. 'Their fidelity is measured by the length of the purse of the seducer, and they transfer their obedience and support from one party to another of their own clansmen, according to the comparative liberality of the donation.'[15] All the more reason, one might argue, to keep the tribesmen sweet.

The position of the recently-raised Jezailchis was entirely changed under the new arrangement. The British Government now merely paid the cost of their maintenance, a sum amounting to 87,160 rupees per year, whereas previously the native levies drew subsidies for items such as firearms. The levies were to be recruited and dismissed by the chiefs of the tribes concerned, who were solely responsible for their management, reporting these arrangements to the Political Officer at Jamrud. This situation was radically altered when Sardar Mohammed Aslam Khan took command of the corps, which in 1887 was redesignated the Khyber Rifles. The trusted corps became the only Pathan militia to be given powers to serve anywhere on the Frontier, not just in their Khyber home territory. The strength of the body at the time was about 550 men, with the usual complement of *subadars*, *jemadars* and subordinate officers. When in March 1881 these arrangements were complete and in working order, the last British soldier filed out of the Khyber Pass and Jamrud Fort became the army's advanced military post.

Tolls of caravans commenced to be levied on 15 September 1881, and the income from these taxes was estimated at about 60,000 rupees per annum. A pittance, it must be said, when measured alongside the precious and exotic merchandise trundling its way across the pass into British India. The camel caravans coming up from Asia brought hides and furs, splendid silks from Bokhara, sacks of gold in bullion and dust, fresh and dried fruits from Kabul, prized thoroughbred horses from Turkistan and other treasures. In short, a sultan's ransom in comparison with what the British offered in exchange to the turbaned traders from Central Asia, which amounted chiefly to indigo, sugar and tea.

With the gradual waning of friction between occupying British forces and the Afridis, a conflict that essentially boiled down to recognition on the part of the former that the tribe was not to be needlessly antagonised, there ensued a period of comparative harmony for nearly twenty years, from the end of the great tribal uprising to the outbreak of the First World War. The Afridis were in fact the only Frontier tribesmen to enlist in any numbers in the regular Indian Army and up to 1914 they presented an almost unblemished record of bravery and loyalty. In the year immediately prior to the outbreak of war, eight infantry regiments had fifteen companies composed entirely of Afridis, Orakzais, Mahsuds or Wazirs. In addition to these class companies, forty-seven companies of Pathans were distributed among twenty regiments of the Indian Army. But the regular army was obliged to deal with cases of desertion and refusal to fight in the war, mostly attributable to religious scruples, or so the offenders alleged. General Sir George Macmunn was one of the very few of the army hierarchy who could spare words of kindness for the Afridis. To this Frontier veteran, the 'jaunty, vain, light-hearted, reckless Afridi' was a man of irresistible appeal for, 'like Saul of Israel, they are choice young men and goodly, if dirty'. Quite remarkably for a military man, Macmunn put forward a justification for their treasonous behaviour. 'It will probably be better to forgive them their sins, both for the excitement of 1919 (that is, their collaboration with the enemy in the Second Afghan War) and the desertion in France,' he writes. 'It has been said that the latter was due not so much to inherent unreliability, serious though that may be, so much as the fact that the destruction of a whole company of, say, Khamber Khel, as might have happened in France, would upset the whole balance of tribal politics unless other clans were to lose equally heavily.'[16] Given the incessant quarrelling among the various clans, the charitable Macmunn argues, it would be unthinkable for one to sustain such heavy losses so as to leave itself outnumbered by a future adversary.

Erring perhaps on the side of prudence, it was nonetheless decided to disband the Afridi units, and virtually all recruitment was stopped until the outbreak of European hostilities in 1939. At that time the Afridi maliks had on many occasions petitioned the Governor of the North-West Frontier Province to reopen enlistment in the Indian Army. Robin Hodson, who was directly involved in recruiting tribesmen into the services, writes, 'The Axis powers had legations in Kabul until 1941 and it was expedient for the general peace of the Frontier to drain away as many of the young bloods as possible and to improve tribal economies by the injection of regular pay packets. Recruitment for the (Afridi) battalion began in 1942.'[17] Hodson points out that the Afridis, who served in the Middle East and other theatres of operations, helped to prevent crucial oilfields falling into German hands during the war.

However, there never was a great deal of enthusiasm for bringing the Pathans into the Armed Forces, and the reasoning behind this was on the face of it quite sound: allowing these men to enlist in the army was tantamount to teaching them the art of modern warfare, an aptitude it was feared would be turned against the British in any subsequent Frontier conflicts. No doubt this was true to an extent, but the Afridis did prove their usefulness to the army in both European wars. Hodson notes, 'During the First World War the Afridis served in various units in France, Mesopotamia, Palestine and German East Africa, and many acts of bravery in action were recognised.'[18] Perhaps the most outstanding example of Afridi gallantry during the war was the action of Jemadar Mir Dast, VC, who 'displayed remarkable courage in helping to carry eight British and Indian officers into safety whilst exposed to very heavy fire'. In some instances the Afridis did transfer their fighting skills back to the Frontier, and used them in defence of the Raj. Hodson says that when the Afghans staged a raid across the Durand Line in 1915 to attack an outpost of the North Waziristan Militia, six former soldiers, Afridis of the Adam Khel clan, were awarded Indian Distinguished Service Medals for successfully defending their post.

Curzon's initiative to carve out a separate North-West Frontier Province was vindicated by an almost total cessation of the cycle of tribal raids and punitive expeditions by the army. For nearly twenty years, an uneasy peace settled on the Frontier, until the outbreak of the Third Afghan War. Caröe, who administered the North-West Frontier Province in the closing days of British rule, acknowledges the success of Curzon's decision.

Since the break-up of the Mughal Empire the whole region had become a sort of corridor for invasion and counter-stroke . . . Durrani and Sikh arms had passed over it in ebb and flow, and nothing had been held or fixed. And when these unstable forces had been replaced by British rulers, the tendency at first had been to treat the Pathans as though they were just an appanage of India, which they never were. Lodi and Sur, Yusufzai and Orakzai, had ruled in India – were they now to become unconsidered trifles on the margin of the Punjab? The separation of the Frontier, then, satisfied this pride . . . Not entirely consciously, Curzon had provided a focus for Pathan self-esteem, and so had done much to consolidate a firm Frontier.[19]

Having a province of their own, with peaceful access to their natural spiritual centre at Peshawar and a government exclusively dedicated to their interests, helped to defuse the Pathans' hostility towards the Government of India. The threat of surprise attack by Pathan lashkars had placed a constant drain on the army's resources and morale. With alarming regularity and with total disregard for constituted order, the raiders would come galloping over the hills, shrieking their war cries, waving their muskets and swords, and scooping up any booty that lay in their path. From the destruction of Elphinstone's army in 1842 to the annexation of the Khyber Pass and its surrounding lands in 1879, right up to the time of Curzon's redrawing of the geopolitical map in 1901, the Afridis staged 'most daring thefts, especially of rifles, and many in the Peshawar cantonments and city'.

The Pathan Muslims are followers of the fundamentalist Sunni sect. Most are uneducated and vulnerable to Koran-waving mullahs, who are themselves only slightly less unlettered than their followers. These religious fanatics, however, are highly skilled in the art of stirring up trouble along the Frontier, more often than not with the connivance of Kabul, as was clearly demonstrated in British India's 1919 war with Afghanistan, which did not by any measure put an end to tribal hostilities. 'The year 1930 vied with 1919 as being the most critical on the North-West Frontier since the Pathan revolt in 1897,' writes Hodson. Radical religious leaders were incensed by the peace terms imposed after the First World War on Turkey, a country held in high esteem by Afghan and Frontier Muslims. In 1930 a gifted Pathan rabble-rouser appeared, Abdul Ghaffar Khan, the founder of the notorious Red Shirt movement. Ghaffar was a tall Pathan, about 6ft 4in, the offspring of an affluent land-owning Khyber family. Throwing in his lot with the fledgling Congress movement, he became a deeply embedded thorn in the side of government, for he demanded nothing less than an independent Pathan state, a homeland by the name of Pakhtunistan.

After the First World War, with India recognised as a separate entity by the League of Nations and the Montagu-Chelmsford reforms in place, introducing a form of political dualism, the subcontinent's march to independence was all but a foregone conclusion. Riding high on this tidal wave of nationalism, it became easy pickings for Ghaffar to fan the flames of chaos in Peshawar, each time he took to the streets to address the followers of his Khudai Khitmatgars (Servants of God) movement, whose mission was to recruit young Pathans for the fight against British rule. By May of that year order had almost totally broken down in the city of 80,000, and the government called in the Gurkhas and other native troops, a move that drove the insurrectionists to a state of even greater frenzy. Murder and acts of sabotage broke out everywhere, spreading from the Khyber to Waziristan and other tribal areas up and down the length of the Frontier. By the end of May the Pathans, and most vehemently the Afridis, were to show how thin and fragile was the thread of coexistence that for two decades had kept the two sides more or less off one another's throats. The British now had a full-scale Pathan revolt on their hands, and even aerial bombardment by the RAF failed to deter an Afridi lashkar from penetrating the Peshawar defences. The bombardments and machine-gunning from the air were effective in temporarily dispersing the lashkars, but the Afridis stubbornly continued to retreat, regroup their forces and launch fresh attacks on the city. In the end, air power eventually carried the day, as it had done a decade before in the Second Afghan War. After the bombing of several Afridi villages as well as a cave complex used as a hideout by the insurrectionists, the tribesmen's fighting zeal began to wane.

The government recognised air attack as a useful tool for spreading confusion and demoralisation among the tribes, and proceeded to draw up detailed instructions for Frontier aerial warfare that remained in effect through the 1940s. In administered territories and Baluchistan – more peaceable areas where the government was firmly in control – aircrews were given specific orders not to return fire from the ground except on recognised operations. When flying missions over tribal territories, on the other hand, crews were allowed 'to retaliate with any armament they possess', meaning machine-gun fire and bombs. It was no-holds-barred with the Pathans, who could not be allowed to stir up trouble on the Frontier at a time when Britain needed all the fighting men the country could muster to deal with the far more deadly threat brewing in Europe. The government was aware of the Pathans' deep hatred of aerial warfare, which of course put the lashkars at a strategic disadvantage. Personnel in military aircraft were required to carry a form translated into Pushtu, stating that the bearer was on duty 'under the orders and protection of the government of India'. The government also knew that this was a worthless piece of paper in the eyes of a people who never accepted the *Sirkar*'s authority. Nobody entertained any illusions about the fate awaiting downed airmen unfortunate enough to be captured over tribal territory. Therefore a postscript was affixed to the form in language the tribesmen were certain to understand: the bearer of the card was to be brought in safely to the nearest government post at once, 'upon which a suitable reward will be paid'.

By August Ghaffar was in jail and the government had placed the Peshawar district under martial law. The threat of a replay of the Pathan revolt had been narrowly averted, but it was a bitter pill for the Afridis to swallow to watch government troops digging in around their tribal lands in the plains west of Peshawar, where the army had advanced its forward defences.

Air power was also deployed against the Mohmands, a tribe inhabiting the lands north of the Khyber Pass, when in 1935 their clans went on the rampage to protest against the construction of the Gandab road, a project which they saw as a threat to their isolation and independence. A Mohmand jirga despatched a 1,400-strong lashkar with knives, axes and metal rods to destroy the road. Once again RAF squadrons were called into action, staging bombing raids on villages and concentrations of tribal forces. 'Air operations on a considerable scale had been going on the whole time and their effectiveness was demonstrated by the approaches made by several clans tendering submission if the attacks were called off,' recalls General Elliott.[20]

The Frontier simmered for a year after the Mohmand campaign, an operation that was never really brought to a satisfactory outcome. By this time nearly a century of almost uninterrupted warfare and skirmishing with the tribes had rolled by and still the Pathans refused to accept the British as their masters. Much less so now, of course, in the waning days of the Raj. So in November of 1936, suddenly, but not unexpectedly, the Frontier exploded. The future novelist John Masters was serving at the time with the 4th Gurkhas on Frontier duty. 'The first incident in what was to develop into the biggest campaign since 1919 took place at Biche Kaskai in Waziristan, where Waziri tribesmen ambushed the Bannu Brigade on a carefully laid, well-concealed and boldly-executed plan,' he writes. 'The brigade suffered one hundred and thirty casualties and lost many arms and much ammunition. The tribesmen, elated by this early success, went on to higher things.'[21] The troubles then followed the customary pattern, with the Pathans stirred into action by a religious hothead, this time the colourful, elusive and Soviet-sponsored *Fakir* of Ipi. Outmanoeuvred by the Nazis in their attempt to carve out a sphere of influence in Afghanistan, the Soviets were only too happy to leap aboard the anti-British bandwagon driven by this Pathan demagogue. The Government of India now had a serious military and political crisis on its hands, as the Fakir of Ipi reached the height of his power in 1941–2, a time when every Pathan knew that Hitler's armies had put the British on the run in the Muslim lands of the Middle East. His pockets lined with ample funds from Fascist Italy as well as the Nazis, the fakir had two advantages over previous insurrectionists such as Abdul Ghaffar. 'First, because he could ration and even pay them, he could keep a hard core of lashkarwals permanently embodied, whose keep was not a burden on the local villagers,' according to Chevenix Trench. 'Secondly, his *Gorwekht Militia* . . . included Pathans of every tribe, even cis-Frontier Khattaks and Yusufzais, with Army and Scouts deserters. They were far better armed than before, having not merely rifles but a considerable number of light machine-guns and at least four guns firing proper 3.7 howitzer ammunition, most of which was probably obtained from Kabul.'[22]

The Fakir of Ipi carried out bold raids on army outposts and was a general source of mischief for Britain and later for Pakistan – this charismatic troublemaker eluded all attempts of capture until his death in 1960. His star went on the wane, however, in 1942 with the failure of his much-trumpeted endeavour to capture Datta Khel, a British fort held by the Tochi Scouts. By that time the Pathans were beginning to wonder if they had cast their lot with the winning side after all. Had not the General Sahibs Montgomery and Wingate set the Germans on the run at El Alamein and thrashed the Japanese in Burma? The forthcoming creation of Pakistan, a Muslim state, allayed the tribesmen's fears of post-independence domination by Hindu factions, so that removed one great source of anxiety.

Agitation for an independent Pakhtunistan was continuously on and off the boil, depending on who was spreading the demagoguery along the Frontier, up to the time of Britain's withdrawal from India. The tribes swore formal allegiance to the co-religionist leaders of Pakistan, but there was no entertaining of fantasies about tribal submission to Islamabad. The Khyber Rifles and other Frontier militias are still called out on a regular basis to deal with tribal grievances. In deference to the Pathans' passionate desire to live independent of government control, or more accurately in recognition that it could never be otherwise, Pakistan accepted a British proposal set out in 1944 for a return to the Curzon system of employing tribal levies to treat with their own people. The Pakistani Government took on board the wisdom of this plan and baptised the operation with the code name 'Curzon'.

In September 1947, one month after Partition, the order was issued for all regular military forces to begin a withdrawal from the tribal areas between the Durand Line and the administered border. So nearly seventy years after the Jezailchis pinned the red tag to their *pagris* in the Khyber Pass, the ribbon that was to become the corps' trademark, the wheel had turned full circle.

CHAPTER FOUR

Kensington to the Khyber: Warburton of the Frontier

November was an auspicious month for Colonel Sir Robert Warburton. The first two momentous Novembers that shaped his life took place before the future founder of the Khyber Rifles was born. The first event was in November 1840, when his father Robert Snr, a Bengal artillery officer, fell in love with and married an Afghan princess, no less a personage than the niece of the Amir Dost Mohammed, the ruler of Kabul who had been deposed and sent into exile by the British invaders of Afghanistan. The marriage deed was quaintly drawn up by the bride's father, Abdul Rahim Khan, who gave away his daughter 'in the matrimonial allowance which is allowable and legal according to the forms of Mohammedan religion to the gentleman of exalted dignity Warburton Sahib'. Warburton's exalted state was no doubt enhanced by a *mahr*, or marriage offering, of 600,000 rupees, along with 'valuable jewellery, including household furniture'.

November of the following year found Warburton's pregnant mother fleeing through the bazaars of Kabul, her cousin Akbar Khan in hot pursuit with murder in his heart. The amir's son had flown into a state of rage when his blood relation refused to give herself up along with other Muslim wives after the Afghans laid siege to the British cantonments in Kabul.

Warburton was a product of that curious breed later to become known, rather scornfully by British expats, as the Anglo-Indian. In the early days of British rule in India, mixed relationships and marriages were unremarkable, as many colonists fresh from their bleak and austere homeland willingly succumbed to the dazzling sensuality of the subcontinent's womanhood. It was only after the trauma of the 1857 Mutiny that these Anglo-Indians came to be treated as outcasts. That was when the English love affair with India started to become poisoned by mistrust and contempt for natives and 'half-castes'.

Warburton's father was one of the six British officers taken hostage in Kabul in 1841 and was thus spared from the massacre of Elphinstone's army on the road to Jalalabad. But Akbar Khan, the chief instigator of the Afghan uprising against the occupying forces, was determined to track down and punish his kinswoman. 'My father's house was burnt down in November 1841 and my mother had to take refuge with her friends and relations,' Warburton recounts in his memoirs. 'For months the troopers of Sardar Akbar Khan followed in pursuit of her. They searched houses and quarters where she was supposed to be sheltered, thrusting in all directions with their lances and swords, trying to find out her hiding place. She had often to run away from one house thus treated to take shelter in another, but a merciful Providence assisted the young wife in escaping from all these dangers.' Had she been captured, at the very least she would have had her nose cut off, the Pathans' customary punishment for infidelity. His mother's eleven month ordeal spent darting from one hiding place to another in the dank, twisting alleyways of Kabul recalls the persecution suffered by thousands of Jews who went into hiding from the Nazis in Occupied Europe. Finally, in September, 1842, Warburton's mother, after giving birth to her son in Ghilzai fort on 11 July of that year, was able to join her husband.

Warburton had embarked on what was to be a lifelong career of service to the empire, serving first in India as a young lieutenant in the Royal Regiment of Artillery. One November morning in 1863, while on a tour of duty at Fort Govindghur in the Punjab, Warburton was handed two telegrams by his orderly. The first, despatched forty-eight hours before the second, was an urgent call to attend his father's sick bed in Peshawar, where Warburton Snr lay seriously ill and in great pain with an unidentified illness, most probably an advanced cancer, judging by the symptoms Warburton describes in his memoirs. With sad irony it was the second Warburton ripped open first, saying there was no need to hurry as his father had died. This was the precursor of even more calamitous news. Warburton soon discovered that he was financially ruined, one of the many victims of the collapse of the Agra and Masterman's Bank in which his father had invested his entire life savings.

Then came 1878, when Warburton was assured a place in the pantheon of Frontier immortals. On 20 November he raised what was the embryo of the Khyber Rifles, the first of the native corps to be formed in the Pathan tribal territories.

Warburton moved among the Khyber tribesmen with the self-assurance of a veteran lion tamer. He was able to do so because he had learnt to receive and administer the sort of rigid discipline that has long since vanished from the British education system. At the age of eight, despite the protestations of his mother, Warburton was enrolled at a school in Mussorie, a hill station outpost run by the Reverend Robert North Maddock, 'a rigid disciplinarian' in Warburton's words, who was fond of using local bamboo rods as rattans that 'created a sensible impression where laid on a boy's anatomy'.[1]

After seven years of enduring this harsh regime Warburton was sent on his first voyage 'home' to England, a country which for all his Victorian schooling he was to find a good deal more alien to his spirit than the wildest corners of the Punjab. Here indeed was the embryo of a worthy role model for Kipling's *Kim*. Warburton and his father embarked on a journey across the subcontinent by dak-gharry horse carriage from Agra to Calcutta, where in April 1857 they boarded a P&O steamer bound for Southampton, leaving behind a tearful mother and a gathering of storm clouds that were a few weeks later to release the horrors of the Indian Mutiny. Of this the young traveller suspected nothing, having stopped en route at Cawnpore to be feted by his father's army friend Major Sir Hugh Wheeler, whose entire family was later wiped out by the sepoy mutineers.

Warburton's first taste of London was less of a shock than one might have envisaged for a lad plucked fresh from the free and easy life of colonial India. Number 27 Kensington Square in fashionable West London is a large brown brick-fronted Georgian mansion now converted into flats, sitting gracefully on the west side of the garden square. In its original incarnation the building was known as Kensington Proprietary Grammar School, which in Warburton's day stood as an institution much favoured by servants of the Raj who sent their offspring back to England to be educated. The school had a special class for the sons of civil servants and military officers, among whom figured the illustrious future Lord Kitchener of Khartoum. In fact its syllabus was especially set to prepare young boys for future service to John Company, as the East India Company was affectionately known. Warburton's uncle Arthur was a 'proprietor' of the school, whose records for 1858 and 1859 list one Robert Warburton as a nominee student, having been proposed for admission by Arthur Warburton. Three years at Kensington did the trick. Warburton emerged from his school cast in the mould of a proper 'Englishman', unlike Kipling's untameable Kim, who despite his mentors' best efforts always managed to escape to the twisted alleyways and shops of Lahore's bazaar traders, in whose company he found himself at ease.

In 1860 Warburton won his school's coveted yearly cadetship award and after one term at Addiscombe and another two at the Royal Military Academy at Woolwich, the fledgling officer was able to fulfil his father's ambition of seeing his son receive a commission in the Royal Regiment of Artillery. After a five-month tour of duty Warburton once more found himself aboard a swift Indiaman, sailing back to India to be reunited with his mother after a six-year absence from his true home.

His father's untimely death at the age of 51 left Warburton in a state of penury, unable to maintain the lifestyle of an artillery officer and its attendant lavish outlay on dress uniforms, horses and servants. With heavy heart, he grudgingly took up an appointment with the 21st Punjab Infantry, having sailed effortlessly through his Hindi and Urdu language proficiency exams. In those days British officers were expected to be able to issue commands to native troops in their own language.

By Christmas 1867 Warburton's regiment was under orders to embark for the Abyssinian campaign, a stroke of luck for the 25-year-old officer who was to receive his first lesson in dealing with truculent tribesmen of the breed that was to become his daily bread in several decades of Frontier service. The British troops were facing a food shortage at Dildee camp, the native porters having run off with the army's pack animals. Warburton was appointed Provost Martial with the remit of finding men and animals to carry stores to the hungry troops at the front. He was always at his best in the company of native tribesmen, thus he had no difficulty in persuading the villagers to provide the necessary transport for the stores. 'So friendly had my intercourse with the natives been that I was able to go out for five or six miles in all directions alone,' he recalls of his days in the African bush. The Abyssinian adventure could be considered a mere warm-up for Warburton's future engagements with a far more belligerent adversary, the Pathans of the Khyber, whose trust and respect he was also able to secure, so that in later days he could boast that 'for upwards of fifteen years I went about unarmed amongst these people'. This, it should be borne in mind, in a territory considered to be the most perilous on India's North-West Frontier, where there was 'absolutely no security for British life a mile or two beyond our border', a view expressed in 1877 by the Viceroy Lord Lytton.

Before he left the Abyssinian campaign Warburton was struck down with the first of the recurrent bouts of severe dysentery that were to plague him throughout his career. Although 'crushed by the blow of being invalided to England', before setting sail on the

Indiaman Warburton managed to pull the right strings at GHQ to secure the backing of his Commander-in-Chief Lord Napier, who recommended him to service in the Punjab on his return to India. His dream of carving out a career on the Frontier was now a reality within his grasp.

During his one-year leave-of-absence in England, most probably spent in Cheshire, the family seat since the thirteenth century, Warburton married Mary Cecil, daughter of 'William Cecil, Esq., late of The Dyffrin and Llanover in the county of Monmouth'. Set against the context of his later life the marriage almost ranks as a non-event, for Warburton is characteristically parsimonious with reference to his sentimental affairs, hardly surprising for the offspring of a Victorian English officer and Muslim Afghan noblewoman. We know that Mary was of delicate health, and therefore unable to join her husband in India until 1870, after a separation of more than twenty months. And that is more or less the sum total of Warburton's recorded allusions to his wife. There are no records and certainly no mention in his memoirs of children, nor is any reference to be found among the stacks of mildewed documents that fill the chambers of the Archives Department of Peshawar, where Mary spent her childbearing years. In a life taken up with soldiering and keeping the peace among the seditious Khyber tribes Warburton did, however, find time to engender three offspring. Frank survived his father by only six years, while daughters Hilda and Marie Cecil married into Irish and English families whose descendants are to be found today living in London and Wiltshire.

Robert and Mary Warburton epitomised the staid Victorian couple, she of solid gentry stock, he the more quirky but nonetheless unassailably proper English officer gentleman – but with not quite so skeleton-free a closet as one might expect.

One character who was intriguingly airbrushed out of Warburton's memoirs is Jahan Dad Khan, *aka* John Paul Warburton. This celebrated detective, attached throughout his professional life to the Punjab police, was born in Afghanistan in

1840, the first son of Warburton's Afghan princess mother Shah Jahan Begum. It therefore emerges that the founder of the Khyber Rifles had a sibling who for reasons unknown was all but deleted from the historical records, save for an obscure pamphlet published privately by one of Shah Jahan's grandchildren, G.D. Martineau of Lyme Regis, the only other reference being an adulatory entry in *The Times* obituary page.

Warburton's mother, disguised in the uniform of a British officer, in fact had made good her escape from Akbar Khan carrying not one but two children, although we are left to guess by what means her sons were smuggled past the mob. Before being sent to a Roman Catholic school at Agra, the elder son's name was changed to John Paul Warburton, and therein lies the root of the mystery: was Jahan Dad wholly Afghan or half British? We know that Warburton Snr was Shah Jahan's second husband. The amir's niece was married to Faiz Talab Khan, a high official in the Afghan court, when she met and fell in love with Warburton Snr, who eloped with his Afghan princess. Talab Khan, realising that his wife was irretrievably lost to him, procured a formal divorce without any mention of children. Warburton's love affair probably bloomed towards the end of 1839, several months after the British made their ill-fated entry into Kabul, thus setting out a good case for Warburton Snr's paternity of both offspring. In spite of his long-held doubts, in later years Warburton Snr came round to the view that after all, he was the father of the two boys, discerning a likeness to himself in the child he had christened John Paul.

The enigmatic John Paul Warburton carved out a distinguished career for himself in the Indian service, gaining the reputation as 'the master sleuth of the Punjab', nicknamed 'Button Sahib', a native corruption of the unpronounceable *Warburton*. The elder Warburton's prodigious success in tracking down criminals and terrorists earned him the unique honour of having an entire village as well as a railway station named after him, now in modern-day Pakistan. 'His reputation as the scourge of evil-doers is known throughout the length and breadth of India,' proclaims

The Times with some poetic licence. In Martineau's account, we find a photograph of John Paul in what must be late middle age, the epitome of a Victorian colonial servant in sola topi and sporting a luxurious handlebar moustache, flanked by his wife and children in front of the long vanished 'Warburton Station'. The exploits of 'Button Sahib' served as an inspiration to no less a luminary than Rudyard Kipling. Having heard of the terror Warburton was reputed to strike in the hearts of *dacoits* (outlaws), Kipling paid several visits to the family and went to some trouble to discuss police methods with the sleuth, whom Edmund Candler later described as 'the Super Detective of the Punjab'. It is generally acknowledged that Warburton served as the model for Kipling's character Strickland, who appears in *Plain Tales from the Hills*, as well as other collections of short stories. 'Now, in the whole of Upper India, there is only one man who can pass for Hindu or Mahomedan, hide-dresser or priest, as he please,' Kipling tells us of his master detective. 'He is feared and respected by the natives from Ghor Kathri to the Jamna Musjid, and he is supposed to have the gift of invisibility and executive control over many Devils.' It is a fact that during his forty years' service in the Punjab, John Paul found himself drawn into intrigues that rang with high romance: the case of the poisoner of Sharuf-ud-Din, the great Ambala Treasury theft, the dacoits of the Sansiyas tribe, plus many other exploits of derring-do.

John Paul, who died in 1919, was a celebrated figure of his day in colonial circles, but of his brother, or half-brother, Warburton of the Punjab, not a word from Warburton of the Khyber.

Lord Napier proved himself true to his word: shortly after disembarking in India, Warburton was despatched to the North-West Frontier as Assistant Commissioner of the Peshawar Division, the tribal region's administrative centre that was to be his home for nearly thirty years, from 1869 to 1898. Whatever acts of savagery Warburton might have witnessed on his tour of duty in Africa, these could have rated as the excesses of naughty schoolboys alongside the barbarism that was to open his eyes to the realities of life and death on the Frontier. He speaks in horror of the routine poisoning of an enemy's cattle, setting fire to the harvested crops of an entire village, brutal murders and mutilations for revenge or on account of the Pathans' three most coveted possessions, *zar, zan, zamin* – wealth, women, land. Yet thanks to his unique identification with Pathan culture, Warburton was able to gain a deeper understand of their ways than did any administrator of the Khyber in the half century after his departure from the Frontier until Britain's withdrawal from India.

There is more than a touch of irony in the fact that Warburton, a legend on the Frontier in his own day, can be accused of hero-worship. But there was a role model Frontiersman whom Warburton never came to know, but whose exploits inspired him. This was Lieutenant-Colonel Frederick Mackeson, who died in 1853 'of a wound inflicted by a religious fanatic' as inscribed on the gravestone that stands in the Peshawar Mall. As Commissioner of the Peshawar Division, Mackeson was given the task of keeping the Khyber Pass open during the First Afghan War of 1838–42. One September evening as he was holding public council outside his house, a Pathan stepped forward to hand him what appeared to be a petition. While Mackeson's attention was distracted, the rogue drew a dagger from his sleeve and stabbed him. Interestingly enough in the context of recent events in Afghanistan, the assassin was identified as one of the religious students known as Talib-ul-Ilm, in other words a Taliban.

'Wherever I have been, in every part of the Peshawar District,' declares Warburton, 'in the Khyber Range . . . the name of Mackeson has been honoured and respected by all the residents of those lands above that of any other Englishman who has been on the Peshawar border.' Warburton was convinced that there must have been something in the character, deeds and life of this exemplary soldier 'to have kept his memory still fresh and dear to the savages of the Khyber Range'. Something indeed worth emulating, on the civil as well as military fronts. If Mackeson was revered for his good works, such as providing clean water to improve the lot of the local inhabitants – 'Take care you fetch my drinking water from Mackeson Sahib's well' was a traditional command to a water-carrier in Peshawar – Warburton was equally determined to leave his imprint as a reformer and innovator in the Khyber region. His one grand scheme, which was put forward to the Viceroy Lord Dufferin on an official visit to the Khyber, was for a parallel road through the pass, ostensibly to ease the flow of traffic between Afghanistan and India. There was, however, another agenda in this plan, and it illustrates that when it came to craftiness Warburton was more than a match for the Pathan. The threat of an enemy closing the pass was a constant obsession during the turbulent years of Warburton's stewardship of the Khyber. He was himself witness to this menace in 1878, shortly before he raised the militia that was to become the Khyber Rifles, when the Afghans stopped General Sir Neville Chamberlain's mission through the Khyber at Ali Masjid outpost, thus igniting the flint that touched off the Second Afghan War. Warburton confided to the Viceroy that a second route from Landi Kotal running north of the Khyber Pass down to Peshawar could never be closed: the reason being that it would pass through the lands of the Shilman and Mullagori, tribes too weak to attempt to take the road. Moreover, he informed Dufferin while on a horseback inspection of the district, the Shinwaris hate the Zakha Khel Afridis, while the Mullagoris detest the whole Afridi race, and both wanted a good road built through their territories to Peshawar that would render them independent of the Khyber Pass. In the end, the government ruled against the project, probably for reasons of economy, as the costs had run about £3,000 over budget before the first paving stones were laid. 'We had cause to regret this act afterwards, especially in 1897,' Warburton laments, having in mind the Afridi uprising that erupted into what he refers to as the 'Khyber débâcle', when British troops failed to relieve the besieged Khyber Rifles garrisons of the pass.

In the years leading up to his decision in 1878 to raise a corps of native recruits to guard the Khyber Pass, Warburton found himself immersed ever deeper in a world of endless intrigues and strife. A particularly awkward problem was the five-year period in which he was obliged to deal with the notorious brigand Ajab Khan. This irksome fellow did his utmost to undermine the Peshawar Commissioner's authority, through constant raids on villages in his district, the massacre of more than thirty coolies employed by the British on a canal construction project, as well as a host of other bloody outrages. Warburton held a degree of respect for his tormentor, this 'remarkable man of a lean frame, standing six feet tall, with a long black beard and a silver toothpick suspended from his neck'. There ensued a cat-and-mouse game between the ranking British administrator of the Khyber and his tribal foe, until in classic Pathan fashion Ajab Khan was betrayed by an erstwhile faithful henchman and Warburton was able to have him convicted and despatched to the gallows. But there were other tribulations on the horizon, notably the Afghan campaign that turned the Khyber into a battlefield before the British troops, forcing their way at bayonet point up the road built by Mackeson connecting Fort Jamrud at the foot of the pass to Ali Masjid, successfully scattered the Afghan troops.

Harassment by outlaws like Ajab Khan and the near military disaster in the pass at the outbreak of the Afghan conflict brought matters to a head: Warburton grasped the futility of attempting to permanently garrison this no man's land with regular troops.

Warburton may have walked among the Pathans like a blood brother, unarmed and bearing the self-confidence of a Daniel in the lions' den, but he was British Army issue to the core. His cadetship was spent at Woolwich instead of Sandhurst and this is important: not only did he fulfil his father's ambition to have his son pass into the ranks of the artillery, but Woolwich was the gateway to a career in the British as opposed to the Indian Army. A Woolwich officer might from time to time find himself serving in India on a tour of duty, but rarely as a career officer. Warburton the solider thus stood out as something of a maverick in the ranks in that he chose to be posted to India as a British Army officer, and on a lower pay scale than his comrades of the

Indian Army. Nevertheless, with his Afghan blood and British military college training, he arrived on the Frontier arguably the ideal man to assess and deal with the intricate geopolitical and cultural threads that ran through the Khyber region.

By this point in Warburton's career, the government had come to value his expertise on the Frontier to a degree that was quite literally to save his life. In the spring of 1879, when Lieutenant Colonel Sir Pierre Louis Napoleon Cavagnari was preparing to march off to Afghanistan, and to his doom as the resident Commander of the Kabul garrison, he summoned Warburton to a meeting at Nowshera. In that balmy outpost Warburton was told that his services 'had been placed at the disposal of the Government of India Foreign Department' for employment under Cavagnari, whom he was to accompany to Kabul as his personal secretary. But the Punjab Government saw things differently. With the Khyber tribes in a state of turmoil, they looked upon Warburton as too valuable an asset to be spared for service in Afghanistan. In April of 1879 the Lieutenant-Governor of the Punjab wrote to the Foreign Department insisting that Warburton's departure for Kabul would be 'injurious to the interest of the public services'. It was noted that the removal of Captain Warburton would leave the district without any officer, civil or military, 'who knows and is known by the headmen of the trans-border tribes' at a time when 'the independent tribes along the whole of the North-West Frontier are in a state of excitement, and, under the guidance, or instigated by, the preaching of fanatical Mullahs'.

This reprieve, as it came to light five months on when Cavagnari, along with all the officers, guides, cavalry, infantry and servants of his party were attacked and slaughtered in the Kabul Residency, was followed by news of a more heartening nature. Before he met his fate Cavagnari, perhaps in part to redress Warburton's disappointment, had lobbied to have jurisdiction of the Khyber Pass transferred from the Government of India to that of the Punjab, a body whose civil administrators were a lot closer to the realities of Frontier affairs than were the bureaucrats of distant Calcutta. Even at this late stage, Warburton held out hope that he would be allowed to join Cavagnari's party – 'a hope,' he later acknowledged, 'which recalled in the light of after events was fortunately, perhaps, not fulfilled'.

Warburton's success in having raised the Khyber Jezailchis the previous year sent his star into the ascendant. One sizzling July morning in 1879, the 36-year-old moustachioed officer was summoned to the office of Colonel William Waterfield, CSI, Acting Commissioner of the Division at Peshawar. In a brief and business-like encounter, Warburton suddenly found his life dream laid before him. 'The Lieutenant-Governor of the Punjab offers you the post of Political Officer Khyber,' quipped Waterfield. 'Will you accept it?' Barely able to conceal his delight, Warburton pulled himself up smartly and replied, 'Yes!' Within a few days he found himself on an inspection tour of the considerable forces massed at Landi Kotal, high on the Khyber Pass. These units comprised two British and three native infantry regiments, three mountain batteries, two companies of sappers and miners, a troop of the 10th Bengal Lancers and, most significantly, two companies of Khyber Jezailchis, who took their name from the jezail, the native soldiers' elaborately ivory-inlaid musket, whose discharge was described by one Frontier soldier as 'a rattling and banging, as of a minor train accident'. As rifles of the day ranked, the jezail was accurate to a frightening degree at long range, but as a weapon of stealth it was as effective as the disintegration of a large mirror over the mantelpiece. The Khyber Jezailchis were now a fully-fledged and accepted unit of the British Frontier forces, accepted because to the astonishment of nearly everyone except Warburton, once employed, the Afridi and Mohmand levies turned out to be exceedingly loyal.

The idea of confiding one of India's most vulnerable invasion routes to a militia made up of wild tribesmen, about whom the British knew little and held in extreme mistrust, must have been a hard sell for Warburton. China, for instance, brought in Han instead of local Cantonese Chinese to guard the Hong Kong

border in the run-up to the 1997 handover. Why not then use
trusted Gurkha, Sikh or other Indian Army regulars to guard the
Khyber Pass? Apart from the expense involved in garrisoning
regular troops on the Frontier, and the harsh conditions they
would have had to endure throughout most of the year,
Warburton convincingly argued that treated with due respect, the
Pathans would respond in kind and remain steadfastly loyal to
their British officers. What the founder of the Khyber Rifles failed
to realise was that this loyalty was bestowed on Warburton
himself, not the Queen Empress. And this was to prove a costly
oversight in the tribal rebellions of 1897.

One outstanding example of this personal allegiance was Malik
Walli Mohammed Khan, an Afridi of the fierce Zakha Khel clan,
who in the previous year had commanded the Afghan troops that
launched an attack on the Khyber outpost of Ali Masjid.
Warburton's relationship with this former Afghan Army officer,
in reality a bond of friendship that lasted the eighteen years he
spent in charge of the Khyber Pass, was a tribute to his servant's
code of honour as well as the prestige Warburton enjoyed among
the Pathans. After the deposed amir's forces had been defeated in
the Second Afghan War, Walli Mohammed journeyed to Kabul to
ask if his monarch had any further commands for him. Yakub
Khan thanked him for his allegiance, but said it would be right
for him to go and make friends with the victorious British. From
Kabul Walli Mohammed made his way eastward over the desert
mountains to Landi Kotal, where he presented himself to the
celebrated Captain Warburton of the Khyber, a name already well
known to the border tribesmen. 'I was drawn to this loyal old
man, the only one of the Khyber Afridi maliks who, having
fought for Yakub Khan, and when he had done all he could for
his old master had desisted from embroiling himself further solely
on the advice given him by the ex-amir,' writes Warburton. Walli
Mohammed swore an oath on the Koran to remain a faithful
servant to Warburton. True to his vow, this battle-seasoned
soldier stood by his English master in every campaign undertaken
to break up tribal attacks against the British Government.

There is no record of so close a friendship between a Pathan tribesman and a British officer as that between these two soldiers from opposite sides of the border. It would be difficult to imagine anyone but Warburton achieving so comfortable a servant-master relationship with a Pathan tribal leader, and an Afghan Army officer at that. Their rapport took second place only to Warburton's lifelong kinship with Sir Aslam Khan, the Khyber Rifles' first Muslim Commandant. Warburton kept an absolute faith in Walli Mohammed's loyalty, so that he had no hesitation in appointing him malik, or chieftain of half the Zakha Khel Afridis, the most warlike and stubborn of the Khyber clans who could muster some 5,000 armed men and in Warburton's estimation, 'every individual being a thief, raider and robber by birth, inclination and habit carried down for many centuries'. He recalls that in later years, on any occasion that Walli Mohammed might be reprimanded for neglecting an order, the devoted Afridi would remind his employer-comrade, 'Did you not secure for me my Maliki? And am I going to work against you after what you have done for me?'

Yet in the very personal nature of this allegiance lay its intrinsic weakness. This truth was driven painfully home with the downfall of Warburton's trusted friend and ally. For years, Warburton tells us, part of his work as Political Officer was to prevent Walli Mohammed falling into the clutches of the fanatical Malik Khwas Khan of the Zakha Khel clan. 'This fate actually happened to him within five weeks of my giving up charge of the Khyber on July 11th, 1897,' he writes. His admired master having departed, Walli Mohammed was cast adrift, once more under the influence of his brethren tribesmen, and one who in this was case ranked as 'the most clever chief' Warburton had come across in the Khyber.

The sizzling month of April, a time of year when temperatures in the Khyber soar to well above 100°F for days as well as nights on end, found Warburton laid low with another of the crippling attacks of dysentery that would eventually end his life.

He was at that time stationed in Jalalabad, having just led his first punitive mission against a Pathan village that had been targeted for sheltering bandits responsible for the murder of a party of unarmed *doolie*-bearers. The Warden of the Khyber now found himself flat on his back on one of these same doolies, transported stage by stage to Peshawar, whence he made his way to Bombay and back to England. Even for an invalid, it was a grand style sea crossing in those days, a month or more on a Peninsular and Oriental Steam Navigation Company steamer to Venice, and from there by rail to Turin, Paris and finally Folkestone. Languid, suffering bouts of 'Peshawar fever', Warburton was confined to bed for eleven weeks in a London convalescent hospital in Fitzroy Square. His recovery was not hastened by the arrival of news from Jalalabad, where troubles had recommenced within days of his departure. For Warburton, the setback in the field was ample proof, as he asserts, that 'to deal with Afghans, officers must be employed who have knowledge of their languages, customs and ways'.

Finally came the day that Warburton, his health tenuously restored, returned to take charge once again of the Khyber Pass. On arriving in the bleak, grey hills, he notes his bemusement at the sight of Afridi tribesmen directing caravan traffic with great aplomb back and forth between Kabul and Peshawar. Only a few years before, when the deployment of 5,000 British and Indian army troops was required to ensure travellers safe passage through the Khyber, the presence of armed Afridis in the defile would have been the warning signal for a tribal raid. But this, after all, had been the *raison d'être* for raising that rag-tag band of Khyber Jezailchis, who carried their own matchlocks, sometimes called *Nikkulsenis* in honour of John Nicholson, the legendary British hero of the Frontier, who himself had come to be known as 'the Lion of the Punjab'. The recruits' one distinguishing piece of kit was a strip of red cloth dangling from their pagris, or turbans, from which was derived the nickname *Sur-Lakkais*, or red tails. They were, in Warburton's esteem, 'an untidy, unkempt band of excellent men'. The Jezailchis, later to be rechristened the

Khyber Rifles, were raised specifically to guard the pass and escort caravan traffic up and down its twisting, dusty road. 'When springtime flushes the desert grass, our *kafilas* wind through the Khyber Pass,' wrote Kipling, who was no stranger to the pass and its menacing yet intoxicating life. The long trains of camel caravans or kafilas, sometimes numbering thousands of men and beasts that required two hours or more to pass a fixed point, plied the route twice a week, on Monday and Thursday under guard of the amir's khassadars, bearing hides, fruit and carpets from Afghanistan and the distant lands of Bokhara and Samarkand to the rich markets of Peshawar. This is how Kipling saw it in *Soldiers Three*: 'There is a pleasant wind among the mulberry trees, and the streams are bright with snow-water, and the caravans go up and the caravans go down, and a hundred fires sparkle in the gut of the Pass, and tent-peg answers hammer-nose, and pack-horse squeals to pack-horse across the drift smoke of the evening.'

The detachment of Khyber Rifles that brought the caravans to Landi Kotal outpost by evening met those at Landi Khana, near the western mouth of the pass, where they settled down for two nights. From Peshawar, the kafilas proceeded westward on the same days of the week, halting at Jamrud at the foot of the pass: once the caravans from both sides converged there the traffic flow became somewhat more complicated. Here the Khyber Rifles had the task of seeing the Afghan caravans safely down to Ali Masjid, where they would wait for the upcoming kafilas with their escort from Peshawar. They then changed hands and were respectively shepherded westward to Landi Khana and down to Peshawar. The mayhem and din of this assemblage of camels and tribesmen resounded on a truly colossal scale. But the experience the Khyber Rifles gained in managing this crush of two-way traffic between Afghanistan and British India served them well for future duties in the pass. Today, the corps still mans the gates at the Torkham border crossing, a scene of constant chaos, with Afghans streaming home to pick up the threads of their past lives, while others struggle to make it across to Pakistan, some to be reunited with relatives, in other cases because there is nothing left to hold them in Afghanistan. And as a backdrop to this migratory flood of humanity, hundreds of lorries rumble through the gates, horns blaring, as drivers high on hashish force a swathe through the crowds with their wildly decorated juggernauts.

A fact that Warburton failed to seize upon was that lions may be taught to crouch on a pedestal at the crack of a whip, or even allow their tamer to poke his head into their mouths, but under that veneer of docility there always lurks a wild and unpredictable beast. This was brought into focus by the veteran Frontier solider Charles Chevenix Trench, who in his book *The Frontier Scouts* highlights the near calamity that took place at Ali Masjid fort four years after the Jezailchis were brought into being. 'In 1882, for purely administrative reasons, it was decided that the fort at Ali Masjid, garrisoned by a company of the Malik Din Khel section of Afridis, should be abandoned and the company moved to Jamrud. Promptly a Subadar and Jemadar (corps officers) concluded that the government was on the run and went round, Koran in hand, urging their men to desert with rifles rather than obey the order. A *havildar* (sergeant) defied them and managed to get the company back to Jamrud.' The lesson should have been plain: an entire company must not be composed of a single section of a tribe like the Afridis, and trans-Frontier Pathans, in their own country, were not reliable when withdrawal was in the wind. The incident was a foreboding of far more calamitous events, in particular the great Pathan uprising of 1897, in which Koran-waving maliks were able to inflame nearly all the Frontier tribes to revolt. Despite these setbacks, in the early days Warburton's tribal militia ensured that the Khyber remained a safe place, and indeed safer than Peshawar. The afternoon the Commander-in-Chief Lord Roberts and Warburton rode across the pass on an inspection tour, escorted only by two troopers of the Khyber Rifles, Roberts' Quartermaster General remarked, 'If this were to be told in England, or to any officer of the old Punjab school, they would never believe it.'

Warburton could take just pride in the fact that from 1878 the Khyber Pass had become a safe highway for civilian traffic for the first time in thirty years: in 1848 it had been declared closed to caravans, trade and travellers, which had to negotiate the much trickier old Tatarra road between Kabul and Peshawar. The British then considered the Khyber far too dangerous a route, with upwards of 20,000 armed Afridis lurking in its treacherous defiles, which often enough would flare up with the crack of musket fire from the tribesmen's own inter-clan feuds. Thirty years later it was the standard route for trade between both countries.

Three years into the job of Political Officer, Warburton was called upon to put his tribal acumen to the supreme test. Early in 1882 the alarm went up at Jamrud, the checkpoint that now stands at the entrance to the pass, when a Khyber Rifles orderly burst breathless into the fort bearing news that the notorious Zakha Khel clan was on the march, poised to launch a massive raid. Their grievance was against one of their own maliks, Khwas Khan – the scoundrel who later was to poison Walli Mohammed against the British. The tribesmen accused Khwas Khan of filching their share of the allowances that the Political Agent paid the tribes to keep the peace in the Khyber. Warburton needed to act swiftly to prevent a localised raid escalating into a full-blown revolt. 'We received timely warning of what was going to happen and the raiders, caught in a trap, lost five killed and about nine wounded,' he writes.

Warburton was well acquainted with the doctrine of the three coveted treasures of zar, zan, zamin. This particular grievance concerned zar, or wealth, so accordingly he sought to contrive a longer term solution to the problem by identifying four other groups within the Zakha Khel clan as potential troublemakers, and setting up a system of paying them their allowances in person, rather than passing the money through the grasping hands of their maliks. Warburton was to employ this stick-and-carrot tactic routinely in his everyday dealings with the Pathans.

Not long after this episode, a freebooter named Kamal, of the Malikdin Khel clan, began menacing the army picquets around

Peshawar and Kohat, murdering a number of cavalrymen and absconding with rifles and loot. So infamous was the mischief he caused that his deeds found a place in Kipling's pen: 'Do you remember that time in Peshawar when Kamal hammered on the gates of Jamrud – mountebank that he was – and lifted the Colonel's horses all in one night?' So the Pathan servant reminisces with his Sahib in *Soldiers Three*. 'Kamal is dead now, but his nephew has taken up the matter, and there will be more horses amissing if the Khaibar Levies do not look into it.'

Taking charge of the case, Warburton's first step was to impose a 8,000-rupee fine on the entire Afridi clan. When the headmen and tribal jirgas take a hit to their pockets, they become unhappy tribesmen. This in itself provided sufficient motivation to spur the men into action, swooping on Kamal's house, torching it to the ground and turning the brigand out of their territory. Nevertheless, the irrepressible Kamal came back again and again to wreak havoc on the British outposts. Warburton, steeped as he was in the ways of the Pathan, knew this was likely to happen. 'The (clans) were again fined for not controlling Kamal, but that individual did not mind in the least, as he had numerous quarters where he could be sheltered when his tribesmen turned against him,' the Political Agent laments. The Pathan social code, known as Pakhtunwali, demands that whatever the circumstances, protection must be granted to those in distress. This is the *nanawatai* (sanctuary) tenet, a practice that turned into a frequent source of trouble for the government. A Pathan who had committed murder or another serious crime in a settled district would slip across the border into tribal territory and seek asylum with an individual or clan of a tribe, often on the strength of no more than a casual acquaintance. Kamal could have quite easily found a safe house in any one of hundreds of villages up and down the Frontier – a noteworthy parallel to the hunt for Osama bin Laden. In the end, the Kamal saga was resolved in classic Pathan style: Warburton placed on the table a 2,000-rupee reward to whoever brought the bandit into custody and 'something less' if he were slain while resisting capture. The

Afridis were delighted to take Warburton up on his offer, but there was one catch that left them slightly puzzled. A cousin of Kamal, who carried one of his kinsman's bullets in his leg, went to visit Warburton with an enquiry: precisely how much was the government prepared to pay for Kamal's body? It was explained to the tribesman that there could be no reward for a deliberate murder, but still he remonstrated: Sahib, how much simpler just to kill Kamal than to drag him before a British court of justice, where he would surely be convicted and hanged. Kamal's angry cousin went away convinced of the superiority of his reasoning. Shortly thereafter, having concealed himself in a mosque in the village where Kamal was sheltered, he patiently crouched in waiting and shot his cousin dead as he went out on his afternoon stroll. A few days later Akbar, brother of Kamal, avenged the murder by gunning down his hapless cousin. Warburton assumes as a matter of conventional wisdom that Akbar must have been assassinated at a later date in the ongoing blood feud, and with that the tiresome Kamal affair came to a conclusion.

The bellicose Zakha Khel clan was always a source of bedevilment, not only to the British forces and Peshawar cantonments, but equally to some of the other, less warlike clans of the Afridi tribe, whose crops, livestock and villages were constantly under threat from these marauding tribesmen. In 1882 Warburton moved a company of Khyber Rifles out of their garrison to protect the villages on a monthly rotation basis. The troops were supplied with a large drum and rockets to sound the alarm in case of attack. Later, the Khyber Rifles began using heliographs, a signalling device by which sunlight is reflected in flashes from a movable mirror, for sending messages across the hills, a practice that still forms part of the drill of this tradition-conscious corps.

The recurring attacks of dysentery that were undermining Warburton's health were by no means his only source of trouble. There were others, 'plentiful enough', in those early days in the Khyber. Warburton spent a good part of the years 1878 to 1883 engaged in settling tribal disputes with the government, as well as among the rival factions of the clans. His time was also taken up with pursuing bandits and raiders, apportioning the euphemistically designated 'Khyber allowances', in reality straightforward bribes to the tribes, levying fines on those same tribes for misbehaviour and hearing the grievances of the jirgas. Some of the tasks lay well beyond the grasp of anyone but a Warburton, with his vast knowledge of the tribes and their idiosyncrasies. When the government decided to undertake the task of repairing the Khyber Pass road, the most recalcitrant of the clans, the Zakha Khels, bitterly opposed the idea of tribesmen from rival clans moving about their territory, even as temporary construction workers. It therefore fell to Warburton to come up with a scheme to keep everybody happy, so to be able to get on with the badly needed road works. The strategy he finally devised must have left his superiors at Punjab government headquarters scratching their heads in bewilderment. From Jamrud to Ali Masjid he ordered the road to be worked by men supplied by the Kuki Khel clan. The section from Ali Masjid to near the hamlet of Gurgurra was allotted to the Malikdin Khels. The stretch from Gurgurra to the fort now belonged to the firebrand Malik Khwas Khan, so this part was covered by his own men. From Khwas Khan's fort to the Shinwari clan's limits was the share of Malik Walli Mohammed Khan's party among the Zakha Khels, while the last tract to Landi Khana and the Torkham border post was to be the domain of the Shinwari workers. The plan might have appeared convoluted on a magnitude worthy of a Medici intrigue but it worked, and the Khyber road, so vital for moving troops quickly up to the Afghan border, was improved and completed without incident, truly a tribute to Warburton's mastery of the ways of the Pathans.

A tribute to the perversity of British colonial administration was soon to follow: in the spring of 1883 the government saw fit to reduce Warburton's salary. There was, after all, cost cutting to consider, just as there had been four decades earlier when the decision to deprive the Khyber tribes of their 'allowances' had led to the Pathan revolt that promptly spread to Kabul, leading to the calamity that befell Elphinstone's army. This was the only moment in Warburton's career, and quite understandably, in which he revealed signs of despair or anger with his employers. A few months after recovering from a major dysentery attack, during which he was evacuated to the Murree hills, this blow to his pride and pocket prompted him to write, 'This was done in the face of a promise made to me in July 1879 . . . and a letter sent by Sir R. Egerton's Government in October 1879, fixing my pay. This was my reward for serving the Government of the Punjab for thirteen years during a fairly troublesome period.'

In spite of this setback, Warburton carried on deepening his relationship with the tribes, only now in the company of Aslam Khan, who had become the Khyber Rifles' first Muslim Commandant. During the summer months Warburton and Aslam Khan rode up to the cool heights near the top of the pass at Landi Kotal, where they spent weeks on end dealing with tribal affairs and hearing petitions from the maliks. 'During the mornings we took our walk, discussed matters with all the headmen and visitors 'till breakfast, when the tribesmen went away for their morning meal,' he recalls. 'From 10 a.m. to 5 p.m. was reserved for work. In the evenings the people assembled once more, and we again had a walk and a talk. Often whilst we were out, the time came round for prayers, when the hillmen would spread their cloths, turn their faces towards the supposed correct quarter, and proceed with their devotions.' During prayer times Warburton waited seated on a rock nearby, after which the party would stroll back to camp and part for the night. These walkabouts were conducted in a setting of tranquillity and harmony, so that all private, public or tribal feuds were put aside in the interest of reaffirming a mutual trust and respect between the Political Officer and the Afridis. 'Hence for six or seven weeks, my camp was full of men having deadly blood feuds with one another, armed to the teeth, each man having his loaded rifle, yet no outrage was ever committed,' he says. 'I may say that this rule was implicitly carried out by me for more than fifteen years.' The only person not armed to the teeth during these sessions was Warburton himself, who says that the people were better pleased when they felt assured he trusted them entirely with his safety. 'I therefore always went about with only a stick in my hand,' he declares.

Warburton's crowning years in the Khyber commenced, appropriately enough, in the month of November. It was 1887, and the Political Officer's official diary was taken up with preparations for a visit to his Khyber region by the Viceroy Lord Dufferin, the Commander-in-Chief in India, Lord Roberts, the entire staff headquarters, the Lieutenant-General of the Punjab, assorted wives, secretaries camp-followers and hangers-on, all of whom had tagged along 'to share in whatever amusements and pleasures might be going on'. Warburton was charged with gathering a deputation of tribal chieftains from Peshawar and surrounding districts, to be paraded before the Viceroy in a splendorous regal *durbar*. As Warburton recalls the event, the pageant was not without its moments of levity, particularly during the tribesmen's march past the viceregal eminence. One tribal elder shouted out for the return of his ornately embossed presentation card, an heirloom to be preserved by his family, when he was wheeled into proper place before the representative of Her Majesty the Queen Empress of India. '*Mira ticket!*' (My card!) the old man bellowed repeatedly at Lord Dufferin, as Warburton had him tactfully pushed out of the tent door. Nonetheless, the persistent Khyber maliks, sensing a jolly in the offing, managed to sweet-talk the Viceroy into organising a junket to visit some of the wonders of India. Thus one morning in 1888 Warburton, who was undoubtedly aware of the futility of this exercise in winning the hearts and minds of the Pathans, assembled sixteen of these grizzled Khyber maliks at the Peshawar railway junction for the journey to Calcutta. 'Nothing that they had seen . . . seemed to have any effect on the stolid minds of the residents of the Khyber Range,' he recalls. 'They passed by everything without a change of feature, as if large stations, broad rivers, magnificent bridges and huge cities were to be seen and met with at every step in the Khyber Pass.'

Warburton was all his life a devoted servant of the Raj, an implacable believer in the empire and the innumerable benefits it had bestowed on India and its unenlightened inhabitants. He had sent his corps off to the front with the words, 'Do nothing that will bring disgrace or discredit on the Khyber Rifles and myself.' Yet if he inwardly grieved, as well he might, that his first nine years at the helm had failed to secure a lasting peace with the Khyber tribes, far worse lay ahead.

Over the next decade, the Frontier tribes staged uprisings at regular intervals and it took all Warburton's strength and considerable negotiating powers – as well as an armed response by the British forces – to plug the holes in the dyke against these sporadic insurrections. 'What I had dreaded and feared, and had done my best to induce the authorities to avoid, was now about to happen,' Warburton laments a few months before the great Afridi revolt that he portrays as the 'Khyber débâcle'. 'We were in for what I had laboured all my years and by every means in my power to avert – a great Afridi war.'

In the years leading up to his retirement Warburton had in vain petitioned the government to provide him with a British assistant, a protégé whom he could teach what was required to befriend the maliks and tribal elders. 'When the time came for my departure he could have stepped into my place, and Government should at once have given him another assistant to learn the work on the same principles and routine,' he says. Alas, the very same box wallahs of the Punjab who had seen fit to reduce Warburton's salary, also refused on the grounds of economy to subsidise a British officer to step into his shoes when he retired. Now that time had come, when he was to bid adieu to the Khyber hills and to those he called his 'wild, savage friends'.

Warburton was due to retire in July 1897, but to escape the heat of the plains around his Peshawar headquarters, he instead took three months' furlough in May, the onset of the hottest season when the thermometer frequently breaks 130°F, to head for the cool uplands of Murree.

There was no evidence in the Khyber of trouble stirring at the time. Peshawar swarmed with hundreds of Afridis who had journeyed down from the hills to collect their allowances and stock up on supplies before migrating to their cooler summer quarters. Warburton himself acknowledges that 'there was no single question troubling their minds seriously which was like to induce them to take up arms against the British Government'. Indeed, when his horse-drawn dak-gharry pulled up at the Peshawar station on 10 May, there stood assembled a throng of Afridi maliks, elders and jirgas crowding the platform to take a last look at the Englishman who had been associated with them for eighteen years. 'It was with a very sorrowful heart that I saw the last of them that evening, as the 5 p.m. train steamed out of the Peshawar Cantonment station towards Rawalpindi,' he recalls. 'I little dreamt then that the Khyber debacle of August 1897 would carry me through every quarter of Afridi land, in the toughest and hardest fought campaign I ever had to misfortune or honour of being associated with.'

The events that brought the tribal lashkars down on the defenders of the Khyber that year were of complex and obscure origins. The Pathans were never short of specific gripes – the salt tax, recent British operations against the tribes, the Durand boundary line. Any one of those issues would have provided an excuse to stir the battle-loving tribes into action. Warburton's assertion that the single catalyst for revolt was an outbreak of religious fanaticism stirred up by the mullahs, who swarmed among the tribesmen calling for a jihad, and with the full blessing of Kabul, is generally accepted as valid. The call to arms had the desired effect: the Afridi lashkars poured out of the hills, storming the Khyber Rifles posts, savagely attacking British forces wherever they were to be found and generally spreading pandemonium up and down the Frontier.

On the evening of 13 August Warburton returned to his bungalow from a briefing with general staff officers commanding the Punjab forces, who had urgently called him in to offer his assessment of the tribal disturbances. Closing the door behind him, he picked up a telegram that had been laid on the entranceway table by his houseboy. The official envelope contained a memorandum from the Foreign Secretary to the Government of India. With sinking heart, Warburton read, 'If Government proposed to re-employ you specially with reference to Afridi affairs, would you be willing?' Wearily casting aside thoughts of a well-earned autumn passage back to England, the Political Officer replied: 'Ready for any Government service if required.'

The Tirah campaign turned into one of the most desperate and hardest fought campaigns mounted against the Afridis, and it required almost seven months of bitter fighting before the insurgents could be subdued. Warburton took an active part in the field operations, from which he emerged more respectful than ever of the Afridis, enemies now as well as brothers. He was equally pleased with the part played by his Khyber Rifles in this operation, particularly the private escort that accompanied him as guides or scouts. 'All proved faithful and loyal, although working against their own countrymen,' he writes. 'When it is remembered that they were carrying their lives literally in their hands, and knew the cruel certain fate which awaited them if they were taken prisoners, I do not think that I exaggerate in saying that such loyalty deserved recognition, and that no men better earned the Victoria Cross or the Military Order of Merit than these.' But they got nothing for their services.

Warburton deeply regretted the government's refusal to provide him with a British assistant, citing this as one of the failures of government policy that might have prevented the Afridi conflict. A protégé would have made friends with the maliks and elders of all the tribes, he argues, and when the time came for Warburton's departure this officer could have seamlessly taken over his role. 'The little extra money required for this purpose would, in the face of what occurred later on, have amply repaid Government in

the end,' he reasons. But other people 'knew better' he laments
with an uncharacteristic twinge of irony, and when the day of his
departure arrived the Khyber charge was entrusted to Sir Aslam
Khan, whose pension papers were already before the Punjab
Government. In the tribesmen's eyes, Khan was at best an
ambiguous character, at worst a traitor to his people for having
taken up service under the British Raj. The Afghan nobleman
could hardly be the ideal candidate to contend with an Afridi
rebellion, being someone who carried the same mercurial
qualities in his blood as did the tribesmen. Consider the task of
mediating with Afridis such as the two tribesmen who
volunteered for the Frontier Regiment in 1914, and were sent to
the trenches in France. One deserted to the Germans, and for his
bravery in fighting against his former employers he was awarded
the Iron Cross. The other gave an equally courageous account of
himself on the British side, and received the Victoria Cross for
Valour. Both returned to their homeland, happy for having had a
chance to fight on a scale that hitherto lay beyond their wildest
dreams. Neither man returned home with the slightest notion of
why the two armies were engaged in this mass slaughter, nor
what it was they had been sent out to defend.

As to what occurred later on, Warburton could never have
envisaged the years of open strife between Government forces and
the Frontier tribes that raged virtually up to the day of Partition.
Racked with illness and deeply disillusioned in spirit, in 1898
Warburton boarded the P&O steamer for the final homeward
crossing. Once back in London he returned to the roots of his
English youth by taking up residence in Kensington, where he
devoted the few remaining months of his life to assembling his
memoirs, a task commissioned by his friend the Prince of Wales.
The job of editing and publishing his papers was left to his widow.
In his final days, tormented by dysentery, he wrote from his London
home to a friend giving an account of his grief over the disastrous
Frontier uprising. 'It makes me quite sad to think how easily the
labour of years – of a lifetime – can be ruined and destroyed in a
few days.' Robert Warburton died on 22 April 1899.

CHAPTER FIVE

Baptism by Fire in the Khyber

Only four years after the Jezailchis had come into existence, their loyalty to the Sahib was put to the supreme test. To no one's surprise, it was the Zakka Khels who, in 1882, provided the men with a chance to cut their teeth in battle against their own kith and kin. As dawn broke over the high granite cliffs of the Khyber Pass one frosty February morning, the narrowest section of the defile erupted in blood-curdling war cries from a lashkar of Zakka Khel tribesmen. Dashing out from behind their sangars, their Khyber knives (weapons capable of disembowelling a victim with a single upward thrust of its twelve-inch razor-sharp blade) glistening in the keen winter sunlight, the warriors swooped down on a caravan coming up from Kabul as it lumbered towards its rest stop at Ali Masjid. Fortunately for the Jezailchis, the Political Agent's native spy network had provided warning of the impending attack. No sooner had the marauders charged into the road, they were met by two companies of Jezailchis and a fusillade from their long-barrelled rifles that swiftly sent the raiders scurrying back to their mountain fastness before they could lay their hands on the booty-laden caravan. Warburton could congratulate himself that his experiment had proved a success, and that his men had come through the test of loyalty with flying colours. What stands out as remarkable about this début field operation of the future Khyber Rifles, was not only the fact that the Afridi recruits showed no hesitation in opening fire on their own tribesmen, but that their native officers had taken the decision to deploy Jezailchis of the very same Zakka Khel clan to do the job.

As anticipated, the Zakka Khels had chosen to dishonour their commitment to the British because of a grievance over money. Historically, this was the catalyst that triggered most tribal raiding. Exculpating themselves on the grounds that their maliks had not been fair in the distribution of the tribal subsidy, a complaint echoed many times over the years in council, the tribesmen who joined the attack offered their submission to the Political Officer. 'Their action is to be attributed more to this cause (money) than to a desire to break the treaty which provided for the management of the Pass by the Afridis,' was the judgement of an official enquiry. 'Measures were taken to remove their causes for discontent by a re-allocation of the Zakka Khel subsidy.'

With this incident resolved, the government was now pleased to confirm that 'The pass has since been protected by Jezailchis, and the arrangements made with the Khyber Afridis have been found to work satisfactorily, and long trains of travellers and pack animals, convoys of treasure, and stores of ammunition for Kabul have come and gone through the pass with safety.'[1]

The Black Mountain was a name that had caused many uneasy stirrings in Indian Army ranks since 1853. The long, narrow forest-clad ridge of this range that sits on the upper border of Hazara District, the most northerly part of the tribal Frontier, stretches north to south for some 30 miles at an average elevation of 8,000 feet. Its name derives from the broodingly dark shadows that cloak its slopes. The lower portion of Hazara possesses an abundant supply of water, produces excellent crops and is inhabited by generally peaceable tribesmen, immigrants expelled some centuries ago from the neighbouring Swat valley, and in the government's view 'a physically weak and contemptible race'. They were traditionally a soft target for raids by their more warlike neighbours to the north, for the Black Mountain proper is the domain of the fearsome Yusufzais, Pathan warriors who prefer to define themselves as Afghans, and who offered the British some of the most fanatical resistance of all the Frontier tribes. As with the Gurkhas of Nepal, the British employed the expedient of recruiting the Yusufzais into some of their most renowned Frontier regiments. But the army found it necessary to mount no fewer than six major expeditions against these recalcitrant tribesmen over a period of nearly forty years before they could finally be proclaimed pacified. The worst troubles took place in 1888, when a number of outrages by Yusufzai clansmen touched off what the British would call tit-for-tat conflicts, and the tribesmen would define as a blood feud, albeit outside their bloodline.

In the early months of that year, two British subjects were killed and two others kidnapped in a retaliatory Pathan raid following the arrest of a seditionist tribal leader. The government stopped short of mounting a full-scale punitive expedition when the situation quietened down, yet it was deemed likely that the tribesmen would be back on the rampage once the snows cleared in the spring. Acting on cue, in March the marauders waylaid two more British subjects, and then in June matters were brought to a head when two British officers and four men of the 5th Gurkhas were killed while on patrol within British territory. The unit came under fire from Yusufzai bandits, and while the main body of troops beat a hasty retreat to regroup, two officers galloped back to the rearguard with a stretcher to recover a wounded havildar. Seeing the British officers cut off from the main body, the tribesmen rushed in and hacked them to pieces with their Khyber daggers. The outraged Political Officer called for the entire tribe to present itself in Peshawar to tender its submission, as well as for the offenders to be handed over for just punishment, that is to be hanged. This demand was ignored. As was the custom when planning military action against the Pathans, the government would fire the first salvo by reading out the Riot Act. Everyone assumed as a matter of course that the maliks would laugh this off as an affront to their honour, and they were right. 'Whereas your clansmen have for years past not ceased to commit crimes in British territory, therefore it is the intention of the British Government to send an army to punish you,' read the proclamation to the tribal chieftains. 'It is hereby made known to you that if you accept and fulfil the following terms you will escape further punishment. Otherwise your country will be laid waste and you will be more severely punished.' The threat was issued in a tone that conjured up a vision of Moses clutching the Tablets, thundering out the Ten Commandments to the Israelites. The offenders were called upon to pay a fine of 4,000 rupees in arms, cattle or cash, 'as you please'. Furthermore, two maliks per section were to be surrendered as hostages, the tribes were to 'suffer troops to march unmolested' through their country, the hamlet of Chapra was to be destroyed 'in any case' and in future no villages or settlements were to be erected east of the crest of the Black Mountain. More than terms of submission, the tribesmen took this to be a declaration of war– which is precisely what it was.

Also in 1888 General Roberts and the Viceroy Lord Dufferin, in the company of their respective wives, ambled off on horseback for an extensive tour of those territories on the North-West Frontier that had been brought under British rule. 'I rode with Lord Dufferin through the Khyber Pass and to the top of the Kwaje Amran range,' writes Roberts, 'our visit to this latter point resulting, as I earnestly hoped it would, in His Excellency being convinced by personal inspection . . . of the necessity for our endeavouring to cultivate more friendly relations with the border tribes.'[2] But if Dufferin, shortly to return to England, was so guileless as to assume that winning the hearts and minds of the Afridis could be achieved through public relations stunts like sending the Khyber maliks on their grand tour of British India, later events were soon to prove him grossly mistaken. Later in the year, the Yusufzai were back on the rampage, falling on rival villages and raiding across the Administrative Border into Hazara District, where the two British officers and native troops had been butchered. No further provocation was needed and there were no more warnings. On 29 August it was decided to despatch a

military force to the Black Mountain within a month. Never one
for half measures, the Governor-General of the Punjab was
'pleased to direct' the mobilisation of a force led by Brigadier
General Sir John McQueen, consisting of three mountain
batteries, thirteen battalions of infantry and one company of
sappers and miners for the ensuing Black Mountain punitive
expedition. 'The Government of India,' fulminated the Governor-
General, 'has concluded that an expedition to punish the
aggressions of the Black Mountain tribes has become absolutely
necessary.' The force was to be assembled by 1 October and the
government wanted the job done in no more than three weeks.

There was a unique feature to this particular campaign in that
it marked the first time a contingent of Khyber Rifles, consisting
of 350 volunteers, was sent into action outside the corps' home
territory. 'His Honour (the Governor-General) has no doubt that
these men would prove very useful', states the Hazara Field Force
expedition plan. The Khyber Rifles, in the ten years since the unit
was raised, had won the government's respect through the native
troops' spirited defence of the pass against marauders and
insurgents of their own tribes. Now the Foreign Department was
anxious to see 'as many of the Khyber Rifles as can be spared
employed in accordance with their offer of service in the Black
Mountain Expedition'. Nevertheless (and one can well detect the
hand of Warburton in this addendum), the government was also
anxious lest the men feel themselves disadvantaged with regard to
their brethren on the other side of the battlefield, who until their
recent misdeeds were drawing handsome tribal allowances. 'It is
hoped that the Military Department will arrange to avoid any
occasion for discontent among the men on the score of expenses,'
the Foreign Department intimated in *sotto voce* in a despatch. In
the final days before putting the expeditionary force on the
march, the government also decided that it was time to upgrade
the Khyber Rifles to the status of a properly equipped corps. The
command to do so emanated from the exalted offices of
Government House, where Lord Dufferin, impressed by what he
had seen during his tour of the Khyber in the company of

Roberts, heartily approved the request for breech-loading Sniders to be issued to the Khyber Rifles, in replacement of their antiquated muzzle-loading jezails. 'Arrange for issue of Sniders and fifty rounds per man, also one blanket per man,' stated the viceregal telegram. General McQueen was happy enough with this arrangement, but shortly after the cessation of hostilities he brought to the Viceroy's attention the delicate matter of what was to become of the Sniders issued for the campaign, as the militiamen, rifle-loving Pathans to a man, were now to disperse to their homeland in the Khyber. 'I would strongly recommend for His Excellency's consideration,' McQueen wrote, 'that looking to the good service done by the corps during this expedition, the Snider rifles now in use be presented to the men under the condition that in the event of death or their quitting the Levy, the rifles will remain with the corps.'[3] Dufferin, whom Queen Victoria once considered 'too good-looking for the post of Lord in Waiting', was a career diplomat who understood the advantages of deferring to the experts. Back came the reply from Simla: 'Chief strongly supports the recommendation.' Having now become an integral part of the expedition, the Khyber Rifles were to be kitted out in 'clothing and carriage' free of charge, in accordance with the Viceroy's instructions. The Khyber Rifles, who had borne their title for less than a year, stepped out of their rag-tag shalwar kameezes into regulation issue khaki tunics and gaitered plus fours, topped by the celebrated red-tagged *pagri*.

The first Commandant of the Khyber Rifles, or the Jezailchis as they were still known in 1878, was Captain Gilbert Gaisford, an Indian-born veteran of the Punjab Frontier Force. Gaisford had served in the Second Afghan War as well as several other Frontier campaigns, and he was selected to command the newly raised corps of sepoys for three rather uneventful years. Gaisford met an untimely end in 1898, aged 48, when he was 'killed by a fanatic at Smallan', reads the inscription on his gravestone at Quetta. But the corps' true guiding spirit throughout the early years of its existence, albeit a soldier who was denounced as a traitor by many radical Pathans, was Lieutenant-Colonel (later 'Sir') Aslam Khan, who took charge of the Khyber Rifles in 1881 as the militia's first Muslim Commandant. Sir Aslam is a name that even today evokes pride in Khyber Rifles ranks, for he was to give two generations of his family to the corps. Warburton treated Aslam Khan as a brother as well as the only Pathan with sufficient prestige to take charge of a corps of tribesmen fresh from the hills. The mullahs tried with some success to stir up hatred for the Khyber Rifles' Commandant, but the men under his command held him in the highest regard as a Saddozai of the royal Afghan Durrani lineage, whose father had been wazir to the ill-starred Amir Shah Shujah. Hence Sir Aslam was in fact an Afghan, his family having taken refuge in Peshawar in 1843 when the British reinstalled Dost Mohammed on the throne. 'Aslam, the son, was in a position to appeal to these old Afridi loyalties,' says Caröe. 'He was moreover in his own person a man of commanding presence and a very great gentleman. Old Sir Aslam was the best-known figure in Peshawar in his day, and his portrait used to look down with eagle eye upon the revelries of the Peshawar Club. He was Warburton's other self and may well have been the predominant partner in the company.'[4] The corpulent, luxuriantly bearded nobleman was the Khyber Rifles' longest serving Commandant, remaining in charge of the corps from 1881 until the outbreak of the Pathan uprising sixteen years later. His tenure as Commandant was far longer than the average two to three years served by most of his successors down to the present day. Caröe notes that the Afridis, who support the Durrani claim to the Afghan throne, gave Shah Shujah sanctuary before his murder, when he was driven out of Kabul by Dost Mohammed, and they twice went so far as to put their whole tribe in motion in his support. 'The effort failed,' he writes, 'but the memory of the Saddozai kings served to stir Afridi loyalty when, nearly a century later, that tribe proved ready to follow the Saddozai, Nawab Sir Aslam Khan.'[5] He was the only Pathan servant of the Raj to be personally awarded a medal by Prince Albert, during a royal visit by the Consort to Jamrud in 1890, and in 1911 he was chosen to serve as aide-de-camp to Edward VII during the king-emperor's coronation durbar.

Sir Aslam, although 50 years old at the time and 'quite unfit for active service', nevertheless insisted on leading his men into battle in the Black Mountain expedition. By that time his tunic was laden with seven military medals and orders, several of them having been earned during active service in the Second Afghan War, 'bearing witness to a life spent in rough service cheerfully rendered'. The Black Mountain action itself was a fairly cut and dried affair, with a British casualty list of twenty-five killed in battle, fifty-four wounded and seven deaths from disease. The government attributed the remarkably low number of disease-related fatalities to 'the men having been specially selected for their physical fitness, the favourable conditions of climate, and good quality of the rations issued'. Moreover, not a single loss was reported among the ranks of the Khyber Rifles, with only five men slightly wounded in the fighting. A good thing, too, for as was laconically reported in a telegram despatched from Simla on the eve of the campaign, 'The Surgeon-General, Her Majesty's Forces, has been informed that, as at present ordered, no medical arrangements are necessary for the Khyber Rifles...which will accompany the Hazara Field Force.' On the other hand, the native Kashmiri unit that marched with the army was provided with rations, clothing and medical supplies fully funded by the Maharajah of Kashmir, a benevolence that the government did not feel compelled to extend to the Khyber Rifles.

The first major action of the Yusufzai expedition was launched shortly after dawn, with a simultaneous frontal assault by three columns straight up the Black Mountain. The troops met with little opposition, while at the same time a fourth column approaching from the rear encountered a more spirited resistance by the defending tribesmen. The Khyber Rifles and several units of regular troops dislodged the last sangars embedded in the hillside and all four columns met cheering at the top, the Black Mountain heights having been taken five days after launching the campaign. The enemy was routed, and for good measure McQueen's forces proceeded to put the torch to a number of hostile villages, along with their stores of fodder, corn and honey. This way, it was estimated that it would take the tribesmen at least two years to rebuild their settlements. Word got through that in some cases, the offenders set fire to their own villages to put the troops off entering their homes, while also saving their chieftains the disgrace of having their settlements destroyed by the British. The final action took place at Thakot, where a flying column carrying only one day's rations cleared the village encountering barely any opposition. The victorious column of Seaforth Highlanders and Khyber Rifles marched into the village to a piper playing 'You're owre lang in coming, lads'. A few days later the Khyber Rifles advanced alongside the Northumberland Fusiliers to subdue the tribesmen holding out at the village of Pokal. It was mid-November and the troops spent a perishingly cold night on the hillside with no blankets before the attack. But the next day the last of the tribesmen submitted and the Black Mountain expedition was at an end. The Governor-General concluded his Black Mountain expedition correspondence on a note of lofty satisfaction: 'A repetition of tribal outrages against the government and wanton violation of our border and slaughter and kidnapping of British subjects, are not likely to happen again.'

Alas, the Black Mountain tribesmen had not quite run out of steam. The government found it necessary to send the troops back in, including the Khyber Rifles, to mount another expedition the following year. Now, the government mistakenly assured itself, the mischievous Yusufzais had finally been persuaded to cease staging raids and terrorising British subjects. Lord Roberts expressed his regret that while the 1888 Black Mountain expedition had been a success from a military point of view, the government's determination to limit the sphere of action of the troops, and to hurry out of the area as soon as the job was done, had prevented the British from reaping any long-term political advantage. 'We lost a grand opportunity for gaining control over this lawless and troublesome district,' laments the general. 'No survey was made, no roads opened out, the tribesmen were not made to feel our power and, consequently, very soon another costly expedition had to be undertaken.'[6] .

The Khyber Rifles covered themselves in glory in this, the militia's first campaign fought alongside Indian and British Army regulars. Six men of the corps were awarded Indian Orders of Merit, the most outstanding recipient being Subadar Major Mirsal Akbar Khan, who was decorated for a number of extraordinary and reckless acts of bravery under fire. In the attack on Abu village, this dauntless, wild-eyed Afridi staged a one-man charge against half a dozen of the enemy tribesmen to save the life of a wounded sepoy comrade. Two weeks later the hulking, bearded fighter was the first man, at the head of his troops, to enter Gori village under heavy fire. From 1 to 4 November Mirsal Khan distinguished himself by leading an attack on the Ghorapur Pass, then in the attack on Pokal he single-handedly cleared the enemy from the column's left flank. During the withdrawal the sturdy Afridi carried a wounded sepoy on his back to a place of safety, and for his finale he led thirty of the Khyber Rifles up the slopes of Chel hill to dislodge a large body of enemy that was dug in on the summit. All this in the space of four days.

Another Khyber Rifles officer, Jemadar Mohammed Ghalli, received the Indian Order of Merit (IOM) for conspicuous acts of gallantry on five occasions. This courageous soldier led the attack on Khund village, drove off more than thirty enemy from a village near Batban, rushed an enemy sangar with a handful of his men, took part in the charge up Ghorapur Pass under heavy fire, and remained behind, covering his comrades, as the last man to leave his position during the withdrawal from Pokal. Four other Khyber Rifles sepoys collected IOMs for their part in capturing a sangar, the attack on Abu village and the taking of Ghorapur Pass.

The newly landed Viceroy the Marquess of Lansdowne distributed the medals on the parade ground during his visit to Peshawar the following year. The ceremony took a dramatic twist when it was discovered, to Warburton's alarm, that no ribbon had been sent with the medal for Subadar Mirsal, who by this time carried thirty battle scars on his body. (The thirty-first, a bullet from an Afridi jezail fired nearly ten years later when Mirsal was defending a Khyber Rifles outpost against Pathan insurgents, was to prove fatal.) At that moment an extraordinary thing happened: one of the Viceroy's Sikh orderlies stepped forward, detached one of his own campaign ribbons and humbly handed it to the Afridi. It was a simple yet extraordinary gesture, recalling the vast quantities of blood that had been spilled by the forebears of all, Sikh, Pathan and British alike, who stood on that spot. Peshawar was hallowed ground to those who took part in the history of the North-West Frontier. It was indeed a veritable Mecca of the Frontier, where in 1834 the Pathans had been driven out by the Sikhs, who were in turn ousted by the Afghans fifteen years later, with the British coming in on the heels of the amir's forces to annex the city and its district to the Punjab. On that October morning in 1889 the Khyber Rifles were officially received into the ministry of the British Empire.

The Black Mountain tribes were yet again to be heard from. In 1891 marauding lashkars began causing the British further headaches by staging raids in settled districts.

So early in the New Year the troops were assembled and put on the march. On 4 February, 300 men of the Khyber Rifles, under Sir Aslam's command, marched down from Jamrud Fort to Peshawar. There the column encamped for three weeks, awaiting a break in the freezing weather that gripped the Black Mountain district. The levies were joined by a detachment of Royal Welsh Fusiliers, and a couple of weeks later the Khyber Rifles and regular troops marched out of the city, heading north towards the troubled region.

It was now Sir Aslam's turn to prove his mettle under fire. The Khyber Rifles had planted a seed to ensure the corps' succession by putting together a kind of boys' company, made up mostly of young Afridis who were drilled, paraded and on special occasions marched out as guards of honour for distinguished visitors. It was an informal contingent that the militiamen encouraged in order to instil in the young warriors the martial spirit of their race. With the campaign fully underway, on 21 March the Khyber Rifles came under fire from a sangar on a hill overlooking the village of Abu. Sir Aslam, ignoring his advanced years and considerable bulk, took the lead at the head of 140 of his Khyber Rifles, with the support of the 5th Gurkhas, to attack the enemy position. As the party advanced, a 12-year-old boy, the Commander of the Boys' Company who had managed to attach himself to the column, rushed forward to help the panting Sir Aslam up the slope. A sepoy moving alongside his Commandant recalls hearing Sir Aslam pushing the boy aside, shouting with gasping breath, 'Get away, boy, get away. You'll be killed!' To which the lad proudly replied, 'Never mind if I am, sir. You can throw my body into the nearest ravine.'

The tribesmen were dislodged from the sangar with little difficulty. By that time it had begun to snow heavily, and some of the men crowded into two large storage sheds which the villagers had built on the hilltop. There they huddled round a small fire, planning to sit out the storm and make their way back down to the main body of the troops at daybreak. It was bitterly cold with the wind howling over the exposed hilltop, so before settling into their blankets, Aslam Khan sent a group of his men outside to gather wood to keep the fire going throughout the night. He remained in the shed with three of his Khyber Rifles orderlies, his horse, a local guide and a few doolie-bearers. By this time a thick layer of snow had blanketed the flat wooden roof. Suddenly, the roof broke loose from its support beams under the weight of the snow. Within seconds, four doolie-bearers, the native guide and Aslam Khan's horse were dead, crushed under the pile of debris, while two of the orderlies suffered broken bones and lacerations. As for Aslam Khan, he could count himself relatively fortunate to be standing in a corner of the room when the shed collapsed. He was pulled to the ground by a broken beam, but escaped the full impact thanks to a two-foot mud platform that broke its fall, leaving him pinned to the earthen floor. The rescue operation lasted twelve hours in a raging blizzard, well into the early hours of the morning when Aslam Khan, along with the dead and injured, were portaged back to Peshawar.

Warburton could justly take pride in the heroism displayed by his close friend Sir Aslam, and the native troops under his command in this, the army's final campaign against the Black Mountain tribesmen. Accolades poured in from distinguished quarters, giving testimony to the gallantry and loyalty of the corps. 'Your Khyber Rifles behaved admirably, and have won the respect and confidence of the General and all the troops,' Colonel John Ommaney, Commissioner of the Peshawar Division, wrote to Warburton. 'You may well feel proud of the good work done by you in the Khyber in managing the Afridis so as to have led to their volunteering and acquitting themselves so well.' From the expeditionary force Commander-in-Chief himself, General McQueen, came this acclaim of the Khyber Rifles:

> Their rapidity of movement over the hills and familiarity of the tactics pursued by the enemy have proved them to be troops of the very best material for the class of fighting in which we have recently been engaged. Their discipline has been excellent, and no instance of misconduct has been brought to my notice, or that of the Column Commanders under whose immediate orders they have served.[7]

The government found it necessary to despatch minor punitive expeditions against the Pathan tribes along the Frontier at the rate of almost one a year, from the close of the final Black Mountain campaign to the outbreak of the great tribal rebellion a decade later. The Pathan rising that swept across the Khyber and other parts in 1897 quickly developed into the greatest ever threat to British authority on the Frontier. In the waning days of summer, an exchange of telegrams buzzed fast and furious between the Viceroy Lord Elgin's monsoon retreat in the cool hill station of Simla and the India Office in London. Almost on a daily basis, Elgin bombarded the Secretary of State for India with a blow-by-blow account of alarming tribal movements in the Khyber district.

19 August: 'Lashkar nation of Afridis including all Khyber clans . . . said to be 10,000 strong, with 1,500 mullahs from Ningrahar advancing on the Khyber. The Khyber posts held by Khyber Rifles only.'

26 August: 'Landi Kotal, held by about 350 Khyber Rifles and 150 tribesmen, taken yesterday . . . garrison have reached (Fort) Jamrud with their arms . . . Afridis in Khyber said to have dispersed, but with intentions of reassembling.'

By the following week, the Viceroy was confidently telegraphing Whitehall that the whole affair had been nothing but a bad nightmare. The Secretary of State could rest assured that the government was now back in control of the Khyber.

8 September: 'All is quiet now. Tribal gatherings have dispersed and confidence is fully restored.'

Four days later, the tribesmen forced Elgin to eat his words.

12 September: Kohat, heavy firing reported . . . enemy in great force . . . enemy attacked rear-guard in determined fashion. Our casualties about 20 killed, wounded and missing.'[8]

The Pathan uprising rapidly gained momentum, which in a perverse way signalled the return to a more normal state of affairs on the Frontier. The word 'peace', as understood on the North-West Frontier, had to be taken at best in a figurative sense. 'Truce' would more accurately describe the uneasy stand-off that prevailed between the government and the Pathans when the two sides weren't actually exchanging rifle fire. On the one hand, the tribes were always resentful of the Kafir roaming about the hills and valleys which they claimed as their ancestral lands. On the plus side, however, the British garrisons and cantonments did present a good opportunity for acquiring booty. This applied particularly to rifles, the Pathans' most esteemed trophy. Tribesmen had been known to crawl naked through the bush to prevent the rustle of their pantaloons against the ground, their bodies sound-proofed with oil, as they crept up on sentries,

springing like tigers on their prey who would be brought down
with one deadly sweep of the Khyber dagger across the throat.
Army records estimate that in the fifteen years prior to the
events of 1897, the Pathans had possessed themselves of 1,250
rifles stolen from the troops, as well as whatever they were able
to obtain through anti-British elements in Kabul. To this arsenal
must be added hundreds of firearms of local manufacture, such
as those assembled in the workshops of Darra Adam Khel, a
Khyber village that even today is entirely given over to
weaponry production. The effectiveness of these home-made
rifles was not to be underestimated. In the 1863 Black
Mountain campaign, regimental records confirm that most of
the enemy were armed with rifles of local manufacture, 'a
deadly weapon at four hundred yards'. The British, on the other
hand, carried the Brunswick two-grooved rifle, a useless firearm
at more than 250 yards, while some of the troops went into
battle with muskets that had been issued half a century earlier
in the Peninsular War.

The Frontier had been simmering with unrest, periodically
boiling up into local skirmishes, since the close of the Second
Afghan War. In the main, these set-tos with the tribesmen were
taken as little more than training exercises, indeed almost
sporting events for the Indian Army, which by the close of the
nineteenth century had greatly improved its firepower superiority
with the issue of the Snider rifle. This firearm was soon replaced
by the Martini Henry, 'twice the fellow the Snider was', recalls
General Andrew Skeen. Then came the Lee Metford and
smokeless powder, used by British battalions for the first time in
1897 and 'startling the tribesmen out of their lives'. Skeen writes,
'All this time the tribesmen had been wallowing along with their
jezails and odd guns and a sprinkling of stolen Sniders and later
Martinis.' It was a time when Frontier fighting was 'a pleasant
enough way of applying peace training, with enough of danger in
it to make it exciting'.[9]

But modern arms were slowly starting to find their way into
the North-West Frontier through the Persian Gulf and

Afghanistan, and dealing with tribal raiders now became a more serious business. In a relatively short period of time, almost 100,000 modern rifles were smuggled through to Kandahar and onward to the Pathans via European dealers, who picked up most of the weapons from stock discarded by Australian and New Zealander troops after the South African war. Arnold Toynbee offers this somewhat convoluted appraisal of the threat that arms smuggling posed to stability on the North-West Frontier: 'It was a striking example of the Empire's subjects doing business with the trans-frontier barbarians to militate against the public interest of the Imperial Government in keeping the barbarians at bay.' In other words, British India was being stabbed in the back by an Arab sultanate that had close treaty relations with Great Britain. 'The barbarians,' Toynbee clarifies, 'could never have attacked effectively without the use of the weapons forged in the arsenals of civilisation.'[10]

The gun-running operation was in the hands of the powerful and warlike Ghilzai tribe, the backbone of the Afghan nation, who had acquired a monopoly on the arms trade through suppliers in Muscat. The Muscat dealers undertook to engage the dhows that ran the guns across the Gulf to the Persian side, where they were landed and loaded onto camels for the arduous trek across Afghanistan to the Frontier. The Government of India despatched a squadron of British cruisers to the Gulf of Oman to harass and chase the dhows, whose Arab skippers eventually refused to transport guns. It was no longer a cost-effective business, with payment from the Afghan traders equivalent to a third of the value of their sailing vessels. They now demanded payment in full, as dhows were becoming scarcer by the day, confiscated or blown out of the water by the Royal Navy. The Afghans were unwilling to acquiesce, having no guarantee of good faith of the Arabs. The blockade proved to be an initial success but it failed to kill off the trade entirely, no thanks to the connivance of the French Government that refused to abrogate its treaty with the Sultan of Muscat, by which some of his subjects were given the right to fly the French flag.

In early spring of 1897 rumours of a most exotic flavour were wafting through the twisting alleyways of Peshawar's bazaar: it was whispered that the Sultan of Turkey was stirring up jihad in the court of Kabul, and also that a miracle-maker had appeared on the Frontier, a great bearded, thundering mullah who roamed the hills assuring the tribesmen that by time of the new moon, their land would be swept clean of the British infidel. Closer to the realm of *realpolitik*, there was growing concern over one of the tribes' chief grievances, namely that the Durand Line and the consequent British advance up to the newly demarcated border signalled an intention to annex this sacred Pathan land. At the same time, the Amir of Afghanistan had just proclaimed himself 'King of Islam' and had published several treatises preaching the virtues of holy jihad. This combination of events led the Frontier tribesmen to believe that an uprising could rely on the active support, as well as the moral blessing, of their spiritual leader in Kabul. Increases in the salt tax and an attempt by the British to promote less barbarous treatment of tribal women were taken as affronts to Pathan honour, with the result that resentment was beginning reach a flash point. All that was lacking to finally ignite the fuse was the appearance of a charismatic jihad-preaching mullah and as if on cue, in stepped the fanatical Sadullah, christened by the British the 'Mad Mullah', the fiery preacher who pitched up in the Khyber fresh from a visit to the court of Abdur Rahman Khan, the self-crowned King of Islam.

The war drums had been sounding for weeks, as one by one the tribes began to rise up in arms against the government. First in Malakand, a campaign in which the young Winston Churchill got a taste of hand-to-hand combat with the tribesmen (and came close to leaving his bones), and later in early August, when the revolt spread to Mohmand territory. Cavalierly brushing aside the warning signals, the government held out the vain hope that Warburton's efforts to cement a relationship of trust with the Afridis would prevent the Khyber tribes from taking to the warpath.

During those summer days Khyber Rifles recruits manning the stone picquets in the pass gazed nervously at the swelling throngs of fellow Afridi and Orakzai tribesmen who filed up the road to listen to the fire-and-brimstone sermons of the Mad Mullah and other hoary-bearded demagogues like Sayad Akbar, Gulandaz and Hadda Mullah. The Afridis crouching behind their sangars, fingers on the trigger, and those patrolling the battlements of the hillside forts, knew full well that when the fanatical battle cry of 'Jihad!' echoed through the defiles of the pass, the Khyber Rifles would be called on to bear the brunt of the attack. As the asphyxiating August heat began building in intensity, so too the atmosphere in the Khyber took on a more menacing air, reinforcing the reflection of a visiting journalist years later that the North-West Frontier was not so much British India as 'enemy territory'.

British agents managed to intercept a number of letters sent by the ringleaders of the uprising to their co-religionists along the Frontier. These inflammatory messages left little doubt of the mullahs' determination to incite the tribes to armed revolt. The Hadda Mullah states in an open declaration to the mullahs and elders of the Afridi and Orakzai tribes:

The Kafirs have taken possession of all Musulman countries, and owing to the lack of spirit on the part of the people, are conquering every region. I have myself informed the people of Laghman and Kunar and the Mohmands, Ningraharis and Shinwaris, and they are all prepared to take part in the fighting. I inform you also that you may try your best to further the cause of jihad which is the best of all devotions and the truest of all submissions, so that we may not be ashamed before God on the day of Judgement and be glorious before His Prophet.[11]

Another missive, this one from two Orakzai mullahs, informed the tribal malik Sinjab Khan that the only possibility of peace was for the British to evacuate the Frontier territories and allow the tribes to keep as fair booty the arms taken in combat from British troops. 'Do not negotiate with the British, and take care that you are not taken in by them,' the mullahs warned. 'Do not believe them.' A third letter, this one from Mir Mohammed Khan in Kabul to his father, carries the terse caution: 'Mind that you do not make peace with the British.' This collection of captured correspondence confirms beyond doubt that the self-proclaimed 'King of Islam' was in it up to his neck, in spite of the amir's feigned attempts to act as mediator between both sides. In early September, the Hadda Mullah writes to his excitable confrères:

On 30th August 1897 I determined with a lashkar to go out for a holy war and defend the religion of the Holy prophet. When I reached Lashkar Killa and was staying there for the night, I received a *firman* from *Zia-ul millat-wud-din* (a letter from the amir) in reply to my petition, and understood its contents, which were to the following effect: You should wait for a few days in your former place, so that I may hold a consultation with the Khans, Maliks, chiefs and respectable men about *ghaza* (battle) and decide what steps should be taken. I will then either come myself or send you my son for jihad, with our victorious troops and supplies, such as rations and food, and will let you know again. I will with the greatest pleasure make exertions in the way of jihad.

The lashkars were roused to a fervour pitch by fantastic tales of devastating blows dealt to British military power and prestige overseas. These reports were being supplied to the tribesmen by a traitorous Indian Muslim, a clerk on the staff of the British Agent at Kabul. The unidentified 'well-wisher of his co-religionists' was feeding the mullahs some spectacular malarkey, and one cannot help but wonder if the fellow was actually being employed as a double agent. 'The British are at present in distressed circumstances,' reads a letter from the Afridi jirga at Kabul to Mullah Sayad Akbar, relaying information obtained from the informer in Kabul.

For instance, Aden, a seaport, which was in possession of the British, has been taken from them by the Sultan (of Turkey).

The Suez Canal, through which the British forces could easily reach India in twenty days, has also been taken possession of by the Sultan, and has now been granted on lease to Russia. The British forces now require six months to reach India. The friendly alliance between the British and the Germans has also been disturbed on account of some disagreement about trade, which must result in the two nations rising in arms against each other. (Accurate enough as prophesies go, albeit nearly twenty years ahead of the event.) The Sultan, the Germans, the Russians and the French are all in arms against the British at all seaports, and fighting is going on in Egypt too against them. In short, the British are disheartened nowadays.[12]

This melancholy intelligence was fed back to the tribesmen in the Khyber, where the jirgas sat in sullen council, the mullahs ranted under the blistering August sun and tension mounted by the day. The storm clouds were rent asunder in the pre-dawn hours of 23 August.

Warburton had received word as early as May that the amir was in league with the Sultan of Turkey, plotting to unleash a jihad in the Khyber. He alerted the Punjab Government to the threat, but Lahore brushed off the warning as uninformed scare mongering. The Governor-General was confident that the army's recent victories in Malakand had once and for all laid to rest the issue of tribal fanaticism. This fantasy continued to hold sway in government even into early August, when reports reached Peshawar that mullahs, brandishing rifles and the Koran, were gathering Orakzai and Afridi tribesmen in the Khyber. The warnings continued to flow in during successive weeks, and were summarily disregarded even by officials supposedly close to the situation, like Sir Richard Udny, Commissioner of the Peshawar District. 'Everything quiet,' read Udny's telegram of mid-August to Lord Elgin, a laconic and melancholy reminder of Cavagnari's memo of eighteen years before, 'All well in the Kabul Embassy.'

The Khyber Rifles now numbered 825 men, under the command of Captain (later Sir) William Barton, a veteran of the last Afghan campaign who entertained no illusions about the nature of the task handed him by the outgoing Commandant, Sir Aslam Khan. Barton was determined to maintain order in the Khyber, by friendly persuasion or by force of arms. He indeed knew what he was up against and had decried the entire North-West Frontier as 'the most lawless country on the face of the earth'. Sir Aslam, feeling the weight of his years and in failing health, nevertheless took up the post of Political Agent Khyber, replacing his old friend Warburton on the latter's retirement.

Barton, with only a few months' experience under his belt as Warburton's assistant, was left on his own to confront the tempest that was shortly to be unleashed on the Khyber. Thanks to the good offices of Aslam Khan, Afridi agents, risking their lives to spy on the movements of their hostile brethren, were able to provide the British with intelligence on tribal stirrings in the Khyber. One morning, a truly disturbing piece of news landed on the new Commandant's desk in his Landi Kotal headquarters: a lashkar of no fewer than 10,000 Afridi warriors, led by 1,500 *ghazi* horsemen from Afghanistan, was advancing on the Khyber Rifles' defensive positions. By that year, nine garrisons had been erected for the corps, from Jamrud, the one closest to Peshawar, to Fort Tyler at the western end of the pass. Of these, the only outposts that in any shape or form bore a resemblance to proper fortifications were Fort Maude, Ali Masjid, and above all Landi Kotal, the massive fortress that stood on the summit of the pass. Landi Kotal was where a protracted defence of the pass could be organised, since Fort Maude lacked an adequate water supply and Ali Masjid was surrounded on all sides by hills, a veritable sniper's dream. The remaining 'forts' were little more than roadside picquets, each manned by seven to twenty troops. Barton never expected them to put up any serious resistance in the face of a massive tribal onslaught, such as the one that was now converging on all the Khyber Rifles' outposts.

Preparations for war took on a marked resemblance to medieval siege tactics. Every morning, loyal Afridi messengers raced breathlessly into Barton's command post at Landi Kotal, bearing menacing reports of tribal movements in the pass. The mullahs were whipping the Afridis into a state of frenzy, haranguing them on the hillsides with fire and brimstone readings from the Koran. By late August it was apparent that the attack could only be a matter of days away, perhaps hours. Barton's first move was to beef up the strength of each garrison, but far more important was the task of laying in quantities of food and water for the men guarding the picquets. On 23 August the Khyber Rifles were distributed at full strength, with 374 men at Landi Kotal and 271 at Jamrud, the two most defensible positions, which were also the pivotal points for holding the Khyber. Scanning the hazy Afghan plains on that morning, the Khyber Rifles sentries at Ali Masjid must have felt their throats go dry when they spotted a huge yellow dust cloud surging up the pass. In its midst there advanced a tumultuous host of several thousand Afridi tribesmen waving rifles and banners, spurred on by the war cries of their mullahs. With the exception of two small sections of the Kuki Khel clan that held aloof from the jihad, the lashkar comprised all the manpower the Afridis could muster. About one hundred loyal Kuki Khel tribesmen, under the command of Malik Kambar, had thrown in their lot with the forty-two levies of the Khyber Rifles garrisoned at Ford Maude. They never stood a chance of holding off the horde. At Ali Masjid, it was too early in the day for the heliograph system to be deployed, so the fort's gallant defenders had no way of knowing that Fort Maude had already fallen to the enemy.

The attackers had surrounded and stormed the Maude garrison, and for some time a desultory exchange of fire took place between the tribesmen sheltered behind rocks and trees and the Khyber Rifles manning the parapets. When Jamrud entered the fray with a heavy fusillade of rifle fire, Maude opened up with its own barrage. But as the morning wore on, the officers commanding the Jamrud garrison took stock of the situation and realised to their dismay that fewer than 300 Khyber Rifles would not be able to hold out for long against the waves of fanatical tribesmen now pressing in for the kill. The order was given for the immediate evacuation of the fort, and this gave a signal to the Fort Maude defenders to beat a retreat down the Khyber road, leaving behind only two Kuki Khel tribesmen killed in battle. This had to be considered a good account on the part of the Khyber Rifles, who through determination and discipline brought down more than thirty Afridis in the attack before being forced to abandon their posts. By this time the lashkar had overrun the sangars at Bagiar and Jehangira, which were evacuated before the attacks as hopeless positions. So now almost the entire length of the Khyber road was in the hands of the tribesmen.

The Afridis' next objective was Ali Masjid, where eighty Khyber Rifles and some forty Kuki Khel tribesmen under their malik Amin Khan were digging in for a desperate defence. The tribesmen massed before the walls of the fort, giddy with their easily gained victories of the day. The troops manning the crenellated parapet surveyed the bellowing mob with deep apprehension, when suddenly the head mullahs stepped forward to demand that Amin Khan and his men abandon the Khyber Rifles garrison. The native troops were branded traitors to Islam, who should be left to suffer their inevitable fate. The loyal Kuki Khel malik inside the fort shouted his defiance to the fanatics clamouring at the gates, and with that the battle got under way.

Fighting raged throughout the day and when darkness began to close in, the weary defenders on the battlements were suddenly startled by the sight of a fiery orange glow several miles to the east. This was Fort Maude, or what was left of the outpost after having been torched by the lashkar. With ammunition running low and the garrison cut off with no hope of a relief column from Peshawar, the defenders realised that the rampaging Afridis would show little mercy to anyone taken alive by the mob. The native officers commanding the hilltop stone fort decided to risk a swift breakout under cover of night, hoping to follow the *nullahs* (ravines) down to safety at Jamrud. So far their losses had been one Khyber Rifles recruit killed and another wounded, while one of Amin Khan's men also lay dying inside the fort. Given the hopelessness of the situation, it was an acceptable tally for the heavily outnumbered garrison. The troops swung open the gates and made a dash for it. No sooner had Ali Masjid been evacuated, the tribesmen swarmed in, unleashing an orgy of looting and burning the fort to the ground. The Khyber Rifles took advantage of the chaos that reigned inside the fort's perimeter to lead the friendly Kuki Khel tribesmen down the pass on a tortuous 3-mile trek, picking their way across broken ground throughout the night. They reached the safety of Jamrud shortly after dawn, exhausted and demoralised. Nineteen of the Khyber Rifles, along with their weapons, were regrettably unaccounted for and it was presumed they had stayed behind to throw in their lot with the victorious lashkar. What fate may have awaited them is a matter for grim speculation, given that the mullahs were more than happy to seize whatever weapons they could lay their hands on and summarily dispose of their owners.

The Afridi insurrectionists, who gathered reinforcements from sections of the Orakzai tribe, were witnessing what they thought must surely be the dying gasp of a half century of British rule in the Khyber. Under the guiding spirit of their mullahs and the mighty sword of Islam, the ghazis had set the feringhees and their traitorous minions on the run. Now the tribesmen turned their savage gaze to the top of the Khyber Pass where the tastiest trophy of all beckoned, Landi Kotal garrison with its great stock of rifles and ammunition.

The seeds of the collapse of the main Khyber Rifles were sown nearly a week before the blood-curdling cries of the lashkar had been heard echoing in the pass. On 18 August Barton, sensing the impending assault, sent word to Peshawar requesting urgent reinforcements to be drawn from the nearly 12,000 British and Indian troops garrisoned in and around the city. The Khyber Rifles Commandant was perplexed by the reply he received from staff headquarters. It was an order to report immediately to Jamrud for 'consultations'. Barton rode down the pass with reluctance, to indulge in what he was certain would be a time-wasting strategy meeting. Nevertheless, he was confident of returning to his post the next day to conduct the defence of Landi Kotal. When Barton reached the sprawling fortress, he was dumbstruck to learn that his orders were to stay put. Moreover, not a man was to be sent from Peshawar to reinforce the beleaguered garrison at Landi Kotal. He looked on aghast as the remaining British officers at Jamrud were hastily withdrawn to the relative safety of Peshawar cantonments. 'While Barton was thus forced by a timorous government to disgrace their name, the Afridis were flinging themselves on their own brethren, who had eaten the White Queen's salt,' writes Macmunn. From that moment, Landi Kotal's fate was a foregone conclusion. The fortress was a solid structure with loop-holed walls and a garrison of 370 men of the Khyber Rifles, reinforced by a number of tribesmen, fighting units made up mainly of Afridis, Mullagoris, Mohmands and Shinwaris.

The much-decorated and wounded Subadar Mirsal, who had become a soldier's legend in his own lifetime among the Afridis, friend and foe alike, was now left in charge of Landi Kotal, whose troops considered themselves betrayed, unable to understand why their commandant had deserted them. Mirsal's predicament was made all the more poignant by the fact that of his three sons, one stood by his side behind the perimeter wall, while two others had joined forces with the lashkar menacing the fort.

Aslam Khan had taken the threat of an Afridi attack on the Khyber very seriously. To this end, on 17 August he had ordered two maliks of the fearsome Zakka Khel clan, Khwas Khan and Walli Mohammed, to send contingents of their tribesmen to reinforce the Landi Kotal garrison. Walli Mohammed, who had been Warburton's faithful servant for many years, dutifully took thirty of his men up to the fort on the Loargi plateau. Khwas Khan declined to go along, sending instead a party of tribesmen with his son, Mir Akbar, who held the rank of Subadar Major in the Khyber Rifles. Sir Aslam would soon have cause to regret this decision. Apart from these two units, some fifty members of the

Mullagori tribe accompanied the corps, but these comparatively dovish tribesmen melted away the moment they got wind of what lay in store on the pass.

24 August fell on a Tuesday, and as far as Mirsal Khan was concerned it was business as usual in the Khyber Pass. The gallant Afridi was totally unaware of the disaster that had taken place the previous day, for nobody had bothered to inform him of the events at Ali Masjid and Fort Maude. So following the weekly routine, Mirsal Khan and his men were carrying out their duties of escorting a kafila from Landi Kotal to Jamrud. When a rider pulled up to warn him of the approaching lashkar, Mirsal Khan acted without hesitation. He ordered the camel caravan turned round and sent to the Mullagori villages for protection. He then rushed his troops back to Landi Kotal to prepare for the siege.

The horde marched up the Khyber behind a stream of banners and war drums, their numbers swelling at each village they passed along the road. Khwas Khan, whom intelligence sources had identified as one of the instigators of the Afridi revolt, along with the equally duplicitous sons of Walli Mohammed, were numbered among the tribesmen who had thrown in their lot with the lashkar. Khwas Khan got a message through to Walli Mohammed urging him to abandon the fort and the Khyber Rifles and join the ranks of the lashkar. Walli Mohammed had been under the firebrand malik's spell since leaving Warburton's service. He unhesitatingly obeyed, taking a handful of his followers with him. Khwas Khan also got a note through to his son Mir Akbar inside the fort, in which he made no pretence to conceal his intentions. The message instructed Mir Akbar to swing open the Landi Kotal gates to his father and his men, using as his pretext the lie that the besiegers wished to negotiate in jirga with the Khyber Rifles. The plan was that once inside the compound, the tribesmen would loot all the ammunition and fight their way out of the fort.

Fortunately Mirsal Khan must have got wind of what was afoot, for when Mir Akbar asked him to hand over the keys to the main gate to admit the 'jirga', he dismissed the treacherous Subadar

Major with the terse warning, 'All and everyone outside who approaches these walls will be fired on.'

On hearing that their ruse had not worked and that the gates were to remain shut, the tribesmen began firing from the open road. They hadn't reckoned on the Khyber Rifles putting up a spirited defence once the attacker had opened up with heavy fire. But they were mistaken. Three of the tribesmen fell in the first volley, that sent the rest of the lashkar scurrying to cover in the low hills about 500 yards south of the fort. In their rage they tore apart the caravanserai, in which the kafilas from Afghanistan put up for the night, along with a blockhouse, and then turned their wrath on a more threatening target, the water pipes that fed the fort. An hour later the Khyber Rifles found themselves totally surrounded by the rampaging lashkar. The heavy exchange of fire continued throughout the day and far into the night, with no sign of a relief column coming up the road from Jamrud less than 5 miles away. The question on all the men's lips was, What had become of Captain Barton Sahib?

Subadar Major Mir Akbar had conspicuously absented himself from the fighting, having instead chosen to take shelter in his quarters. He would have nothing to do with the tooth and nail defence being put up by his brothers in arms, who without respite had been holding off the fanatical lashkar for the better part of twelve hours. In the early hours of the following day, 25 August, Khwas Khan, Walli Mohammed and the local Shinwari maliks held a hurried consultation to seek some way to drain the ranks of the Khyber Rifles, which meant getting their clansmen out of the besieged fort. They slipped a message into the garrison instructing Mir Akbar to make a run for it, not omitting on his way to gather up all the valuables he could lay his hands on. The Shinwaris, who co-inhabit part of the Khyber Pass with the Afridis, were only too happy to obey the call to desert their posts. The tribesmen began jumping down from the fort's north wall and scampering back to their villages. As they ran for it, a Khyber Rifles havildar, and what is more one from the Zakka Khel clan that had little charity for cowardice, shouted to the Khyber Rifles sepoys defending this wall, 'Don't fire on them, your cartridges can be used for better advantage.'

It did not take long for the rot to take hold. A nephew of Khwas Khan was admitted to the fort under a flag of truce. He entered the courtyard claiming to be message bearer from Sayad Akbar, to the tribesmen one of their most revered mullahs, and to the British an arch troublemaker. The messenger said he was authorised to make peace terms with the exhausted garrison. Sweeping the air with his arms, the Afridi proceeded to spout off a torrent of lies in the name of Sayad Akbar, to the effect that the British had abandoned the impregnable citadel at Jamrud and that there were serious doubts the Sirkar could even hold Peshawar. The gullible and exhausted recruits fell into despair. The Khyber Rifles officers knew that Fort Maude and Ali Masjid had been put to the torch, and what was worse, that no attempt had been made to march a relief column from Peshawar. They recalled Barton's last words before setting off to Jamrud, when their Commandant had promised to send assistance to his men. The troops now gave up hope of holding out for another night against the lashkar, so they started to bargain their way out of Landi Kotal, agreeing to march down to British territory through the district of the peaceful Mullagoris. (The men were cheered wildly by the hamstrung British troops when they eventually filed past the Jamrud garrison. On the other hand, the soldiers from Fort Maude spat as they passed the regulars, on a day of 'shame and humiliation for every Briton'.) Meanwhile, no sooner had the Khyber Rifles removed their guards from the walls, a party of Afridis and Shinwaris broke cover from a nullah and in a flash were helping themselves to stores of ammunition and loot from the officers' quarters, including Barton's personal possessions, notably the Commandant's silver. This so enraged the sepoys that they returned to the battlements and commenced firing into the mob at point-blank range.

The Khyber Rifles, led by Subadar Mirsal, who was in no mood to see the honour of the corps besmirched, brought down more of the enemy in those few minutes than in the previous twenty-four hours of combat. A chaotic battle now flared up, with close range firing inside the fort. In a momentary lull Subadar Mirsal discovered the treacherous Mir Akbar opening the taps of the fort's 60,000-gallon water tank in order to drain the troops' supplies. He ordered Mir Akbar back to his quarters, to be dealt with later. More pressing tasks were at hand. Subadar Mirsal rushed to the officers' mess to dislodge the looters and shot dead six of the tribesmen. More tribesmen poured into the room and in the exchange of fire a bullet found its way into Mirsal's head. It was his thirty-first and final battle wound. This was the moment Mir Akbar was waiting for. With the Khyber Rifles leaderless, he took advantage of the confusion to snatch the keys to the magazine and divide the spare ammunition among his tribesmen. Next he flung open the main gates, and while the lashkar charged in, led by one of Subadar Mirsal's sons, Mir Akbar carried off Barton's silver plate on a charpoy covered with a sheet, saying it was the body of a dead comrade.

It was a ragged and sullen troop of Khyber Rifles that wound its way down to Jamrud, while at the same time a five thousand-strong lashkar took possession of the pass from Ali Masjid to Fort Maude. In all, 134 militiamen returned with their rifles, with 274 left unaccounted for. The final sting was when the government disarmed the levies and sent them back to their villages. The men's names were kept on the rolls, but all were informed that they would draw no pay pending re-employment. This desertion of the Khyber Rifles was later mourned by a senior Army officer as 'a day of pain, shame, grief and humiliation for every Englishman in India'. Another Frontier veteran, General Elliott, argues that the failure to reinforce the Khyber Rifles 'does not stand up to objective scrutiny'. He points out that 'Indian soldiers eat very much the same food as Pathans, so the supply difficulties were not as great as all that. The anxiety expressed that no aspersions must be cast on the loyalty of the maliks and the Khyber Rifles would ring more true if it did not run directly counter to the advice given by both Barton and Aslam Khan who were, after all, the best men qualified to judge.'[13] It was presumptuous of the government to assume that the native levies and friendly tribesmen would fight to the last man against their kith and kin, leaderless and with the knowledge that several brigades of troops were standing idle in Peshawar.

Sir Richard Udny, who several weeks earlier had cheerfully brushed aside the repeated warnings of tribal unrest, as the Peshawar Polo Club carried on enjoying a quiet summer season, summarised the Landi Kotal disaster in a report to the Government of India. He described the heroic stand put up by Subadar Mirsal as 'a smart little fight in which Mirsal was shot through the head and killed on the spot'. Udny laconically deemed it 'not improbable' that a good many sepoys of the Khyber Rifles would turn up 'sooner or later' with their rifles, while others might send in their weapons 'when the excitement has subsided'.[14]

Warburton's reaction was of a less detached nature. 'My mind is quite heavy over this hideous disaster, which I feel could have been staved off even up to the day of mischief,' lamented the only man who, had he been allowed, stood a chance of persuading the Afridis to call off their jihad. In fact, Warburton's labours of eighteen years to build up a tenuous foothold in the Khyber were being unravelled in less than a week.

The army had enough manpower to protect its key stronghold of Peshawar, 'in the then excited state of the city', with its population of hundreds of wives and children. With memories of the Great Mutiny and the tales of slaughter of civilians still sharply-etched in the minds of many senior Army commanders, there was never a question of sending troops into the Khyber. 'There was considerable reason to fear that the rising of the Khyber Afridis would be followed by a rising of the Kohat Pass Afridis, and the Jawakis, and to have committed our only available troops to the Khyber would have left the Peshawar Valley open to attack from the south and south-east', concludes an official military memorandum. The report then acquires the flavour of an exculpation of the government's failure to bail out the besieged Khyber Rifles and the decision to recall their

Commandant. 'Captain Barton from Landi Kotal and the Commissioner of Peshawar asked that troops might be thrown into the Khyber. General Officer Commanding Peshawar, General Edward Elles, wired that he did not think this advisable. The danger (to Peshawar) was immediate. The Commissioner held that in the face of such a rising, no reliance could be placed on the Khyber Rifles. As regards Captain Barton, an immediate decision had to be arrived at. If, as Sir Richard Udny believed, the Khyber Rifles were not to be trusted and regular troops could not be sent to his support, the course followed in recalling him at once was the only one to adopt.' Army Command acknowledges that at least two battalions of infantry and a mountain battery could have been spared to relieve the beleaguered Khyber Rifles. But to do so, it was argued, 'would have been a grave military risk, having regard to the numbers and armament of the Afridis'. The report then drifts into a slightly baffling twist of logic by suggesting that since no British troops were stationed in the Khyber Pass at the time of the Afridi attack, there was no need to send reinforcements to rescue them.

> Had there been troops or officers in the pass who had to be brought away, the matter would have been different, but the Khyber Rifles could get away at any time. In any case it would have been necessary for our troops to have replaced rather than supported the Khyber Rifles, for the danger of treachery from within would have been too great if mixed garrisons, partly of regular troops and partly of Khyber Rifles, had been made use of.[15]

The government's dismissive attitude towards the men who had been recruited to do a job the Army knew was beyond its capacity, namely to keep the peace in the Khyber, must have been an extremely bitter pill for Aslam Khan, or any of the native levies to swallow. The report neatly sums up its defence: 'Therefore the withdrawal of Captain Barton was justified, and leaving the Khyber Rifles in the Pass rather than withdrawing them was justified under our agreement with the tribes and that, on the whole, Sir Richard Udny's decisions, in view of the fact as known to him at the time, were justifiable.' Never mind the assurances given in good faith to Barton by Aslam Khan, and by Barton to his men of the Khyber Rifles, when the Afridis were massing for the attack, that troops were advancing into the pass. 'These facts were not known 'till long afterwards and therefore could not affect our action,' states the memorandum. 'What we might have done had we known this, is now a mere waste of time to consider.'[16]

A powerful dissenting voice came from Lockhart himself, who showed no sympathy for the official whitewash. 'However loyal and well-disciplined irregular native troops may be, they can hardly be expected to fight against overwhelming odds of their own kinsmen, after their British Commandant has been withdrawn, and they have been warned that no support or assistance is to be looked for,' the General summed up in a memo of his own to the Secretary of State. 'Under such trying conditions, the best mercenary troops in the world might be expected to waver, and I think it highly creditable to the Khyber Rifles that, when left to their own resources, they fought as well as they did.' Lockhart was convinced that had reinforcements been rushed to the pass from Peshawar, the Khyber Rifles would have stood their ground, the water supply at Landi Kotal would have been saved from destruction, 'and that the formidable tribal gathering would have melted away'. The Afghan war veteran realised the need 'to inspire these levies or irregulars with the fullest confidence that, in time of emergency, they will be as fully and as promptly aided and reinforced by the army behind them as regular troops would be.' Lockhart conceded that the government's agreement with the Afridis did not oblige the army to assist the Khyber Rifles. 'But these wild mountaineers,' he pointed out, 'are unacquainted with the niceties of political jurisprudence, they had for many years filled their part of the agreement, some of them had been employed by us as irregular troops in Frontier warfare elsewhere, and they may reasonably have hoped for the assistance which, technically speaking, they had no right to demand.'[17]

Meanwhile, Sayad Akbar's claim that the British were about to be routed from Peshawar was not so fanciful as might have been imagined. The fall of Landi Kotal left the city almost hopelessly exposed to attack, with only mighty Jamrud standing between the cantonments and the tribal hordes. The mullahs could easily boost their 10,000-strong lashkar tenfold or more, merely by promising the tribesmen the capture of Peshawar as their trophy of war. The Orakzai clans were now fully committed to the Afridi-led jihad and had begun launching attacks on the posts along the crest of the nearby Samana ridge, while alarming reports came in of Orakzai raiding parties penetrating into the strategic Kurram valley to the south. The government was treating this as a most serious threat to Peshawar's security, if not the very survival of British control in the city. Once the defences west of the Indus were breached, the probable consequences were be too dire to imagine. The loss of the Khyber dredged up painful memories of General Sam Browne's battle to push his column through the pass in the last Afghan War twenty years earlier. And what signal would the fall of Peshawar immediately send to jubilant seditionist elements across the rest of India?

By early October the government reluctantly saw no alternative other than swift and decisive military reprisals against the tribesmen. Operations were set in motion on a scale hitherto unseen in Frontier warfare. To the exaltedly named General Sir Bindon Blood fell the task of dealing with the Mohmands and several other rebellious tribal groups on the Frontier. The brunt of the campaign involved putting together the largest force since the Mutiny and these troops were placed under the leadership of Lockhart, at the time Commander-in-Chief of India and a soldier who had rendered valiant service to Roberts in the last Afghan war. Having been recalled from leave in England, Lockhart made immediately clear his no nonsense intention of bringing the lashkar to its knees on one set of terms only, that of unconditional surrender. 'The British Government has determined to despatch a force under my command to march through the country of the Orakzais and Afridis and to announce from the heart of their country the final terms that will be imposed,' the General proclaimed in a statement to the rebels. Lockhart, a seasoned veteran of Frontier conflict, expressed himself in equally blunt terms when apprising the 34,500-strong Tirah Expeditionary Force under his command of the sort of enemy they could expect to encounter in the field. 'It must be remembered that the Force is opposed to perhaps the best skirmishers and best natural rifle shots in the world, and that the country they inhabit is probably the most difficult on the face of the globe,' Lockhart warned his men. 'The enemy's strength lies in his knowledge of the country, which enables him to watch our movements unperceived by us, and to take advantage of every rise in the ground and every ravine.'[18] The Indian Army manual stressed that these nullahs were to be avoided at all costs. General Andrew Skeen once warned the cadets at Sandhurst of the perils of succumbing to the temptation to seek shelter in a nullah. 'When an enemy, however few, spots a party in such a position, you can sure that it will be rounded up and shot down with a minimum of trouble to the enemy and a minimum of chances for the sinners.' As far as Lockhart was concerned on the eve of battle, the Indian Army trump card was its 'discipline, controlled fire and mutual support'.

Overkill was very much the order of the day. Assembling the Tirah Expeditionary Force at Peshawar must have resembled putting Napoleon's Grande Armeé on the march. Lockhart put together two divisions made up of six mountain batteries, two companies of sappers with two printing sections (sic) of the Bombay Sappers and Miners, four British and four native field hospitals, a machine-gun detachment, three battalions of light infantry, one regiment of infantry, two cavalry units and an artillery battalion. The 1,010 British officers and 33,496 British and native troops were supported by 19,934 non combatants and 71,800 mules, ponies, bullocks, donkeys and camels. The Afridis were in for a rough ride.

Warburton had been recalled to the Khyber too late to negotiate a peaceful settlement with the Afridis. Instead, he was seconded to

Lockhart's staff at Jamrud, where he worked from dawn to midnight doing his best to repair the damage by using his good offices with the tribesmen. But he met with little success at this late stage. Warburton's knowledgeable hand can be seen in the second part of Lockhart's message to the troops, for this covers the delicate tactical issue of extricating the troops from Afridi territory. The General set out a complex list of instructions on how to conduct an orderly retreat, almost always the moment when British and Indian regulars would come to grief at the hands of the tribes attacking their rearguard. 'Bodies of troops holding a crest, knoll or spur must show cunning and activity in retiring,' he cautioned. 'A few men without exposing themselves must first slip away and get down the hillside, while the remainder extend and thus lead the enemy to believe that the original number is still present.'[19]

The government had no intention of keeping an occupation force in Tirah, the forbidden land of the Afridis that no European had ever before entered. It was sufficient to bring the lashkars to submission, and this task Lockhart accomplished by January of the following year, almost five months to the day after the first shots were fired in the Khyber. Lockhart's assurances that British Army discipline would win the day were vindicated. The lashkars were driven back on all fronts and capitulated rather than face the hardships that awaited them under the traditional scorched earth policy of the advancing army. An officer attached to the force sums up the operation: 'One after another, the Afridi clans recognised the futility of further resistance, and complied with the British demands.'

Lockhart set a precedent in Frontier warfare that was to stand the government in good stead in future conflicts with the Khyber tribes, of which there were aplenty up to 1947. For this was the first time that a Pathan guerrilla force had been defeated by a regular army. The terms of surrender obliged the Afridis to reopen the Khyber Pass, deliver all the weapons stolen from the Khyber Rifles (or in certain cases, by them), surrender twelve mullahs who had taken a prominent role in inciting the tribes to rebel, pay a fine of 50,000 rupees in cash and, a final detail not to be overlooked, the tribesmen were to return Captain Barton's looted silver to its rightful owner.

Although the Khyber Rifles were not officially disbanded after the fall of Landi Kotal, the corps was in a state of disarray, with the troops scattered throughout the Khyber villages or biding time in the cafés of Peshawar waiting for their wages to be renewed. However, a contingent of the levies served in the Peshawar Column of Lockhart's expeditionary force, and these men were in fact in the vanguard of the troops that retook Ali Masjid in December. By March 1898 the Khyber was back in British hands and the Khyber Rifles were formally re-established.

CHAPTER SIX

Another Century, Another Uprising

The dawning of the twentieth century brought a flourish of hope for political progress on the North-West Frontier. The new Viceroy, Lord Curzon, was focusing more attention on the region than had any of his predecessors at Government House in Calcutta. Creating the North-West Frontier Province, with a Chief Commissioner reporting directly to the Viceroy, was a first step toward acknowledging the territory's strategic value. Political Agents were appointed in each of the five districts in the new province, and these were invariably men with an intimate knowledge of the tribes under their jurisdiction, including fluency in their language. Curzon designated Lord Kitchener Commander-in-Chief of the army. The hero of Khartoum was to Victorian England a figure of enormous prestige whose exploits in the Sudan and South Africa had also reached the ears of the Pathans, a people who revered martial prowess. Kitchener was instrumental in reshaping martial policy on the Frontier, which basically entailed replacing regular troops with tribal levies like the Khyber Rifles. In fact, two battalions of Khyber Rifles under British officers had already been stationed in the pass, this time with support from a regular army unit raised by Kitchener himself, the 1st Peshawar Division. This was also a period of modernisation as well as political and military reform for the

Khyber Agency. The first stage of the Khyber Railway was laid from Peshawar to Jamrud and a telegraph line was installed in the pass, all without interference from the Afridis, a development that led some to speculate that the tribe might be making determined efforts to remain loyal to their engagements. But in case they weren't, a new metalled road was also extended to Landi Kotal, allowing troops quick and easy movement up the pass in the event of trouble. Sooner or later, this was inevitably to happen. Roos-Keppel had forewarned as early as 1902 that if there was at that moment no sign of trouble from the Afridis, this was based more on the awareness of their impotence than any feeling of loyalty towards the government. 'Whatever their feelings may have been before 1897,' the Khyber Rifles Commandant wrote to Lord Roberts, 'there is I think no doubt that the Afridis generally are now hostile to us in heart. The mullahs are always preaching to them that government means to attack them when convenient and to crush them once for all, and many of them believe this. The consequence is that they are always in an agitated and nervous state and ready to believe any nonsense, however ridiculous, which may be current in Tirah or Peshawar.'[1]

Only one of the Khyber clans had flatly refused to accept Lockhart's terms of submission when the Pathan rebellion was put down in 1898. This was, of course, the Zakka Khels. Roos-Keppel was mistaken on one account: this time it was straightforward banditry, not religious fanaticism, that triggered the crisis. The first stirrings of unsavoury behaviour by these tribal brigands came about under Curzon whose term of office, the longest of any Viceroy, stretched from 1899 to 1905. It fell to Curzon's successor, Lord Minto, to deal with the outbreak of serious violence and atrocities committed by these bellicose clansmen. Minto had served as ADC to Roberts during the Second Afghan War and thus brought to the job an enviable grasp of the Pathans and Frontier politics. Unfortunately, Minto was hamstrung by the politicians in Whitehall, mainly in the person of John Morley, the Secretary of State for India, who dictated a 'go softly' policy to the Viceroy at a time when Whitehall was becoming acutely sensitive to Indian nationalist agitation.

Towards the end of 1904 a large delegation of Afridis paid a visit to Kabul, where they were warmly received by the Amir Habibullah and his brother Nasrullah. No sooner had the tribesmen returned to the Khyber, and not by coincidence, the Zakka Khels went on the rampage, launching a series of raids into British territory. They were assisted in carrying out these attacks by other Pathan clans and even by bands of Afghan outlaws, such as the notorious Hazarnaos, a gang of cut-throats who lurked about both sides of the border. The firepower that these raiders could muster took the villagers living near Peshawar totally by surprise. Most of the incursions were directed at markets and villages beyond the jurisdiction of the Khyber Rifles, who were garrisoned in their forts. So it fell to the Border Military Police, armed with nearly 40-year-old Sniders, to confront the raiding parties.

The extent of Afghan duplicity in the campaign of hit-and-run violence waged in the settled areas was revealed in a campaign of devastating raids, and in particular by the quality of the rifles carried by the tribesmen. From 1906 onwards the number of rifles smuggled in through Afghanistan grew at an alarming rate, rising from 15,000 in 1907 to almost 40,000 by the time the army, now wholly fed up with the mischief, was preparing to launch a punitive expedition against the Zakka Khels. During the 1897–8 Tirah expedition only one Afridi in every ten was armed with a Martini Henry rifle. By 1908 these weapons were the rule, not the exception. The significance of this volume of trade is reflected in the price of one of these prized rifles, which dropped from 500 rupees to 130 rupees between 1906 and 1908. Armed with their Martini Henrys, the Zakka Khels were able to keep their pursuers, who carried the less powerful Sniders and Enfields, at a distance and thus almost always make good a swift escape into the hills. The British eventually set up an effective blockade of the Gulf to stop the arms traffic, but not in time to stop the sporadic clashes being met by a full-scale punitive expedition. Roos-Keppel was convinced that the spread of these outrages was a deliberate act of defiance aimed at undermining British authority. 'Every man, woman and child in the (Zakka Khel) clan looks upon those who commit raids, murders and robberies in Peshawar or Kohat as heroes and champions,' he complained to the government. 'They are the crusaders of the nation. They depart with the good wishes and prayers of all, and are received on their return after a successful raid with universal rejoicing and congratulations.'[2] Roos-Keppel was also concerned that his Khyber Rifles' morale was rapidly being subverted, as the men knew that their obsolete weapons could be easily outranged by the Martini Henry-wielding Zakka Khels. And lurking somewhere in the shadows was the infamous mullah Khwas Khan, Warburton's arch-enemy and a chief instigator of the Pathan uprising. It was through this Zakka Khel's intrigues that the marauders were spurred on to ever more daring deeds.

The insolence of the Zakka Khels reached unparalleled heights one morning in 1907, when the Afridi clans friendly to the government were summoned to Landi Kotal to receive their allowances. Roos-Keppel, whose duties were now split between acting as Political Agent as well as Commandant of the Khyber Rifles, saw fit to omit the Zakka Khels from the guest list. He reasoned very sensibly that to reward these outlaws for their criminal behaviour would be an act of perversity. The Zakka Khels saw things differently. Khwas Khan had little difficulty persuading his clansmen that they had every right to take this as a deliberate snub by the feringhee. So it was with some astonishment that on the appointed day, Roos-Keppel found himself confronted with a Zakka Khel delegation demanding entry to Landi Kotal. The party was led in person by the infamous Khwas Khan. Under the watchful eye of the Khyber Rifles sepoys, many of whom had to endure the taunts of their outraged Zakka Khel cousins, the mullah strode up to Roos-Keppel in the courtyard and let fly a rant of abuse over the government's alleged unfair and discriminatory treatment of his recalcitrant clansmen. He then presented Roos-Keppel with a list of demands, insisting that the system of deducting fines from the tribal allowances must immediately cease. The decision to withhold the Zakka Khel allowances and proportionately increase those paid to the other Afridi clans was an initiative taken by Roos-Keppel himself, in his role as Political Officer. Khwas Khan also refused to accept responsibility, in the clan's name, for raiders passing through their territory and insisted that the government remove all restrictions on their visits to Kabul. The Khyber Rifles Commandant cursorily dismissed the mullah and his gate-crashing jirga, and returned to the business of the day, which was to dole out the Afridis' annual allowances. A few weeks later Khwas Khan and his followers were to be found around Kabul's Bala Hissar, where in the shadows of the market stalls they conspired with the amir's brother Nasrullah, who also happened to be the leader of the most virulent anti-British faction in the Afghan court hierarchy. The Zakka Khels departed Kabul happy men. If the despised British had excommunicated them from the community of Afridi worthies, not so their Afghan brethren, true friends who knew how to reward loyal ghazis. Not only did Nasrullah top up the illicit allowances the Zakka Khels were collecting from the amir's coffers, he also afforded them facilities for purchasing large numbers of rifles through the Persian Gulf arms connection.

No sooner had the tribesmen made their way back to Tirah, the attacks on villages within the British administrative border were renewed with increased frequency and boldness. The pattern was a familiar one, as Roos-Keppel was to inform the government with depressing regularity. A small group of unarmed Zakka Khels would appear in a village, usually on the pretext of shopping for provisions. This enabled the bandits to familiarise themselves with the place without arousing suspicion. By evening the rest of the gang would ride in, guns blazing, and make off with whatever took their fancy. The village alarm drum would be beaten, the Border Military Police rushed in to join the armed villagers in the firing, but almost always too late to confront the raiders, who were by now picking their way home through the intricate network of nullahs. Quite often it was parties of military police as well as regular Army troops that were caught in an ambush. After wreaking havoc among the recruits, the Afridi outlaws would scamper back to the hills with an armload of precious rifles. On one occasion the raiders even attempted to abduct the Assistant Commissioner of Peshawar, and in January 1908 a party of some eighty hell-for-leather desperadoes staged a daring lightning attack within the very city limits, looting the house of a Hindu banker of some half a million rupees' worth of valuables.

The government was determined to take retaliatory action, but it was a decision taken with great pain and reluctance for fear of inciting the Afridis to a replay of the great Frontier rebellion a decade before. It took Roos-Keppel and his supporters at Government House nine months to convince Morley that the only hope of putting the brakes on the rampaging Zakka Khels was to mount a full-blown punitive expedition. The Secretary of State was reminded that in the previous seven years, the offending Zakka Khel clan had murdered no fewer than thirty-two British subjects and kidnapped thirty-seven others in the Peshawar district. Morley at first demurred, suggesting as an alternative greater vigour in exacting fines from the Zakka Khel. Roos-Keppel calmly pointed out that the 33,546 rupees the clan already owed as compensation for their misdeeds was a sum greater than three years' worth of allowances. He explained that the real risk of provoking a general uprising would be the failure to take immediate reprisals, which would be interpreted as an obvious sign of weakness on the part of government. The Zakka Khels' apparent immunity from punishment was beginning to infect the rest of the Afridi clans as well as other tribes. The question was how far it would be prudent to go in punishing the offenders. Roos-Keppel held that nothing short of permanent occupation of the Zakka Khel heartland, the Bazar valley of Tirah, would bring lasting stability to the region. After subduing the clan by force of arms, the next step would be to set up permanent posts in the valley manned by the Khyber Rifles, a plan that was to take nearly another century to bring to fruition. He was determined to deploy his native levies against the tribesmen instead of regular troops, which he held to be the only realistic solution. It was on this issue that the Khyber Rifles Commandant and Lord Minto parted company. The Viceroy fired off a letter to Morley expressing his grave reservations about Roos-Keppel's unorthodox plan. Forcing a British administration on Tirah flew in the face of the government's traditional hit-and-run policy. Then followed the customary exchange of telegrams between Minto and Morley, proposing the construction of military roads in the valley, with perhaps the establishment of a few advanced posts, or a blockade of the area, and other pie-in-the-sky schemes from two men sitting many miles removed from the realities of the Frontier. Minto positioned himself on the side of the 'doves'. He told Morley the government had no intention of launching a punitive expedition 'on the old lines, which included the burning of villages, blowing up houses, cutting down and ringing fruit trees and other acts of destruction'.[3]

Meanwhile, Major-General Sir James Willcocks had arrived in Peshawar, where he busied himself with the more practical business of mobilising three brigades that were to make up the Bazar Valley Expeditionary Force. Willcocks's plan was to launch a direct attack on the Zakka Khels' stronghold, while Roos-Keppel was to lead a flying column of 800 Khyber Rifles in an encircling movement from Landi Kotal, thus cutting off the tribesmen's escape route into Afghanistan.

The morning before putting his native levies on the march, Roos-Keppel ordered the Khyber Rifles to line up on the drill ground at Landi Kotal. He surveyed the stern, hawk-like faces of his trusted Afridis, and wondered just how trustworthy they would prove themselves in the coming encounter with the feared Zakka Khels, for among the men standing at attention before him, he recognised many members of the same hostile clan. He offered the men under his command a choice: they could take up arms against their own people or be granted six months' leave, no questions asked. A tense silence fell over the parade ground. After an anxious moment or two, the Commandant, concealing a smile of satisfaction, acknowledged with a nod. Not a man had stirred in the ranks.

Within twenty-four hours of setting out from Peshawar, all the key Khyber posts had been secured by loyal militiamen and on 14 February Willcocks's force was concentrated at Ali Masjid, ready to move into action. The Khyber Rifles advanced the next day, sealing the entrances to the Bazar valley, while hammering a very surprised enemy force with the army's new ten-pounder guns. Within a week the Zakka Khel resistance had crumbled in disarray. The Khyber Rifles had successfully closed the Khyber Pass, thus cutting off the main route used by Afghan reinforcements trickling across the border. The mercenaries, laden with heavy boxes of ammunition and sacks of flour, now had to negotiate the more circuitous and difficult Thabai Pass. On the 25th, a detachment of loyal Afridis sat down with the Zakka Khel in a marathon jirga, a gathering that lasted throughout the night. The peace talks were pierced by the howls of hundreds of Afghan mullahs clustered on the hills overlooking the jirga, who shouted abuse at the Afridis and called on the Zakka Khel not to heed the lies of the 'feringhee dogs'. The Zakka Khel maliks shouted back to the Afghans that they would have been delighted to have seen them ten days earlier, while the Afridis themselves threatened to attack the taunting fanatics if they failed to return immediately whence they came. The Afghans sulkily drew back across the border and in short order, the remaining pockets of Zakka Khel resistance were routed from the valley. On 28 February the Zakka Khels sent a delegation to the British tents to sue for peace. In less than a fortnight, what *Punch* dubbed the 'weekend war' had ended, with the loss of three British soldiers. Enemy casualties numbered in the scores, at the very least, although this was always difficult to ascertain with any accuracy since the tribesmen quickly removed as many dead or wounded they could from the battlefield. The total cost to government for subduing the Frontier's most obstinate clan came to £57,000.

Willcocks, in a memorandum to the Secretary of State for India, cited several chief factors that had contributed to his victory. High on the list was the exemplary conduct of the Khyber Rifles, as well as the services rendered by Roos-Keppel and the rapidity of the advance. Once more, British force of arms had prevailed where diplomacy had failed, in this case the reforms put in place by Curzon, and victory was achieved more 'along the old lines' than government had contemplated. Roos-Keppel was pleased to report at the conclusion of the campaign that

> every fort and watch tower in the valley has been razed to the ground, large supplies of wood and fodder have been obtained, and the losses due to exposure among the sheep, goats and cattle (which are always, in Bazar, kept in caves in the winter) have been very great. The Zakka Khel have entirely exhausted their supplies of ammunition and cash and every individual in the tribe has felt the sharp punishment inflicted and will continue to do so for some time.[4]

It was no more than what the offenders had expected, and certainly a lot less than what they would have inflicted on the British had the battle gone the other way. Men like Roos-Keppel, a soldier with many years of first-hand dealings with the Pathans under his belt, knew that once the sword was out of the scabbard, half measures were not on the agenda.

Captain Hugh Nevill, a contemporary of Roos-Keppel, was of the same mind as his comrade-in-arms regarding the matter of retribution against the tribes, although he was less sympathetically disposed towards the Pathans, whom he considered deceitful by nature. 'The destruction of villages and crops may seem at first sight a barbarous method of carrying on war, but it is generally the only way of meting out punishment for raids in British territory committed by our predatory and elusive neighbours on the North-West Frontier,' he writes. 'They have no trade to dislocate, no stocks and shares to depress, and the Hague Convention is to them not even a name. War with uncivilised enemies must be waged with the methods they understand.'[5]

No sooner had the Zakka Khel maliks pressed their thumb prints to the terms of surrender, accolades came pouring in praising the Khyber Rifles for the corps' sterling performance under what was for many of the men an extremely trying campaign. Roos-Keppel was first in with the plaudits, acclaiming as 'a point of great political interest' the Khyber Rifles' behaviour in the field. 'This corps, which is composed mainly of Afridis, including some 350 Zakka Khel,' his despatch to government stated

> had to take part in an expedition against a people to whom the men were bound not only by race and religion, but by the closest ties of blood. Indeed in many cases during the expedition, brother was fighting against brother and son against father. The experiment was viewed with mistrust by many and with misgiving by all, but it has been more than justified, as throughout the expedition the Khyber Rifles gained universal praise for their keenness and willingness, not a man deserted, and not a rifle was lost.

The Commandant and Political Officer went on:

> I mention this particularly in this report, as I consider it of great political importance. The Khyber Rifles were in 1899 merely an armed rabble without cohesion or discipline, and the tribesmen themselves have fully shared the doubts of the authorities as to whether the men could really be employed against their own relatives and countrymen. The political effect of the satisfactory conduct of the Corps cannot but be considerable, not only among the Afridis but throughout the border tribes.[6]

Roos-Keppel also considered it 'little short of marvellous' that the elders and chiefs of the other Afridi clans were able to restrain their clansmen from joining the Zakka Khel insurrectionists. Here one is tempted to bear in mind that cutting the Zakka Khel scallywags out of the tribal allowances left a larger slice of the imperial pie to share out among other clans.

Willcocks followed up with a glowing ratification of Roos-Keppel's words. 'I can endorse every word regarding the Khyber Rifles,' he wrote in his report to Morley.

> I have already reported to His Excellency the Commander-in-Chief in India (Kitchener) on the good conduct and discipline of the corps throughout the operations. It has indeed been an object lesson and proves what good leading and example can do in a battalion enlisted from among the very people they are sent to fight against. The services rendered by Sahib Zada Abdul Qaiyum (a Khyber Rifles officer), Assistant to the Chief Political Officer (Roos-Keppel), are deserving of the highest praise. He accompanied me in my first advance from Ali Masjid to China (a Zakka Khel stronghold), while Lieutenant-Colonel Roos-Keppel was commanding the Landi Kotal column and his advice at Chora was most useful. He is a very hard-working, loyal and zealous servant of the State.[7]

It now fell to Morley to stamp Whitehall's seal of approval on the corps. 'It only remains to join in the tribute which all concerned have paid and justly paid to the Khyber Rifles,' wrote the Secretary of State to Roos-Keppel. 'They have once more shown to their own people their loyalty to the British Government, which is not less proud of them than they are of their service. It cannot fail to be gratifying to them to read of the estimation in which they are held by the General under whom they have served, and by the Commanding Officer whom they know so well.'

How different this chorus of praise for the Khyber Rifles was to the tune government would be singing in ten years' time.

Within two months of routing the Zakka Khel bandits, the Peshawar bazaars were once again buzzing with rumours of tribal unrest. This time the focus was on the Mohmands, who inhabit the mountains north of the city within an area under Khyber Rifles jurisdiction. The British always held this tribe to be too treacherous by nature for regular army service, although some of the tribesmen served well in several of the corps of Frontier Scouts. The Mohmands had been lured into the Zakka Khel conflict by their mullahs, but the Bazar valley operation was wound up too quickly for the small lashkar raised by the Mohmands to join in the fighting. By late April, however, things began to take an unpleasant turn. There were now confirmed reports, no longer rumours, filtering through to Roos-Keppel's office of Mohmand lashkars staging attacks on Khyber Rifles and Border Police outposts. The ranks of these lashkars were swelling rapidly, with reinforcements slipping across the Afghan border on a daily basis. The Zakka Khels were still licking their wounds from their recent beating and had little stomach for a another encounter with the British, while the other Afridi clans that inhabit the Khyber Agency held to the undertakings agreed with Willcocks, that is to keep their unruly brethren on a tight lead. So it was the Mohmands' turn to have a go at the Sirkar, and this was brought about solely as a result of religious agitation by the mullahs. The tribe required little incitement to rise up, even in April, the harvesting season and thus a critical time for these mountain folk to be tending their fields. The Mohmands had been virtually on a war footing for some five years over the construction of a railway line that was to run north of the Kabul river, cutting straight through their homeland. These plans were subsequently abandoned, but the Mohmands continued to send raiding parties against military outposts.

It suddenly began to look like there was a deadlier time bomb lurking beneath the Mohmands than had been the case with the Zakka Khel troublemakers, as the lashkars now constituted a not insignificant force of 10,000 men.

The first attack took place on the night of 23 April, when a mob armed to the teeth launched a mounted assault on a constabulary post at Matta, an area that had been placed under army control. Willcocks' troops drove off the attackers, with the unexpected help of some runaway horses. When the firing began some of the police cavalry horses took fright and stampeded into the barbed wire entanglements surrounding the fort, as a result of which ten were killed and several others had to be shot. The Mohmands, seeing the rampaging horses, thought they were being attacked by mounted infantry and hastily decamped. Many of the tribesmen involved in this raid had been on the receiving end of a devastating charge by the 11th Bengal Lancers in 1897, which took place on the very same spot.

Before the troops had time to draw breath the lashkar regrouped for an attack on Landi Kotal, the crucial garrison that was held by 600 men of the Khyber Rifles under the command of Roos-Keppel. Willcocks's reserve brigade was swiftly despatched up the pass from Peshawar to relieve the Khyber Rifles. But the defenders of Landi Kotal once again proved themselves more than willing and able to take up arms against their fellow tribesmen. This time the clash took on a delicate political as well as military factor. Many of the Pathans gathering for the attack on the Khyber outposts had marched eastward across the Afghan border to join the Mohmand lashkar. This added another dimension to the coming engagement, for in the eyes of government it raised the spectre of a full-fledged conflict with Afghanistan.

The crunch came on 1 May when the Mohmands began concentrating their forces before the crenellated walls of Landi Kotal, waving their tribal banners and beating their war drums in the hope of drawing the Khyber Rifles, at least those levies who were from their own tribe, out of the grasp of the infidel Sirkar. Far from defecting to the enemy, the defenders held off the lashkar in three solid days of determined fighting. The Khyber Rifles stood firm behind the fort's formidable battlements and were only relieved on 4 May by Willcocks's 3rd Brigade, which smartly drove the interlopers back across the Afghan border. The most remarkable act of valour of this campaign took place at Michni on 2 and 3 May, where a handful of some fifty Khyber Rifles under Subadar Torkhan held off an attacking force of 4,000

Mohmands for seventeen gruelling hours of non-stop firing. The enemy actually managed to place one scaling ladder against the wall before they were beaten off, and this was to become a cherished Khyber Rifles trophy of war. By 5 May Willcocks was so confident that the situation had been brought under control that he ordered his army columns back to Peshawar, leaving the pass once more in the hands of the Khyber Rifles.

The tenacious defence of Landi Kotal effectively broke the Mohmands' fighting spirit. The action also averted complications with British India's neighbour to the west. The threat of Afghan intervention was taken seriously enough for the government to have recalled almost all Northern Army officers who were on leave and draw up emergency plans to buttress the Frontier defences. In Nevill's judgement, 'It is only too probable that matters would have been very different if anything in the shape of a reverse had occurred . . . at Landi Kotal.'

It was time for reprisals. Willcocks, leaving the Khyber Rifles in charge of the defence of the pass and its immediate environs, launched a punitive expedition against the Mohmands, quickly chasing the wild clans right up to the Durand Line. The expedition followed the usual pattern of scattering the tribesmen by day and putting up with their sniping by night, with on this occasion with the added physical hardship of appalling thunderstorms. In twenty days' time the operation was wound up at a cost of £10,000, but not without considerably worse than usual losses of ninety-seven British and native troops killed in action. The Mohmands and their Afghan allies, whom it must be said put up a desperately courageous stand against superior firepower, lost at least 400 men. Thus in keeping with military logic of the day, victory went to the Government of India.

The Mohmands saw things in a somewhat different light. Unbroken in spirit, for years thereafter, in fact almost to the end of British rule in India, this Frontier tribe continued to visit trouble on the Khyber. The Mohmands in fact stood in the vanguard of the Afghan invasion of 1919 that was to bring about the demise of the Khyber Rifles for the next quarter of a century. More than half a century after independence, the Mohmand Agency formed by Pakistan in 1947 continues to be the focal point of violent conflict on the Frontier. The Mohmands' tribal settlements straddle both sides of the Durand Line, in an area where geographical watersheds and tribal boundaries do not coincide. In any event Afghanistan does not recognise the Durand Line as its legitimate border with Pakistan, and as Caröe observed with prophetic insight, 'An international line that divides the allegiance of a tribe is a fertile cause for disturbance.' A few years ago, while US forces in Afghanistan scoured the hillsides in search of Taliban remnants and the elusive Osama bin Laden, Mohmand tribesmen backed by Afghan Government elements hostile to Pakistan launched an offensive on border positions at Salala Pass using Kalashnikovs, 12.7mm machine guns and rockets. Pakistan rushed in around one thousand Frontier Scouts, backed by armoured personnel carriers, heavy artillery pieces and helicopters to eventually regain control of the Mohmand homeland. But Pakistan and Afghanistan were briefly drawn to the brink of war over mutual charges of border violations.

The First World War provided the detonator for a renewed outbreak of hostilities on the North-West Frontier. Turkey's entry into the European conflict on the side of Germany gave the mullahs an excuse to take to the hills, spreading the gospel of jihad with renewed vehemence. The Sunni tribesmen held Abdul Hamid, the Sultan of Turkey, in great awe, and many regarded him as successor to the prophet Mohammed. The mullahs were encouraged in their fanatical endeavours by a Turco-German mission that arrived in Kabul to do what it could to incite the tribesmen to revolt. Tribal attacks on Frontier militia outposts were launched as early as November 1914, much to the consternation of the Chief Commissioner Roos-Keppel, who had to deal with a Fifth Columnist propaganda machine that was broadcasting to the world at large dire warnings of an imminent invasion of India by a Turco-German army, in league with Persia and Afghanistan. The Border Military Police, now reorganised as the Frontier Constabulary, lacked sufficient firepower to hold the lashkars at bay. The mullahs were quick to take advantage of this weakness and the following year they took their clarion call to Mohmand country, where the tribesmen required little encouragement to go on the march once they got the scent of booty up their noses. The Khyber Rifles found themselves manning the frontline defences against the Mohmand raiders, whose descent on Peshawar district came within a whisker of cutting off the city's water supply. The corps fought off a determined attack on Michni Fort, although their numbers were so thin and their weapons obsolete, that Roos-Keppel prevailed upon the government to re-arm the Khyber Rifles, as well as the other Frontier militias, with the new .303 rifle as a replacement for the Martini-Henry, and also to increase the men's fighting strength by a quarter, to include mounted infantry and artillery. The government agreed as well to raise a new corps modelled on the Khyber Rifles, known as the Mohmand Militia, specifically to see to the rebellious tribesmen north of Peshawar and thus help take pressure off British Army fighting units that were badly needed in other theatres of war.

This was how the situation stood in the months leading up to 3 May 1919, when Afghanistan launched a surprise attack on the Khyber that touched off the Third Afghan War. Hostilities came about as a result of the usual intrigues between rival religious and political factions. The British had in the Amir Habibullah a reasonably enlightened ruler who promoted social reforms at home and amicable relations with the Raj. This in itself rendered him fair game for ultra-religious and nationalist elements in Kabul, who despatched a hired assassin to gun down the amir while on a shooting trip near Jalalabad. The gunman crept into the amir's tent at night and blew off the top of his head with a rifle shot. The killer's identity remains a mystery to this day, but public opinion had to be placated so one unfortunate Afghan colonel, considered dispensable, was charged with the murder and hanged on flimsy evidence. There ensued a sharp, delicate power struggle for succession to the throne of Kabul. The late king's brother Nasrullah immediately proclaimed himself Amir, without taking into account the cunning of his nephew Amanullah, the amir's third son who had his own designs on the throne. Taking care to ensure that his proclamation took place in the presence of the country's notables and military commanders, Amanullah declared himself the preferred candidate for the job, and graciously accepted Nasrullah's homage. This wily 27-year-old Afghan nobleman was described by a British contemporary as 'a man of strange character, conceited, arrogant, and with a somewhat empty precocious mind'.

There is nothing like a good patriotic scapegoat to mobilise flagging public support. Some influential army elements suspected Amanullah of having a hand in his father's murder, thus the new amir saw the need to distract his subjects' attention from recent events. His most conspicuous ploy was to hitch his star to the rising swell of nationalist agitation across the border in British India. Few Afghans would have argued with the demand that the right to set foreign policy, for instance, which had been placed in British hands forty years ago at the end of the second Afghan War, be returned to its rightful owner. There was also the question of Peshawar, a highly inflammable issue for most Pathan Afghans, who resented British claims to sovereignty over the city. Amanullah bowed to pressure from his generals, who after all were the men who had placed the young amir on the throne.

One of the more picturesque incidents in this Afghan escapade was the case of the Peshawar postmaster. Amanullah summoned this British civil servant to Kabul and after a briefing from the amir, the man was sent whence he came weighted down with copies of a proclamation, signed by Amanullah, calling on all Muslims to rise up in aid of Afghanistan in a war against the infidels. Once back in Peshawar the postmaster, who drew his salary from the North-West Frontier Government, had these documents distributed far and wide by Afghan agents. The uprising was timed for 8 May but here the duplicitous plot thickens, for the postmaster was betrayed by one of his own men, who reported the conspiracy to Roos-Keppel. The Khyber Rifles Commandant promptly called in troops to surround Peshawar and threatened to cut off the city's water supply if the rebels moved so much as a finger. It was then the turn of the ringleaders to be double-crossed and handed over to the authorities, after which the city was declared safe.

Undeterred, Amanullah made his opening move on 4 May. The Afghan Commander-in-Chief Saleh Mohammed speedily deployed 150 of his troops across the Durand Line to occupy the village of Bagh at the western entrance to the Khyber Pass. This was within British territory and the incursion thus constituted an act of war. So for the third time in eighty years, general mobilisation was called and on 6 May the Government of India was at war with Afghanistan.

The village of Bagh was in itself of no strategic importance, save for the threat this action posed to the 500 men of the Khyber Rifles stationed up the road at Landi Kotal, who relied on the settlement for their water supply. The act of sabotage was carried out the next day by a larger party of Afghan kassadars and Shinwari tribesmen, who arrived at Bagh and cut the water supply to the Khyber Rifles garrison. For the Afghan forces, speed and surprise were of the essence. British and Indian Army forces back from the carnage of the trenches in the First World War were in a battle-weary condition, but they were still a far superior fighting force to anything the Afghan military could hope to put in the field. General Mohammed was able to muster 50,000 troops around which the tribal lashkars, numbering as many as 80,000 fighting men, could join battle. On paper it looked like a significant threat. Fortunately for Britain, the Afghan units were ill-trained, ill-paid and mostly under strength. Few infantry units even had bayonets, and ammunition was in short supply. But the picture was far more worrisome in the Khyber, where the amir was able to gather 20,000 to 30,000 tribal fighters who, in contrast to the Afghan regulars, were of excellent fighting quality, well armed and with plenty of ammunition of local manufacture or looted from the British.

At this point, a general Pathan uprising was Roos-Keppel's worst nightmare. 'A greater danger than Afghanistan is the tribes,' he says in a letter to the Viceroy. 'That they have not risen against us yet is extraordinary, as we have always counted on the almost certainty of their rising should the Amir declare war. Things in Tirah are looking ugly but the leading men and the majority of the tribe are still on our side, but are afraid lest they may be committed by their young men, in which case they say that it is as well to be hung for a sheep as a lamb.'

The main thrust of the Afghan invasion fell on the Khyber Pass. Bands of Afghan tribesmen swooped on the roadside picquets at Khairgali that were manned by Khyber Rifles on kafila days. The party of sepoys detailed to escort the camel caravans were met by a large party of armed Afghans under a notorious raider, Zar Shah, who spotted a freelance opportunity for booty and rode in on the back of the Afghan Army's advance, falsely boasting that he was acting under orders of the Afghan Commander-in-Chief.

This time the government was swift to relieve the beleaguered Khyber Rifles garrisons in the pass. Roos-Keppel, who hoped to avoid a replay of the fiasco at Landi Kotal twenty-two years earlier, when Barton was prevented from sending aid to his militiamen, despatched a motorised column of two companies of Indian infantry, one section of mountain artillery and another of sappers and miners to assist the Khyber Rifles.

The first assault came up against stiffer resistance that had been expected. The British forces were unable to dislodge the Afghans from Bagh, despite the concerted efforts of the Khyber Rifles, Sikhs and Gurkhas, that is, the toughest fighting units available on the British side of the Frontier. The Afghan troops, and especially their allies from the tribal territories, were worked to a fever pitch over their successful invasion of British-held territory and they fought like madmen. General Arthur Barrett, who was in command of the North-West Frontier Forces, stationed himself at Khyber Rifles headquarters at Landi Kotal to direct the operations. The first warning signs of trouble among the Khyber Rifles came on 10 May. The failure to oust the enemy, who had always been depicted as an assemblage of uniformed rustics, provided food for thought for the Pathan levies. Even Roos-Keppel treated the invaders with contempt as a fighting force. 'I do not look upon the Afghans as a very serious danger,' he wrote to Lord Minto. But he also confesses his surprise as 'the sample of the Afghan Army that we have had to fight in the last few days has fought better than I expected, in fact they have fought with great bravery and tenacity but they have no organised commissariat or transport and are incapable of conducting a campaign on a large scale.' Several Khyber Rifles sepoys, however, were led to believe that the Afghans were about to overwhelm the defenders and rout the British, and so they deserted the corps.

The Afghans by now had in place at Bagh a powerful force of up to 8,000 regulars with at least a battery of mountain artillery and some quick-firing machine guns. The amir was bent on making this the great jihad against the infidel and threw everything he could muster at the Khyber, the gateway to Peshawar. 'Enemy reinforcements were undoubtedly arriving, the indecisive attack on the 9th had not depressed the enemy, the tribesmen in independent territory needed but little to make them go over to the enemy,' Barrett reported. 'Finally a picquet of the Khyber Rifles deserted.' The following day the incident was being treated as a regrettable but minor side issue, as Barrett prepared a fresh and definitive assault on Bagh, this time with air cover as well as artillery. At this point the regular army was still fighting side-by-side with the Khyber Rifles, as Barrett highlights in his summary of events. 'The artillery followed up the retreating enemy with their fire, ably assisted by the Khyber Rifles, who throughout the day had been co-operating on the north of the main (Khyber Pass) road,' says the official despatch.[8]

By 13 May the Khyber Rifles as a unified corps was beginning to show serious signs of wavering. With the breakdown of reliable information that is the inevitable companion of warfare, reports began filtering into the militia's Khyber outposts via Afghan agents in Peshawar of an imminent uprising in the city, that the

Afghan forces were winning all along the Frontier and would shortly be at Landi Kotal, that the Khyber Rifles garrisoned at their headquarters had shot their officers and gone over to the Afghans, along with many other tales of heroic Pathan victories. The illiterate Afridis, who in those days made up the bulk of the Khyber Rifles, were highly susceptible to this sort of propaganda. Recruits were beginning to desert in large numbers and Roos-Keppel was obliged to take decisive action to head off a full-scale mutiny. 'The Khyber Rifles have behaved very badly, and you can imagine how it distresses me to have to say this as I practically made them and am their Honorary Colonel,' he later explained to the Viceroy. 'The men at Landi Kotal who had the British officers with them did well and fought well, but the officers were so occupied with battle fighting in front that they neglected the outposts and did not visit them. As day after day went past, the Khyber Rifles became more and more agitated, and from deserting by single men they began to desert in large batches. I have now handed over all these outposts to the Regulars and have told the Commandant to speak to all the men there and discharge any man who does not wish to go on.'

The officers remained loyal to the government, but 1,180 sepoys opted for discharge. Nearly 150 of the loyalists were posted to a military police unit, while 200 of the men, with the intention of keeping them gainfully employed on government's side, were redeployed as an irregular force called the Khyber Levy Corps. This rag-tag bunch of tribesmen wore no uniform and were expected to provide their own rifles. Roos-Keppel continues, 'I am afraid it will be the end of that was a fine corps, which in the Zakka Khel expedition did not lose a man or a rifle, although we had three companies of Zakka Khels with us.' Roos-Keppel makes no attempt to exculpate the deserters, but after a quarter century's service on the Frontier, he was fully cognisant of the religious and tribal pressures that had been brought to bear on the Khyber Rifles levies. 'The militia system grew up as a cheap expedient to relieve regular troops from irksome and arduous duties in a country where service is unpopular,' he later writes.

The militia outposts were located far off in tribal areas, and miles of hostile and dangerous country separated them from the nearest posts of regular troops. In such circumstances, and particularly when there were no regular troops to support them during the Afghan War, the militia men could hardly have been expected to remain loyal to the British Government in the face of the cry of jihad in Afghanistan and of the aggravated anti-British feelings in tribal territory.[9]

The first thirty-five years of this unique and original native levy of the North-West Frontier was brought to an inglorious end on 19 May. The Khyber Rifles as a corps was disbanded, not to be raised again until after the Second World War.

As for the conflict in hand, Roos-Keppel had persuaded the government to carry the advance deep into Afghan territory, capturing Dakka and Jalalabad, as well as several other key positions, and forcing the amir to the negotiating table in Rawalpindi. For a defeated leader who could hardly be considered in a position to dictate terms, Amanullah managed to walk away from the negotiating table with a key demand under his belt, the granting to Afghanistan of autonomy in foreign affairs, thus effectively achieving full independence for his country. Small wonder that, though beaten on the field of battle, he marched home proclaiming victory to his jubilant followers. After all, the wily Afghan king had achieved all that his father and grandfather had in vain demanded of the British. Nor was it any surprise that Amanullah took advantage of the occasion to build a grand palace, erect a massive triumphal pillar and distribute medals to his defeated troops to commemorate his victory over 'the greatest empire in the world'. True, the British refused to renew their subsidies to Afghanistan as well as the licence to import arms. But this was a trifling matter, for the amir well knew to whom he could turn for assistance. Within a few weeks of ratifying the peace treaty an Afghan mission pitched up in Moscow, thus stoking the Government of India's smouldering fears of Russian, and now Bolshevik, intrigues in Central Asia.

Roos-Keppel retired shortly thereafter to return home to London, where he died soon after. Sir Abdul Qayyum, who had served as Political Agent in the Khyber during the Afghan war and almost filled the role of Roos-Keppel's second self, recalls that on a visit to Britain he found his former chief lying ill and in a state of despondency. The Yusufzai nobleman believed that Roos-Keppel's demise had been hastened by a sense of emptiness in retirement, and that this feeling of severance from the people he had worked for had emptied his life of meaning. Like Warburton, after playing out a swashbuckling career of high adventure on the North-West Frontier, there was little to sustain him in the stifling quietude and orderliness of the country he had spent his life defending.

When war broke out in Europe in 1939, the Government of India found its eastern land border threatened by the Japanese advance through Burma. The North-West Frontier, on the other hand, posed a different type of security threat. Nazi agents were on the prowl in Constantinople and Kabul, plotting to stir up trouble by spreading anti-British propaganda and promising 'liberation' for the oppressed Muslim victims of imperialism.

The government was therefore forced to deploy army units to the Frontier that were badly needed in other theatres of war. From the Commander-in-Chief General Sir Alan Fleming Hartley to the Political Agent of the Khyber, Major Roger Bacon, an idea began to crystallise, that encouraging the Afridis to enlist for active service the army might kill two birds with one stone. On the one hand, hundreds of armed Afridis, potential insurgents in the eyes of government, with little else but time on their hands would be removed from Peshawar and the Khyber villages, out of the line of fire of German propaganda. It was also argued that the Afridis had a long history of fighting for Britain in far-flung places. Therefore, the argument ran, it would make perfect sense to tap into their martial experience in the war against Hitler. Renewing Afridi enlistment, which had been suspended in 1919 after several desertions in the trenches, was by all means preferable to the restless tribesmen distracting the regulars from their wartime mission. For Germany was not the only threat to stability in India. The ex-Khyber Rifles sepoys were no longer drawing a pension from the British Government, so there were economic pressures on these men, who were quite adept in finding other ways of filling their pockets. The unrest was exploited by the Hindu-dominated Congress Party, for which the Pathan Muslims had absolutely no sympathies. Yet the Congress subversives were able to score a number of successes in rousing the Khyber Afridis to action, mainly by supporting armed raids on Peshawar and other cities during the period of nationalist agitation in the 1930s, right up to the outbreak of war. A battalion of Adam Khel Afridis was sent to Africa in the 1867–8 Abyssinian Campaign. They also served in British East Africa in 1898 to help deal with mutinous Sudanese troops. The Afridis also took up arms on the government's side in campaigns fought outside their home territory, such as in the Black Mountain and Chitral expeditions. During the First World War Afridi soldiers were to be found in units sent to the front in Egypt, France, Mesopotamia, Palestine and German East Africa. Roughly since the time of the Third Afghan War, the armed forces had provided a conduit for tribal integration into the Raj. By 1930 nearly 15 per cent of the Indian Regular Army was recruited from the Pathan tribes, along with the more traditional people beyond the limits of the Government of India's administration, such as the Gurkhas.

By the end of 1941 the die was cast. Sir George Cunningham, one of the Government's most efficient and perspicacious administrators, a career Frontiersman who had served as Governor of the North-West Frontier Province for eleven years and was asked by newly-independent Pakistan to stay on until 1948, had prevailed upon the Viceroy to reopen enlistment in the Indian Army. The unit raised was the 1st Afridi Battalion, made up of former soldiers of the disbanded Khyber Rifles under the command of six British officers. When Cunningham proudly rose to his feet at a luncheon with the Afridi maliks to announce the decision, the news was greeted with whoops of jubilation from the assembled tribal leaders. This was nothing less than what the chieftains had been demanding from government for years, a way to restore pride in their young fighters while at the same time providing them with gainful employment. Once the serious discussions got under way, the maliks made it clear that certain conditions would have to be agreed before they would let their men march off to fight for the Sirkar.

Critical among these undertakings was the demand that if any of the men who enrolled for active duty had problems with blood feuds back home, he would be granted leave, no questions asked and transport provided, so that he could go and settle matters. This reconciled the Afridi recruits to travel abroad, which had not been the case when they were sent to the trenches in the First World War. The army agreed the terms, but this turned out to be a tricky business, for there was always the fear that a member of the other feuding family might be serving in the battalion, someone who could get a message back to the Frontier to warn his kinsmen of their enemy's imminent return. To prevent the soldier going off on 'compassionate' leave from walking into a death trap, his date of departure was always kept secret.

The establishment of the Afridi Battalion was a political decision, since the government wanted to release as many troops as possible for frontline service elsewhere. But it worked well for both sides. The Afridis were happy to have the money coming in from their sons earning army pay abroad, while in return the tribesmen promised to keep the peace in the Khyber. In June 1942 some 700 ex-Khyber Rifles sepoys and a handful of British officers boarded the train to Bombay, whence they embarked for the Middle East theatre of operations to spend the best part of five years in Persia, Iraq and Syria. The British officers set sail with some trepidation over the thought of several days in close quarters aboard a small Mecca pilgrim ship with several hundred heavily armed Afridis. The moment had come to put the men's discipline to the test. The battalion was marched alongside the ship about to set sail for Aden. One of the officers shouted, with more hope than conviction, the order 'Ground Arms', and then very quickly, 'Two Paces Forward'. To the officers' relief and amazement, the Afridis dropped their precious weapons to the ground and the rifles were collected and stored for safe keeping.

It was a strange enough war for the Afridis, who travelled to the Middle East fired up with enthusiasm for engaging in what they love most in life, a good fight. Instead, in the three years spent overseas where the tribesmen were attached to the 10th Army, the men of the former Khyber Rifles not once engaged in battle with the enemy. One of the battalion's first roles was to guard the army's base ordnance depot in Iraq against theft by local Arabs, a task for which the Frontier tribesmen were eminently suited. The Afridis were also stationed on the Turkish border, a delicate business given that the sultan had yet to decide whether to throw in his lot with the Allies. 'The coup de grâce against any active role came . . . when the Afridis were ordered back to Persia and Iraq Force (PAIFORCE),' recalls Robin Hodson. 'By December 1943 the battalion found itself occupying thirty-eight posts on the trans-Iranian railway.'[10] This was the line of supply for aid to Russia, and it needed to be heavily guarded against the threat of German or pro-German saboteurs based in the Iranian tribal areas. So for the Afridis life was not all that different from their traditional role of protecting the kafilas on their journey through the Khyber Pass. The years spent abroad with the army brought benefit to all concerned. By training the Afridis in commando tactics, the men gained valuable experience for their future role as recruits in the newly formed Khyber Rifles. The tribesmen, alas, served the army as human guinea pigs for experiments with anti-malarial drugs. In September 1943, half the battalion were administered the drugs (mepacrine) and the other half came off the treatment. One platoon was placed on pammequin, another anti-malarial prophylactic. The two drugs were introduced as substitutes for quinine when supplies of the latter fell into the hands of the Japanese after their conquests in South-East Asia. At the end of September, the total number of malaria cases noted was twenty-three, with only half the battalion under suppressive treatment. This appeared to furnish the medical authorities with all the information their required, and in early October the army ordered the Afridi Battalion back to the Syrian-Turkish border to resume frontier control.

By the time the Afridi Battalion returned home in 1945 self-government for India was all but a done deal. Earl Wavell, as wartime Viceroy had seen his proposed strategy of gradual withdrawal from India washed aside by the surging tide of events. It was obvious to all that British troops would soon be departing the North-West Frontier. This was the moment to reactivate Curzon's strategy of empowering native levies as border guardians. On 1 March 1946 a dual ceremony took place on the parade ground at Sialkot, a former garrison town north of Lahore. Two tables were set up under canopies, a British officer standing at each behind a stack of documents. The Afridi Battalion was formed up and the men, some 700 of them, marched one by one past the first table to be handed their discharge papers from the Afridi Battalion. They then moved five yards ahead to the next table to pick up their enlistment papers in the Khyber Rifles. Lieutenant-Colonel John Birch was appointed Commandant of the corps, with Captain Karamatullah Khan as his adjutant. Two days later the levies and their four officers entrained for the North-West Frontier and Landi Kotal, at last their permanent home in the Khyber Pass.

CHAPTER SEVEN

Guardians of a Frontier Ablaze

It was fitting that the North-West Frontier, this stubborn, hostile and most remote outpost of Britain's Indian Empire, should have been the last place in the subcontinent to see the sun set on the Raj. In August 1947, the Union Flag was lowered at Khyber Rifles headquarters in Landi Kotal, to the air of the 'Last Post' and to the supreme indifference of the Pathan tribesmen squatting in their hilltop eyries, as uninvited observers of the solemnities. 'As the sun dropped behind the peak of Sikaram at the far end of the Safed Koh range and the shadows of night crept through the Khyber Pass with the stealth of Afridi bandits, the gathering darkness seemed to swallow the naked staff atop the battlements of Landi Kotal fort in one swift gulp,' noted Charles Miller. 'The final notes of Last Post echoed faintly in the overhanging hills. Then a great silence came down like a blanket, enveloping the Khyber Rifles bugler and colour guard as they returned to their barracks.'[1]

The general salute had been given and the flag broken, but it was not yet endgame for Britain on the North-West Frontier. When George Cunningham drove through the streets of Peshawar following the ceremony, he found his car mobbed by nearly a thousand people, all shouting 'Pakistan Zindabad!' and 'Jinnah Zindabad!' But to the newly sworn-in Governor's astonishment, the crowd then began to cry 'Cunningham Governor Zindabad!' 'Indeed, it was rather like the Rectorial

installation in St Andrew's all over again,' recalls Cunningham.
'At one point a band, rather surprisingly, struck up 'God Save the
King!''[2] So the British had not, for the time being, fully
relinquished responsibility for this burdensome yet compelling
corner of their lost Indian Empire, for as one soldier who
remained behind noted, 'At that time, the Pakistanis were happy
to have us stay on for as long as we wished.' Without a doubt,
most British military stationed in Peshawar carried more
Frontier experience under their Sam Brownes than the officers of
the newly formed Pakistan armed forces.

Sovereignty over the tribal territories passed to the Government
of Pakistan, but nobody was under any illusions that this was
anything but a continuation of the chimerical state of affairs that
had existed for centuries past. The Pathan homeland might be
administered, albeit to a very limited extent and only with the
consent of the tribesmen, but it was not to be ruled.

As far back as 1907 the Government of India had begun
mulling the creation of a system to co-ordinate the seven corps of
Frontier tribesmen that had been raised since the Khyber
Jezailchis came into being nearly thirty years before. In that year
the various units were grouped together under a new
organisation called the Frontier Corps, also known as the Frontier
Scouts, whose headquarters were permanently shifted two years
after Partition to the imposing hilltop Bala Hissar fortress that
towers over the main road leading into Peshawar. The brigadier in
command of the Frontier Corps held jurisdiction over a huge
swathe of territory from the Karakorum range at the northern
extreme of the Frontier to the Mekran coast 2,500 miles to the
south. The Pakistani Government, or more accurately the Punjabi
élite that rules that country's military, was uncomfortable with
what it perceived as the threat of a fledgling army taking root
within the armed forces. Hence the Frontier Corps was later
dismembered and the units stationed in northern areas were
placed directly under army control. Baluchistan province was
given its own Frontier Corps, headquartered at Quetta, with a
strength of twelve militia units. The Khyber Rifles came under the

Peshawar command and their ranks were now filled not only by Afridis, but also by Mahsuds, Wazirs and other tribes of renowned fighting qualities.

Pakistan, unlike its neighbour India, does not give the impression of being unduly troubled by its colonial past. More than half a century after Partition, politicians in Delhi perplexingly still feel compelled to assert their Indianness by changing venerable names like Calcutta, Bombay and Madras to the irritating Kolkata, Mumbai and Chennai. In Pakistan, on the other hand, far from striving to erase the vestiges of the Raj, there is almost a manifest pride in conserving quaint relics of empire such as the Civil Lines and cantonments, posted on street signs in Peshawar and in other cities. This may be a reflection of the fact that Pakistan maintained friendlier relations with the West during the Cold War days, or it could well be the legacy of the many years the country has been ruled by the army, a breed notoriously addicted to the status quo. In any case, British administrators and military personnel were a familiar sight in Pakistan for some considerable time after Independence, and the Khyber Rifles were no exception. The job of commandant started to go exclusively to Pakistani nationals only in 1949 when Lieutenant-Colonel Iftikharuddin, the youngest of Sir Aslam Khan's three grandsons, followed in the footsteps of his distinguished forebears.

The reincarnated Khyber Rifles that emerged in the aftermath of the Second World War bore little resemblance to the corps that had been disbanded only a quarter century before. The steely-eyed warriors crouched behind their sangars, guarding the braying and clanging kafilas that plodded up the Khyber Pass, or the men shrouded in the smoke and clamour of battle defending the walls of Landi Kotal, a mere twenty-seven years on seemed as remote in time as a square of British redcoats on the fields of Waterloo.

The post-1947 Khyber Rifles took up positions as the second line of defence in the pass. In the event of invasion, they were (and are) to be deployed in support of the Pakistani Army, much in the same way that the original Jezailchis had been engaged by the British as a stopgap force. But it would be wrong to assume that the corps had been recast in a mere ceremonial capacity, kitted out in smart militia uniforms to entertain luncheon dignitaries at the Landi Kotal officers' mess. Nothing, in fact, could be further from reality.

The first armed conflict between the newly independent states of Pakistan and India broke out in October 1947, with the ink barely dry on the document of transfer of sovereignty, and it was the Pathans, always itching for a good fight, who could take a bow for having ignited the fuse. It was pretty much a foregone conclusion that the Muslim dominated principality of Kashmir was ordained to become the bone of contention between both countries. Thus less than two months after independence, the Princely State found itself divided and invaded. Pro-Pakistani historians, as well as most former Frontier Corps officers, avow that the incursion was a spontaneous act of religious patriotism. More sceptical chroniclers have few doubts that the events of October were meticulously orchestrated by the Pakistani military. The latter school of thought gains some plausibility on the basis of personal diaries kept by some of the leading characters on the scene. Cunningham, for instance, as Governor of the North-West Frontier Province, sent for his chief minister on 25 October to inform him that he 'knew, or suspected, pretty well who had been instigating the tribesmen to go to Kashmir. He (the Minister) grinned.'[3] Whoever was behind the invasion, the fact is that on 22 October a motorised force of several thousand Pathan tribesmen swarmed into Muzaffarabad, now the capital of Pakistani Kashmir, where they embarked on an orgy of arson, pillage and plunder. The Pathans met with little resistance, most of the Indian Muslim troops having deserted, the rest fleeing in terror before the onslaught. The tribesmen rapidly approached the gates of Srinagar, almost unopposed, and by 26 October the Government of Pakistan was receiving reports that the city would fall into their hands by nightfall. With his Princely State in mortal danger of being torn apart by rampaging tribesmen from the North-West Frontier, the Maharaja Sir Hari Singh was persuaded the very next day that any hope of continued independence for Kashmir was a pipe dream and that accession to India, whose army was massed on his eastern border, was the realistic option. 'In the special circumstances mentioned by Your Highness, my Government have decided to accept the accession of Kashmir State to the Dominion of India,' wrote Lord Mountbatten, the last Viceroy and first Governor-General of India, on 27 October. Mountbatten conceded that Kashmir's accession to India had been brought about by violence, a fact that in Pakistan's view discredits the operation, but at the same time he insisted that 'the violence came from the tribes, for whom Pakistan and not India was responsible'. Mountbatten was also concerned over the fate of several hundred British residents in Kashmir, and concluded in a report to George VI that to save Kashmir from complete pillage and safeguard British lives 'Indian troops would have to do the job'.

The battle for Kashmir raged on for a year, until the state was divided roughly along the lines in which it finds itself today. A United Nations resolution calling for a plebiscite was at first embraced by both powers and later rejected by India, and as a result the Kashmir dispute motivated another costly war between both countries in 1965.

Meanwhile, in April 1948 four platoons of the Khyber Rifles under the command of Major Aziz Khan arrived in Kashmir. This was the first time that the militia had been sent into action outside tribal territory. The venue may have been shifted from the scrub hills of the Khyber to the fabled lush valleys of the vale of Kashmir, but the time-honoured fighting qualities of the Pathans were most effectively brought into play. Prior to the assault and eventual capture of Pandu village and its surrounding strategic objectives, there was a no man's land that needed to be patrolled. It was also vital to gather intelligence on enemy strength and troop dispositions in the area. In short, grist for the stalking and surveillance skills that had made the Khyber Rifles such a valuable asset to the British. As an added bonus, from the tribal levies' point of view, there was also an ambush to be laid. But in official reports, all we are told about the corps' activities in the Kashmir conflict is that, 'In this operation the Khyber Rifles showed their worth and proved themselves second to none.' On the other hand, one could hardly expect the Pakistani military to be too forthcoming about a campaign that set the scene for half a century of stalemate warfare. Likewise, a contingent of Khyber Rifles 'took a prominent part' in the 1965 war, in which a motorised company of levies fought its way across the Indian border to come within a few hours of Srinagar. The men, however, were recalled at the last minute 'due to a change in battle plans'.

Pakistan's records of most of its military operations against India are classified as secret. In fact, in the 1971 disaster which deprived Pakistan of its eastern territory, now known as Bangladesh, the Khyber Rifles and all other units involved in the action were ordered to destroy their war diaries. Concerning the Khyber Rifles' role in that conflict, the official reports make reference, without much effort at enlightenment, to a contingent of three companies that was flown to Dacca in April 1971, where 'they performed various duties and were attached to different army units, and gave a good account of themselves during the war'. Another three companies went to Gilgit on the Western Front, to be deployed mainly in patrolling a rugged and inhospitable mountainous region that, albeit on a grander scale, in many ways was not dissimilar to the Khyber.

The experience gained fighting under the command of Pakistani regulars in Kashmir not only enhanced the profile of the Khyber Rifles, but also prepared the corps for more sophisticated duties, well beyond its original role as guardian of the Khyber Pass. In recent years Khyber Rifles units have been deployed in quelling civil disturbances in Peshawar, and they have taken part in drug busting operations as far afield as Karachi.

Pathan youths continue to flock to the ranks of the Khyber Rifles today as they did more than 125 years ago, when Robert Warburton conceived the idea of turning poachers into gamekeepers. In 1878 the tribesmen volunteered for service in the Khyber Pass because enlisting in the Jezailchis provided them with an income, but more importantly because it gave them an opportunity to fire their rifles with impunity. The scent of cordite and adventure still exercises a powerful influence on recruits, as would be expected in a corps garrisoned on one of the world's most explosive international borders. But a salary and a rifle are no longer the chief incentives for enlistment: in fact, the Khyber Rifles' pay scale is lower than the regular army's, and the traditional rifle that gave the corps its name is now shouldered only for ceremonial purposes. A Khyber Rifles sepoy earns 2,000 rupees a month (some £20), about 1,000 rupees less than an army conscript. The militiamen are financially disadvantaged in other ways, too. A Khyber Rifles trooper, if wounded in battle or simply down with flu, must pay for medical treatment out of his own pocket and then submit a claim for reimbursement. A regular soldier simply walks into his regimental infirmary and is treated free of charge. The Khyber Rifles are today armed with light automatic weapons and mortars, not as glamorous as a lovingly oiled and polished Martini Henry, one might argue, but a lot more effective in dealing with the sort of adversary they are likely to meet on the 60-mile front along the Durand Line that falls under Khyber Rifles jurisdiction.

Despite the apparent disadvantages with regular army service, when the English daily *Frontier Post* publishes its annual list of vacancies for the Frontier Forces, the Khyber Rifles are besieged with applications from hundreds of eager young tribesmen. The corps recruits some 200 volunteers a year. The men are selected in accordance with a tribal quota system. Whereas in the past it was taken for granted that the ranks would be filled with local Afridis, the five wings are now made up of men from ten Pathan tribes: Afridi, Yusufzai, Bangash, Khatak, Wazir, Shilmani, Mohmand, Mullagori, Yusufzai and Orakzai. The Afridi contingent, however, continues to outnumber the others given the proximity of their villages to the Khyber Agency. The only tribesmen excluded from enlistment are the Shinwaris, who are deemed to pose a greater security threat than any of the others as a large proportion of their families lives on the other side of the Durand Line in Afghan territory. The fear is that if a border conflict were to break out in their homeland, the Shinwaris would be rendered untrustworthy for action. The levies are quite happily segregated into platoons along tribal lines, and they are deployed by taking into account each tribe's particular skills: the Afridis for their unmatched fighting capabilities, the Shilmanis as expert marksmen, and so on.

'In one recent year, we received more than five hundred applications to fill eighteen vacancies allotted to the Yusufzai tribe,' recalls Captain Shafi Ullah Khan, a tall, bearded Khyber Rifles officer who sits on the Frontier Corps' examining board.

The appeal of the Khyber Rifles is so strong that we get university graduates from Peshawar competing to enlist as sepoys. I recall one in particular who said that one evening he was listening to a popular romantic ballad on the radio, 'Mung yuu da Khyber Zalmi' ('We are the Young Men of the Khyber'), and presented himself the very next day at Frontier Corps headquarters asking to volunteer for the Khyber Rifles. People here are very much aware of the militia's history and traditions. We even get requests for transfer from men serving in other Frontier Corps units.[4]

The Khyber Rifles is today made up 3,500 men serving in five wings. These units are in effect light infantry battalions, each one under the command of a major or lieutenant-colonel. The Jamrud wing is deployed at the entrance to the Khyber Pass, with others stationed at outposts in adjacent areas – Shilmani and Charbag tribal territory, and of course the corps' hallowed headquarters at Landi Kotal. The fifth is in Tirah, and the advent of this wing, which was transferred from Ali Masjid to the hitherto forbidden mountainous tract between the Khyber Pass and the Khanki valley, may prove to have far-reaching geopolitical implications in the current war on Al Qaeda terrorism.

On a crisp December morning, two months to the day after the 11 September attacks in the US, the Afridi villagers of Tirah south of the Khyber Pass woke to the clatter of helicopter rotor blades closing in on their mud homes. The vanguard of the taskforce was led by the Khyber Rifles, followed by a regular Pakistani Army unit, a section of paramilitary khassadars in black shalwar kameez uniforms, and a detachment of Swat Scouts. In the days leading up to the invasion Khyber Rifles agents had quietly cut a deal with the local maliks, so the troops landed under the guise of a peaceful mission. Nevertheless, given that this marked the first time in North-West Frontier history that soldiers were despatched to Tirah as a permanent occupation force, the men went in armed to the teeth with light automatic weapons and back-up from two artillery batteries.

Captain Ullah Khan went in with the first wave to hit the ground that day. 'We gathered the tribal maliks and made it clear that our mission was to cordon off the territory, as it was being used by al-Qaeda militants as an escape route into Pakistan,' he explained. 'The villagers could hear the American B-52s bombing in the nearby Tora Bora range, where Osama bin Laden was thought to be in hiding. We told the headmen in no uncertain terms that if they didn't want some of the same, they would let our troops enter their land unopposed.'[5]

The occupation of Tirah had a twofold objective. Apart from depriving the terrorists of a safe haven, the Khyber Rifles launched an all-out offensive on the drugs trade that is rampant throughout the region. Tirah in particular has long been a prime heroin-producing centre. The land is a cul-de-sac in the mountains, miles from the nearest roads, and the difficulty of its passes, some rising to 8,500 feet, combined with the fierceness of its inhabitants has throughout history rendered it inviolable. Tirah covers an area of some 600 square miles, comprising all the hidden valleys lying round the source of the Bara river. In this mountainous stronghold some of the most savage Afridi and Orakzai clans operate the drug connection, from poppy growing to sophisticated cottage industry refining operations, and finally to smuggling the finished product across the border, through Afghanistan to Western markets. That was the cosy and profitable state of affairs until the arrival of the Khyber Rifles in December 2001. The troops laid waste to hundreds of acres of poppy fields and shut down the area's refining facilities so that now it is estimated that about 75 per cent of the region's poppy cultivation has been eradicated.

The Tirah campaign had a third objective, which one could argue in the longer term will prove to be the most significant. This was to drag the local villagers out of centuries of backwardness and isolation. So deep-rooted is this state of darkness that some of the local tribesmen had never ventured into Peshawar, a day's journey from their homes. Within weeks of occupying Tirah, the Khyber Rifles had rounded up a number of Al Qaeda militants and sealed off the terrorists' escape channel through these rugged hills. The next task was to make good on the Pakistani Government's often promised but never fulfilled pledge to improve the tribesmen's lot. A motorable track was laid through Tirah that cut the journey time to the market town of Landi Kotal from eight to three hours. The villages were connected to the grid, schools and hospital facilities were made available, and by all accounts the villagers have reacted with enthusiasm to their first taste of Western-style progress. It remains to be seen whether the tribesmen have genuinely embraced their new-found domesticity, or are simply waiting for the first opportunity to turn on their self-appointed benefactors. The largest British military force ever assembled in India, after all, lingered for three unsuspecting years in Kabul before being driven out to perish in the snow.

It is tempting to believe that the Khyber Rifles will make a success of their efforts. Should this turn out to be the case, the occupation of Tirah could have major historic implications, in that it will have set a template for the eventual pacification of the Frontier. A sad milestone, perhaps, for those inclined to romanticise a way of life that in almost every respect is best summed up in Churchill's definition of 'nasty, brutish and short'. A more enlightened observer might argue that these reforms are long overdue. There is no evidence to suggest that improvements in healthcare or education undermine a people's cultural traditions. Spain, a country that virtually leapt from the nineteenth to the twenty-first century without any request stops, is today endowed with one Europe's most modern transport systems and national health schemes. Yet Spaniards still flock to bullfights and enjoy their late night suppers. A national culture suffers when the motive for intervention is one of repression, as was the case in China's invasion of Tibet.

Perhaps the greatest single shortcoming of Britain's Frontier policy was the failure to extend to the Pathans the same Victorian benevolence that benefited other Indian subjects of the Raj. With some notable exceptions, and here the names of Warburton, Roos-Keppel and a handful of other worthy Frontiersmen come to mind, the British preferred to dismiss the tribesmen as barbarians and savages. For more than a century, the only contact between the Government of India and the Pathans was almost always on the battlefield. During these years the threat of Russian aggression, more fanciful than real, struck terror in the heart of the Raj, to the extent that Britain was incapable of seeing the North-West Frontier as anything but a buffer zone. There is fertile ground for speculation on what the outcome might have been had General Lockhart, who led the punitive expedition into Tirah following the 1897 Pathan uprising, had made an attempt to win the Afridis' loyalty in the same way the Khyber Rifles are undertaking to do it more than a century later.

'I Wonder What Happened to Him'

Every October, when the chill autumn winds descend on Salisbury plains, a group of elderly men gathers for an informal luncheon at the Rose & Crown Hotel. They are easily recognisable as 'gentlemen of the Old School', soft-spoken, courteous to a fault, smartly turned out in tweed jackets, twill trousers and spit-and-polish brogues. Much of the animated conversation round the crowded table would leave the casual listener totally bewildered, peppered as it is with expressions like gasht, *barampta* or lashkar, words of a language that few in the West have ever heard spoken. What would the other diners in the room make of Major John Girling rising to his feet to solemnly pronounce, '*Da ter shawai kar arman mah kawah, chi biyartah puh las nah rashi?*' The Pushtu proverb truly reflects the convivial mood of this annual gathering: 'Grieve not over what is past, for it will not return'. Their past will certainly not return, for it forms part of Britain's bygone imperial glory, a legacy that is systematically being excised from school syllabuses. Yet there is no remorse in evidence at the table, only good-natured banter and anecdotes about a life that today, in the early twenty-first century, seems almost unimaginable outside the film sets of Hollywood epics. As the afternoon wanes, one might hear them 'vivaciously speculating as to what became of who', as in Noël Coward's classic of the Indian Army, 'I Wonder What Happened to Him?' One might also hazard a guess, taking note of the soldierly bearing and squared shoulders of the men seated at

the table, all well into their seventies and eighties, that they are
ex-Services. And that would be correct. But it is unlikely that the
various corps in which they served so many years ago would
mean much to the average person. Regimental names like the
Gordon Highlanders or the Black Watch resound with glory and
deeds of gallantry to anyone with the most cursory interest in
military history. When it comes to high romance and gallantry,
arguably none of these units can hold a candle to the South
Waziristan Scouts or the Zhob Militia. The handful of men
assembled for their yearly luncheon are the surviving members of
the Frontier Corps Association, a brotherhood of old soldiers
officially disbanded in 1997 before, as its secretary Major Girling
noted on that occasion, 'it died a natural death'. For a few
adventurous years, these veterans of India's North-West Frontier
led a remarkable *beau geste* existence, before retiring to tend their
English gardens in the rain.

Colonel Tony Streather, very much a portrait of the spit-and-
polish military man, with regimental moustache and precision
speech, could hardly be accused of retiring to a humdrum life
after serving on the Frontier until 1950. A former officer in the
Zhob Militia and ADC to the Governor of the North-West Frontier
Province, Streather distinguished himself shortly after departing
Pakistan as a member of the first British team to climb
Kangchenjunga, the world's third highest mountain. Albeit now
well into his seventies, Streather radiates a Churchillian vitality,
seeming poised to move on to his next activity. 'As ADC in
Peshawar, one of my jobs was conducting people up the Khyber
Pass,' he says. 'In those years it was a full day's journey to go up
the Pass. We would stop off along the way to show visitors some
of the sights, such the spot where Alexander the Great's horse
was reputed to have kicked a rock, or where the elephant got
stuck going through a gorge in Kipling's *Soldiers Three*.'[1]
   Streather was one of many British officers who stayed on after
Partition, and who did so because the new Pakistani Government
was keen to draw on their experience and skills in keeping the

peace on the Frontier. Even then, when out on gasht British officers would wear the same turbans and pantaloons as the tribesmen. 'You'd have to, otherwise you could too easily be picked off by snipers,' recalls Streather.

In those days before Partition, the Great Game was still very much a live issue. There was the fear that Afghanistan could be influenced by Soviet Russia, and that was really why we were all there. After independence it went on just the same, but they pulled the army out and increased the fighting strength of the Khyber Rifles and the other Frontier militias. The problem that crept up after 1947 was the threat of Pakhtunistan, a revival of the scheme espoused in the 1930s by the agitator Abdul Ghaffar Khan, who campaigned for a united Pathan movement, along with the Afghan tribes, to carve out a chunk of Pakistan for themselves under the guise of a Pathan state. That heated things up a bit and we all rushed to the Frontier, as it looked like the Afghans were about to stir up trouble. This is still one of the big worries today, that the Pathans will attempt to take the Frontier.[2]

Graham Wontner-Smith spent some three decades of his life running a large department store in London's Oxford Circus. But before settling into his career in retailing, the still-sprightly former soldier led a rather more exotic existence. A veteran Frontiersman, he is the last known surviving British officer to have served in the Khyber Rifles when it was re-formed after the war. Wontner-Smith was in his final year at school, when he found himself looking for a way to join the army. One evening, the opportunity to fulfil his dream fell into his lap, in the person of an Indian Army officer who turned up at his school to give a lecture about the adventurous life to be had serving the Raj in uniform. Wontner-Smith approached the officer after the lecture and said he would like to volunteer. Soon afterward, with war declared, events began to happen in rapid succession. Wontner-Smith was called up for a medical, became an officer cadet, enrolled in Aldershot, later to be shipped out to India by convoy and from there to an officers' training school in Mhow for six months.

At one point during my time in Mhow this business of the Frontier Corps came up,' he says. 'I made it known that I was very keen to join the unit. There was this mystique about the region, in particular the Khyber, as it has been the route for invasion since time immemorial. So I was finally commissioned and I went to the Rajputana Rifles, thinking no more about it. About that time, the Afridi Battalion had just been raised with an establishment of six officers. They had only managed to get five and were desperate to find another officer. The Commandant and the Adjutant came round to GHQ to get them to cough one up. In the process, they recorded my interest in the Scouts and that was how I came to be transferred to the Afridi Battalion.[3]

From there it was off to the Middle East, spending the best part of five years in Persia, Iraq and Syria. Wontner-Smith returned to India to witness the ceremony at which the Afridi Battalion was transformed into the reincarnated Khyber Rifles. 'We were affiliated to the 12th Frontier Force whose regimental headquarters were at Sialkot,' he explains. 'So we were six British officers in the Khyber Rifles commanding some seven hundred men. We had two wings that were in fact double companies, and I served as commander of one of the wings. We rotated in those days, and the idea at the beginning was that one wing would be based at headquarters at Landi Kotal and Landi Khana on the Frontier, while the other was stationed at Shangay and Ali Masjid, the two forts south of the Khyber road.'

There was still a lot of gashting going on in those closing days of empire, and chasing after troublemakers, too, with the countdown to independence having begun and tension building by the day across the Frontier, where a perilous question mark hung over the tribal lands. Would the Pathans come out stirring up sedition in armed defiance of forced accession to Pakistan? 'Yes, we did a lot of gashts, and of course always to the north of the Khyber Pass, never to the south, which was the forbidden land of Tirah,' recalls Wontner-Smith.

> The agreement through the Political Agent was that we would never go south into this sacred Afridi territory. We had to man all the various picquets, but our principal aim was simply to be a presence in the Khyber, and to keep the peace. During our time, in fact, there was no trouble. The peace didn't need to be kept, it just remained. The fact is that we never worried much about which way the men's loyalty would swing had fighting broken out with the tribes. The Afridis were happy to fire on one another to settle their blood feuds, so it wasn't difficult to get them as Khyber Rifles recruits to fire on their own people.

Girling, formerly of the South Waziristan Scouts, can gloriously lay claim to having commanded the last British cavalry charge in India – in a rather unconventional fashion, as he tells the story. 'You would often be out in a convoy that got shot up and when that happened you'd get out and chase the raiders away,' he recalls sixty years on, comfortably ensconced on a farm deep in the Dorset countryside.[4]

> You might find yourself on patrol, which we called a *gasht*, somewhere out in the unsettled tribal districts. That is what happened one Sunday afternoon in 1949, when I set out with a troop of mounted infantry in pursuit of a gang of raiders who had made off with a herd of cattle from a neighbouring village. The quarry escaped, but on the way back to our post a fusillade of shots rang out from a low knoll some three hundred yards away. I couldn't think of what order to give, so I shouted to my men, 'Right into line – *Charge!*' It sounded pretty good at the time, but it suddenly occurred to me, a bit too late of course, that we weren't supposed to do that with mounted infantry. I rode at what was meant to be a controlled canter to the centre

front, but the pony I was riding decided this might be a novel variety of the game of polo in which he had recently been schooled, and he was off in an uncontrolled gallop. My pony was urged on by the thunder of the hooves of the rest of the troop following behind. At this point it flashed through my mind that it might be a good idea to draw my pistol, but both hands were occupied trying to restrain my mount, who was determined to be first to the goal. By the time we reached the top of the knoll, I spotted half a dozen or so black *pagris* rapidly disappearing a couple of hundred yards away. When we returned to our barracks I reported the affair to the acting Commandant, who was singularly unimpressed. However, he did forgive me to some extent a few years later after marrying my sister, and thereafter he was really quite civil about the whole incident. We all shared a special moment in history.

The soldiers who campaigned on the North-West Frontier for nearly a century, and the administrators who ruled this remote corner of British India, were responsible for defining that moment in history. They left their mark, then passed on to join the ranks of the other conquerors, from Alexander onwards, who crossed swords with the Pathans.

But the British episode was unique for the enduring heritage it left behind, from a prestigious school of higher learning in Peshawar, to a modern road network, a system of jurisprudence and a language. The British also bequeathed a military tradition, a legacy much in evidence today in the Pathan levy raised by Robert Warburton more than 125 years ago, that today still stands guard over the Khyber Pass.

Table of Hostilities on the North-West Frontier 1839–1947

Hostilities on the NWF 1839–1947	Causes and Outcome	Dramatis Personae
1839–1842 First Afghan War	Fearing the surge of Russian influence on Afghanistan the British take Kabul. The army agrees to leave in January 1842. The column is massacred on the march to India in the worst defeat ever suffered by British troops.	Ranjit Singh, Sikh conqueror of Peshawar, dies. Shah Shujah installed as Afghan amir to replace Dost Mohammed. Sir William Macnaghten and Sir Alexander Burnes murdered in Kabul. Mohammed Akbar Khan, favourite son of Dost Mohammed, incites tribesmen to slaughter British Army. Later eludes capture. Major-General William Elphinstone, commander of British troops in Kabul, taken hostage on the retreat

Hostilities on the NWF 1839–1947	Causes and Outcome	Dramatis Personae
		and dies in captivity. Brigadier Sir Robert Sale, defender of Kandahar, and Major-General Pollock lead the Army of Retribution against Kabul.
1845 First Sikh War	British forces are attacked by the Sikhs who cross the Sutlej river. The war lasts two months and ends victoriously for the British with the capture of Lahore, Kashmir, Gilgit and Ladakh.	Sir Henry Lawrence reduces the Sikh Army, later made President of the board of administration of the newly annexed Punjab.
1848–9 Second Sikh War	Two British officers are murdered in Multan and the Sikhs take Peshawar. They are defeated in the battle of Gujerat. The Government of India annexes the Punjab. Peshawar is re-taken and the Sikhs' Afghan allies are driven back across the border.	Dost Mohammed takes Peshawar with Sikh allies. Colonel Frederick Mackeson installed as first Commissioner of Peshawar. Sir Colin Campbell commands Peshawar Cantonment.
1863 Ambela Campaign	British forces defeat native agitators after a month of intensive fighting in the Ambela Pass in Swat.	General Neville Chamberlain crushes Pathan fanatics at Ambela Pass

Hostilities on the NWF 1839–1947	Causes and Outcome	Dramatis Personae
1878 second Afghan War	Reacting once again to Russia's eastward expansion, British forces invade Afghanistan and take Kabul in July, 1879. The Afghans attack Kandahar and General Roberts marches to relieve the garrison. Hostilities end with an inconclusive British victory.	Sir Louis Cavagnari, British representative in Kabul, murdered by Afghans. Sher Ali, amir who invited Russian mission to Kabul, flees the capital ahead of the British advance, leaving his son Yakub Khan in his stead Frederick Roberts, later created Earl Roberts of Kandahar, leads Kabul Expeditionary Force, conquers city and then undertakes his legendary 313-mile Kabul-Kandahar march in 21 days. Abdur Rahman Khan installed on throne by British.
1895 Siege of Chitral	The British are besieged for 48 days in Chitral fort by tribesmen from the neighbouring state of Jandul, as well as rebellious Chitralis. Two British columns come to their relief and the siege is lifted.	Umra Khan of Jandul joins forces with the Chitralis to attack British. Major George Robertson puts up desperate defence of Chitral fort. General Sir Robert Low and Colonel James Kelly ride to the relief of Chitral garrison.

Hostilities on the NWF 1839–1947	Causes and Outcome	Dramatis Personae
1897 Malakand Campaign	Hostility towards the British grows along the Frontier. Several Pathan tribes join in a jihad to rid the Frontier of the infidels. The revolt is put down by General Sir Bindon Blood with the Malakand Field Force.	Sadullah, the 'Mad Mullah' leads jihad against British. General Sir Bindon Blood comands Malakand Field Force that puts down rebels. Winston Churchill covers Malakand campaign as reporter for *Daily Telegraph*.
1919 Third Afghan War	Native soldiers under British command join with the Afghans to avenge General Rex Dyer's massacre at Amritsar. After a month of skirmishing in the Khyber Pass and other Frontier areas, the Afghans surrender and the Treaty of Rawalpindi affirms Afghanistan's independence.	Amanullah, Afghan amir, declares war on British. General G.D. Crocker leads British forces. General Nadir Khan commands Afghan Army, ordered by Amanullah to surrender to British.
1929–47 Border Skirmishes	The Pathan freedom movement gains ground and the British are subjected to frequent attacks along the Frontier. The situation calms down by 1932, but operations continue against the tribes up to Partition in 1947.	Religious fanatic Fakir of Ipi leads an uprising by Wazir and Mahsud tribesmen. Rebellion put down but he escapes into mountains.

Glossary

babu	civil servant, or office worker
badap	revenge
barampta	round-up
bara	smugglers' market
charpoy	light bedstead
dacoit	outlaw
dak-sharry	horse-drawn trap
doolie	covered litter
durbar	court of audience
fakir	holy man
feringhee	foreigner
gasht	a patrol
ghazi	defender of the Faith
Ghilzai	Afghan tribe
havildar	sergeant
jemadar	similar to Second Lieutenant
jezail	flintlock musket
Jezailchis	original name for Khyber Rifles
jirga	an assembly of tribal elders or dignitaries
kafila	camel caravan
khan	lord or chief
khassadar	a tribal policeman
kotal	the flat summit of a pass
lashkar	tribal army
mahr	marriage offering
malik	headman
masjid	mosque
mullah	a religious leader or priest

naik	corporal
nullah	dry watercourse or ravine
pagri	turban
Powindah	Afghan nomad
sangar	a stone breastwork
sepoy	Indian soldier
serai	the courtyard of an inn
shalwar kameez	long tunic and loose trousers
sirdar	leader or chieftain
sirkar	the government
sowar	Indian cavalry trooper
subadar	lieutenant
wazir	chief minister or adviser
zamin	land
zan	women
zar	wealth

Notes

Chapter One: 'To stop is dangerous, to recede ruin'

1 Vincent Eyre, *Journal of an Afghan Prisoner*, Routledge & Kegan Paul, London, 1976, p. 30.
2 *Ibid.*, p. 31.
3 *Ibid.*, p. 29.
4 Florentina Sale, *A Journal of the Disasters in Afghanistan*, John Murray, London, 1843, p. 23.
5 Herefordshire Record Office, Garnons Collection, Airey Papers.
6 Eyre, *Journal*, p. 244.
7 Earl Roberts of Kandahar, *Forty-one Years in India*, Macmillan, London, 1914, p. 578.
8 *Ibid.*, p. 535.
9 *Ibid.*, p. 388.
10 Robin Hodson, *The Story & Gallantry of the North-West Frontier*, Clio Publishing, Southampton, 2002, p. 375.
11 Quoted from *Daily Telegraph* obituary, 17 April 1987.
12 *Ibid.*

Chapter Two: 'The Earth is full of anger'

1 John Fox, *Afghan Adventure*, The Adventurers' Club, London, 1958, p. 83.
2 Crocker, Henry, 'The Khyber Pass', *Royal Central Asian Society Journal*, 1931, p. 430.
3 *Ibid.*, p. 425.
4 Lowell Thomas, *Beyond Khyber Pass*, Hutchinson, London, 1934, p. 22.
5 Lockhart, William, Letter to Secretary of the Government of India, OIOC, 1898.

6   Charles Allen, *Soldier Sahibs*, John Murray, London, 2000, p. 37.

7   Crocker, 'Khyber Pass', p. 425.

8   *Ibid.*, p. 430.

9   Olaf Caröe, *The Pathans*, Macmillan, London, 1958, p. 413.

10   Francis Ingall, *The Last of the Bengal Lancers*, Leo Cooper, London, 1988, p. 42.

11   George B. Scott, *Afghan and Pathan*, The Mitre Press, London, 1929, p. 111.

12   William Fraser-Tytler, *Afghanistan*, Oxford University Press, London, 1950, p. 188.

13   Caröe, *The Pathans*, p. 382.

14   William Barton, *India's North-West Frontier*, John Murray, London, 1939, p. 87.

15   Ian Hay, *The Great Wall of India*, Hodder and Stoughton, London, 1933, p. 31.

16   Susan Maria Farrington, *Peshawar Cemetery*, Basca, London, 1988, p. 12.

17   Crocker, 'Khyber Pass', p. 428.

18   George Roos-Keppel, Notes to the Secretary of State, OIOC, 1905.

19   Victor Bayley, *Permanent Way Through the Khyber*, Jarrolds, London, 1939, p. 17.

Chapter Three: 'These misguided, ignorant yet plucky barbarians'

1   *Official History of Operations on the North-West Frontier, 1897–8*, OIOC, 1898.

2   *Ibid.*

3   *Ibid.*

4   Winston Churchill, *My Early Life*, Charles Scribner, London, 1930, p. 133.

5   John Masters, *Bugles and a Tiger*, Michael Joseph, London, 1956, p. 199.

6   Charles Chevenix Trench, *The Frontier Scouts*, Jonathan Cape, London, 1985, p. 246.

7   Caröe, *The Pathans*, p. 408.

8   George MacDonald Fraser, *The Steel Bonnets*, Barrie & Jenkins, London, 1971, p. 3.

9   James G. Elliott, *The Frontier 1839–1947*, Cassell, London, 1968, p. 69.

10   Hodson, *Story & Gallantry*, p. 375.

11   Scott, *Afghan and Pathan*, p. 175.

12   Hugh Lewis Nevill, *Campaigns on the North-West Frontier*, John Murray,
      London, 1912, p. 7.

13   David Dichter, *The North-West Frontier of Pakistan*, Clarendon Press,
      Oxford, 1967, p. 130.

14   Robert Warburton, *Eighteen Years in the Khyber*, John Murray, London,
      1900, p. 210.

15   Frederick Mackeson, European Manuscripts Collection, OIOC, 1853

16   George Macmunn, *The Romance of Indian Frontiers*, Vanguard Books,
      Lahore, 1998 (reprint), p. 138.

17   Hodson, *Story & Gallantry*, p. 395.

18   *Ibid.*, p. 386.

19   Caröe, *The Pathans*, p. 420.

20   Elliott, *The Frontier*, p. 183.

21   Masters, *Bugles and a Tiger*, p. 190.

22   Chevenix Trench, *Frontier Scouts*, p. 241.

Chapter Four: Kensington to the Khyber: Warburton of the Frontier

The quotes in this chapter are taken from: Robert Warburton, *Eighteen Years in the Khyber*, John Murray, London, 1900 and G.D. Martineau, *Controller of Devils*, privately printed at Lyme Regis (undated).

Chapter Five: Baptism by Fire in the Khyber

1   *Official History of Operations on the North-West Frontier*, 1882, OIOC.

2   Roberts, *Forty-one Years*, p. 521.

3   *Official History*, OIOC.

4   Caröe, *The Pathans*, p. 380.

5   *Ibid.*, p. 272.

6   Roberts, *Forty-one Years*, p. 524.

7   Nevill, *Campaigns*, p. 104.

8   OIOC, Lord Elgin papers.

9   Andrew Skeen, *Passing it On*, Gale & Polden, Aldershot, 1932, p. 14.

10   Arnold Toynbee, *A Study of History*, Oxford University Press, 1957, p. 125.

11   OIOC, L/MIL/17/13/19, p. 388.

12   *Ibid.*, p. 391.

13 Elliott, *The Frontier*, p. 198.
14 *Official History*.
15 *Ibid.*
16 *Ibid.*
17 *Ibid.*
18 *Ibid.*
19 *Ibid.*

Chapter Six: Another century, another uprising

1   *Official History*.
2   *Ibid.*
3   *Frontier Disturbances: diary of events April–May 1908*, OIOC, 1908.
4   *Ibid.*
5   Nevill, *Campaigns*, p. 347.
6   *Frontier Disturbances*.
7   *Ibid.*
8   *North-West Frontier Policy*, OIOC, 1920.
9   *Ibid.*
10 Hodson, *Story & Gallantry*, p. 398.

Chapter Seven: Guardians of a Frontier Ablaze

1   Charles Miller, *Khyber*, McDonald & Jane's, London, 1977, p. 368.
2   George Cunningham, Private Correspondence, OIOC, 1947.
3   *Idem.*
4   Captain Shafi Ullah Khan in conversation with the author.
5   *Idem.*

Epilogue: 'I Wonder What Happened to Him?'

1   Colonel Tony Streather in conversation with the author.
2   *Idem.*
3   Graham Wontner-Smith in conversation with the author.
4   Major John Girling in conversation with the author.

Bibliography

PRIMARY SOURCES

Herefordshire Record Office, Garnons Collection, Airey Papers
British Library Oriental and India Office Collections (OIOC)
Lockhart, William, *Letter to Secretary of the Government of India*, OIOC, 1898
Military Operations on the North-West Frontier of India, 1897–8, OIOC, 1898
Imperial Gazetteer of India, North-West Frontier Province, Calcutta, 1908
Government of India, Secret Despatches to Secretary of State, 1919
Army Chief of Staff Instructions to Government of India, 1941
North-West Frontier Policy, L/MIL/17/13/11, 1920
Frontier Warfare, L/MIL/17/13/12, 1922
Frontier Disturbances: diary of events April–May 1908, OIOC, L/MIL/17/13/23, 1908
Official History of Operations on the North-West Frontier, OIOC, L/MIL/17/13/30, 1945
Military and Levy Corps, NWFP, L/MIL/17/13/48, 1943
Operations of the Tochi Field Force in 1897–8, L/MIL/17/13/101, 1900
Proceedings of the Government of India Military Department, Hazara 1888–89, P/3484

SECONDARY SOURCES

Abdullah, Morag Murray, *Valley of the Giant Buddhas*, Octagon Press, London, 1993
Ahmad, Aisha, *Pashtun Tales*, Saqi Books, London, 2003
Allen, Charles, *Plain Tales from the Raj*, André Deutsch, London, 1975
——, *Soldier Sahibs*, John Murray, London, 2000
Barthorp, Michael, *Afghan Wars and the North-West Frontier*, Cassell, London, 1982

Barthorp, Michael, *The North-West Frontier*, Blandford Press, Poole, 1982

Barton, William, *India's North-West Frontier*, John Murray, London, 1939

Bayley, Victor, *Permanent Way Through the Khyber*, Jarrolds, London, 1939

Beaumont, Roger, *Sword of the Raj*, Bobbs-Merrill, Indianapolis, 1977

Blinkenberg, Lars, *The History of Unsolved Conflicts*, Dansk Udenrigspolitisk Instituts, Copenhagen, 1972

Bruce, Richard, *The Forward Policy and its Results*, Longmans, Green, London, 1900

Caröe, Olaf, *The Pathans*, Macmillan, London 1958

Chevenix Trench, Charles, *The Frontier Scouts*, Jonathan Cape, London, 1985

Chowdhry, Jai Krishna, *The Gate-Keepers of India*, Rama Krishna, Lahore, 1932

Churchill, Winston, *My Early Life*, Charles Scribner, London, 1930

Cloughley, Brian, *A History of the Pakistan Army*, Oxford University Press, Oxford, 1999

Collin Davies, Charles, *The Problem of the North-West Frontier*, Cambridge University Press, London, 1932

Condon, William, *The Frontier Force Rifles*, Gale & Padden, Aldershot, 1953

Crocker, Henry, 'The Khyber Pass', Royal Central Asian Society Journal, 1931

Davey, Cyril J., *A Handbook to the North-West Frontier*, J. Ray, Rawalpindi

Davies, Collin, 'British Relations with the Afridis of the Khyber and Tirah', The Army Quarterly, Vol. XXIII, 2, January 1932

Da Costa, John, *A Scientific Frontier*, W.H. Allen, London, 1981

Dichter, David, *The North-West Frontier of Pakistan*, Clarendon Press, Oxford, 1967

Elliott, James G., *The Frontier 1839–1947*, Cassell, London, 1968

Eyre, Vincent, *Journal of an Afghan Prisoner*, Routledge & Kegan Paul, London, 1976

Ewart, James, *Story of the North-West Frontier Province*, Government Printing and Stationery, Peshawar, 1929

Farrell, Thomas, The Founding of the North-West Frontier Militias, Asian Affairs, 1972

Fox, John, *Afghan Adventure*, The Adventurers' Club, London, 1958

Fraser-Tytler, Kerr, *Afghanistan, a Study of Political Developments*, Oxford University Press, London, 1950

Gregson, James Gelson, *Through the Khyber Pass*, Elliot Stock, London, 1883

Harris, John, *Much Sounding of Bugles*, Hutchinson, London, 1975

Hay, Ian, *The Great Wall of India*, Hodder and Stoughton, London, 1933

Hensher, Philip, *The Mulberry Empire*, Flamingo, London, 2003

Hodson, Robin, *The Story & Gallantry of the North-West Frontier*, Clio Publishing, Southampton, 2002

Holdich, Thomas, *The Indian Borderland*, Methuen, London, 1901

Hopkirk, Peter, *The Great Game*, John Murray, London, 1990

Ingall, Francis, *The Last of the Bengal Lancers*, Leo Cooper, 1988

James, Lawrence, *The Rise and Fall of the British Empire*, Little, Brown, London, 1994

Keppel, Arnold, *Gun Running and the North-West Indian Frontier*, John Murray, London, 1911

Khan, Azmat Hayat, *The Durand Line*, University of Peshawar, Pakistan, 2000

Khan, Imran, *Warrior Race*, Chatto & Windus, London, 1993

Khan, Mohammad Nawaz, *The Guardians of the Frontier*, The Frontier Corps, Peshawar, 1994

Khan, Teepu Mahabat, *The Land of Khyber*, Uzbek Publishers, Peshawar, 2001

Lal, Baha, *North-West Frontier Administration Under British Rule, 1901–1919*, National Commission on Historical and Cultural Research, Islamabad, 1978

Lamb, Christina, *The Sewing Circles of Herat*, HarperCollins, London, 2002

Lawrence, George, *Reminiscences of Forty-three Years in India*, John Murray, London, 1874

MacDonald Fraser, George, *The Steel Bonnets*, Barrie & Jenkins, London, 1971

Macmunn, Sir George, *The Romance of Indian Frontiers*, Vanguard Books, Lahore, 1998, (reprint)

Martineau, G.D., *Controller of Devils*, privately printed at Lyme Regis, (undated)

Masters, John, *Bugles and a Tiger*, Michael Joseph, London, 1956

Mersey, Viscount, *The Viceroys of India*, John Murray, London, 1949

Miller, Charles, *Khyber*, McDonald & Jane's, London, 1977

Mitford, R.C.W., *To Cabul with the Cavalry Brigade*, W.H. Allen, London, 1881

Moorhouse, Geoffrey, *To the Frontier*, Hodder and Stoughton, London, 1984

Morison, J.L., 'From Alexander Burnes to Frederick Roberts', Raleigh Lecture on History, 1936

Nevill, Hugh Lewis, *Campaigns on the North-West Frontier*, John Murray, London, 1912

O'Ballance, Edgar, *Afghan Wars, Battles in a Hostile Land*, Chrysalis Books, London, 2002

Qaiyum, Abdul, *Gold & Guns on the Pathan Frontier*, Hind Kitab, Bombay, 1945

Rashid, Ahmed, *Taliban*, I.B. Tauris, London, 2000

Richards, D.S., *The Savage Frontier*, Macmillan, London, 1990

Roberts, Earl of Kandahar, *Forty-one Years in India*, Macmillan, London, 1914

Sale, Florentina, *A Journal of the Disasters in Afghanistan*, John Murray, London, 1843

Schofield, Victoria, *The Plain Tale of the North-West Frontier and Afghanistan*, Buchan & Enright, London, 1984

Schofield, Victoria, *Old Roads, New Highways*, Oxford University Press, 1997

Scott, George, B., *Afghan and Pathan*, The Mitre Press, London, 1929

Shafi Sabir, Mohammad, *The Story of Khyber*, University Book Agency, Peshawar, 1966

Singer, André, *Lords of the Khyber*, Faber & Faber, London, 1984

Skeen, Andrew, *Passing it On*, Gale & Polden, Aldershot, 1932

Spain, James, W., *The Pathan Borderland*, Mouton, The Hague, 1963

Starr, Lilian A., *Tales of Tirah and Lesser Tibet*, Hodder & Stoughton, London, 1924

Stein, Sir Aurel, *On Alexander's Track to the Indus*, Vanguard Books, (reprint), Lahore, 1998

Swinson, Arthur, *North-West Frontier*, Hutchinson, London, 1967

Tanner, Stephen, *Afghanistan, a Military History*, Oxford University Press, 2002

Thomas, Lowell, *Beyond Khyber Pass*, Hutchinson, London, 1934

Toynbee, Arnold, *A Study of History*, Oxford University Press, 1957

Warburton, Robert, *Eighteen Years in the Khyber*, John Murray, London, 1900

Wilkinson-Latham, Robert, *The North-West Frontier, 1837–1947*, Osprey, London, 1977

Younghusband, Major-General Sir George, *The Story of the Guides*, Macmillan, London, 1908

Index